The Dream Culture
of the
Neanderthals

The Dream Culture
of the
Neanderthals

Guardians of the Ancient Wisdom

Stan Gooch

Inner Traditions
Rochester, Vermont

Inner Traditions
One Park Street
Rochester, Vermont 05767
www.InnerTraditions.com

LIBRARY OF CONGRESS CATALOGING-IN-PUBLICATION DATA

Gooch, Stan.
  [Guardians of the ancient wisdom]
  The dream culture of the Neanderthals : guardians of the ancient wisdom / Stan
Gooch.
     p. cm.
  Originally published: Guardians of the ancient wisdom. Great Britain : Wildwood
House Ltd., 1979.
  Includes bibliographical references and index.
  ISBN 1-59477-093-X (pbk.)
  1. Occultism—Miscellanea. 2. Curiosities and wonders—Miscellanea. I. Title.
  BF1999.G627 2006
  001.9—dc22   2005032568

Printed and bound in Canada by Transcontinental Printing, Inc.

10   9   8   7   6   5   4   3   2   1

Text design and layout by Virginia Scott Bowman
This book was typeset in Sabon with Techno and Avenir as the display typefaces

To send correspondence to the author of this book, mail a first-class letter to the author
c/o Inner Traditions • Bear & Company, One Park Street, Rochester, VT 05767, and we
will forward the communication.

In memory of Ruth Issacharoff,
the dark lady

Contents

Acknowledgments

I would like to thank a group of people who do not get thanked often enough. They are called librarians and we never discover their names. Especially, I would like to thank the staffs of the University of London Senate House Library and of Camden Central Library for the unstinting research help they have given me over the years.

I would like specifically also to thank David Sawyer of David Sawyer Associates for access to his private library of esoteric literature, and Peter Redgrove, Penelope Shuttle, and Robert Temple for a continuous stream of information.

There are two kinds, the white and the black.
The white is weak and easily decays, the black is
stronger and less liable to decay.

THEOPHRASTUS

Introduction

Many writers, some with good reason but others with none, speak of an "ancient wisdom"—of some great body of knowledge and of great civilizations that produced and enshrined it—now lost to us. Fragments of this knowledge, it is said, are found all over the world and they are proof that the complete body of knowledge once existed.

It is an interesting enough proposition, certainly. But is it merely some attempt at wish fulfillment, some general flight from our not always appealing reality? This is what its severest critics suggest. Or if it is not that, what exactly is it?

A few serious and highly qualified writers (as opposed to a much larger number of well-meaning dabblers) have concerned themselves with attempts to rediscover or define specific aspects of this alleged ancient wisdom. Some of the first kind are Robert Graves, Margaret Murray, J. G. Frazer, Robert Temple, and Geoffrey Ashe.

What precisely is it that drives these seekers?—for make no mistake, there is a greater intensity and sense of longing in their pursuit than can be explained by any purely intellectual curiosity. They, along with the readers that devour their books, are illumined by a sense of quest. What is the quest, and where does it take us?

I also said a moment ago that serious writers as well as others are engaged in this enterprise. What is it that justifies the use of the word "serious?" Or, rephrasing the question, what is it we are left with when all the obvious nonsense of the unreasonable answers has been stripped away?

We are left, I think, with something very crucial indeed. It is not just the clue to our real past, as opposed to the empty answers of the history books, but the key to our only hope of a future. In my own opinion, nothing less is at stake. The detailed quest of this book will involve us crossing many apparently fixed boundaries. We are certainly not going to let anybody tell us where or where not to look. Everything, therefore, is potential grist for our mill—biology, legend, sex, superstition, evolution, deviation—so too are the entire areas of religious, scientific, and magical belief. Whatever else is true of any search for understanding today, one thing is certain: the time of studying particular aspects of man's life in isolation is over. Man is a totality (all of whose attributes coexist and interact continuously). He should never have been studied as anything else.

As everyone knows, we are currently witnessing a great revival in occult thought and practice. One of my aims will be to show that this revival and the still earlier ones are only the sporadic outward signs of a continuous, though hidden, tradition. These revivals are like the apparently isolated single volcanoes, which are nevertheless sustained by continuous subterranean energies.

Discovering the hidden energies and traditions of the occult is one of the great adventures of our time. And absolutely definitely, orthodox knowledge and orthodox history are going to have to change to accommodate them. There is no question about that.

But a word of caution is also in order. Modern science and conventional thinking are not so much wrong—although in some areas they are very seriously wrong—as incomplete. They tell only *part* of the human story and they tell it from only one angle. But in turn, in bringing the occult wisdom and psychology into play, we must take great care not to claim (a) that occult wisdom is always right and never wrong, or (b) that it does not have to take account of the orthodox view. These are two points on which many occultists and alternative seekers go wrong.

So it is perfectly permissible, for example, to postulate visitors from outer space and then assign consequences to such alleged visits—but in the continued absence of one single fragment of actual, manufactured material from an extraterrestrial source, this view has to remain only a hypothesis, only an idea. It is not the same as fact. It is also permissible to propose lands and civilizations swallowed up by the waves, if you think you need to. But still you cannot claim this idea as a fact until, and unless, the actual remains of that civilization are found.

And then, meanwhile, what of the mass of traditional archaeological and fossil finds (and the chronologies and hypotheses that are, reasonably enough, based on them)? These finds *are* fact. The high-flying, or low-flying, occult theorist cannot ignore them. And what also of our knowledge of conventional biology and evolutionary mechanisms? Somehow your theory of ancient civilization or ancient psychology has to square with all of these. You *must* account for those *also*. Actually this is a very useful proviso, because it acts as a check or safeguard against complete anarchy, against the silly position of "anything goes." As I usually say, where anything goes, nothing goes.

In my own theories I try to take equal account of both the adequacies and inadequacies of occult thought; and of both the adequacies and inadequacies of conventional thought. I personally want a picture that does justice to both and I think anything less has the seeds of its own failure built into it.

So, unconventional and indeed revolutionary though my own proposals are, they yet do not essentially violate the observed fossil, archaeological, and historical record. They add to that record the forgotten, or rather deliberately repressed, dimensions of the occult. My proposals also take good account of modern biology and psychology. And why not? Surely it cannot be bad for us to gain on the swings *and* the roundabouts?

What my book precisely offers is very strong evidence of a hidden, lost civilization. But this was more a civilization of the mind than of buildings. For the lost ancients built not cities of stone, but cities of dreams. And, moreover, their beggered inhabitants, reduced now below the level of animals, still live *at this moment* at the edges of our civilization. I hope with all my heart we can yet save some of them.

If we will now pay our debt to these people and what they stood for, my book then offers us also a new evolutionary prospect—surely we need that? It offers us a joy of sex, which is joy of creativity, and a whole range of clairvoyant and paranormal abilities: the whole now neglected storehouse of the intuitive mind.

There is, finally, the subject matter of chapter 14. But I will let that speak for itself.

With these inspiring enough prospects in front of us, let us not lose any further time, but get straight down to specifics and the starting point of our quest—the number thirteen.

1
Thirteen

It is said that when Merlin faded from the world
he took thirteen magic treasures with him.

—Welsh Legend

At the time of coming to write the present book, my own position on the number thirteen was as follows. I had considered it of great importance that the moon, in any given year, has either thirteen full moons or thirteen new moons. These two possibilities alternate regularly, year by year. Ancient peoples, I felt, worshipping the moon—and there is plenty of evidence that they did so—might well have taken this fact to be of some importance, already by itself and in its own right. The alternation of a new or a full moon at the end or turning point of the year (again an event of great importance in itself), after a procession of twelve full moons and twelve new moons, might perhaps have suggested to them something of the enduring *duality* of our universe—of the alternation or opposition, say, of the male and female principles in human life. We do, in fact, see such a philosophical position enshrined in the elaborate yin yang symbology of ancient China.

Incidentally, the strong similarity of the yin yang symbol to a moon, and in a general sense to a moon that passes through phases, should not be overlooked. So far in occult studies I think it has been.

However, I did have still more urgent reasons for considering the "thirteen moons" of the full year to be important. From S. P. Grossman's

Figure 1. The Yin Yang Symbol

Textbook of Physiological Psychology I learned that the *average* (as opposed to the individual) menstrual cycle of human females is twenty-eight days. Now, 28 x 13 happens to be 364 days, almost exactly the length of the full year.

Here matters do, in fact, get very interesting. On the figures so far a skeptic might simply say: "OK. Women menstruate on average once a month. There are thirteen months (or moons) in the year. So all you are really saying is that thirteen months equal thirteen months." Where that simplistic view breaks down, however, is in the false assumption that there are thirteen *complete* moons, i.e., thirteen complete *lunations* in a year. There are not. There are only either thirteen full moons or thirteen new moons.

A lunation—the name given to the complete cycle of the moon through all its phases—is 29½ days long (actually 29.53059 days). However, 13 x 29½ gives us a year of 383½ days, which is quite hopeless.

Primitive moon-calendars were not, in fact, based on the true lunation of the moon at all. They were based on an arbitrary month of twenty-eight days, and twenty-eight days, as we saw, just happens to be the average menstrual cycle of modern woman.

As we also saw, 28 x 13 gives us 364 days, almost a full year. But a true full year is 28 x 13 *plus one,* that is, 365 days. This, it appears, is actually why, in the oldest European fairy tales, whenever people set out on some mythical or quest journey they undertake to return in "a year and a day." Robert Graves remarks that "in both Irish and Welsh myths of the highest antiquity 'a year and a day' is a term constantly used."

I was, meanwhile, already aware of books like Louise Lacey's *Luna-ception*, which reported that individual women's menstruation cycles, which often vary widely on either side of the twenty-eight-day mark, could be regularized by the woman sleeping with the bedroom light on during certain days of the month. The firm implication was that the bedroom light was the "moon," and that, therefore, female menstruation was in some way literally linked to moon-cycles.

Finally, again still before undertaking the present book, I was further impressed by the fact that the Jewish coming-of-age ceremony for males (the Barmitzvah), when a Jewish boy officially becomes an adult, takes place at the age of thirteen. And at that point, of course, he is 13 x 13 months—that is, menstrual months—old.

IN SEARCH OF THIRTEENS

Anyone who has not actually undertaken the appropriate research might imagine that there exists a vast literature on the subject of the number thirteen.

The truth is dramatically different. Hours of patient research, in both orthodox and unorthodox libraries, leave one with a mere handful of notes. The majority of dictionaries and encyclopedias of the occult do not even contain an entry on thirteen! When an entry does occur, it is just a few lines of more or less gossip. Any hard facts mentioned are likely to be repeated from other reference books, with the wording slightly altered. How can it be, one wonders, that a number like thirteen, still with its firm hold on the public imagination, can have so little background?

In time and with patience, however, a picture does begin to emerge. It is a fascinating one that justifies all the effort. These findings, further linked with speculations of my own and of others, then become a firm plank in the enterprise of identifying the ancient knowledge—and finally in the resurrection of magic itself.[1]

UNLUCKY FOR SOME?

Everyone in our culture knows that thirteen is unlucky. We learn it at our mother's knee. Almost, it seems, we take it in with our mother's milk. In our society this belief is as universal as air.

Nor is it a matter for taking lightly. In their *Encyclopedia of Superstitions,* E. and M. A. Radford report a recent case of a woman whose house was involved in a renumbering exercise by a local authority. Her house was to be renumbered thirteen. She took the case to the High Court, claiming that her house was now reduced in value. Several house agents testified, under oath, that this number is definitely damaging to the value of a property. Other encyclopedias report similar legal cases resulting in similar verdicts in favor of the litigant.

All commentators are agreed that still today the large majority of apartment buildings and hotels avoid the number 13, either skipping it altogether or substituting the number 12A.

Already one might feel that such widespread and persistent reverberations in our modern society could not but result from some once important source of influence.

However, since I do not wish to seem to be constructing a case on mere hearsay, we turn immediately to evidence of a far more solid and tangible kind.

ROBERT GRAVES AND THE WHITE GODDESS

Robert Graves is a distinguished novelist and scholar, whom many best know as the author of *I, Claudius.* At the beginning of his book, *The White Goddess,* he tells us:

> My thesis is that the language of poetic myth anciently current in the Mediterranean and Northern Europe was a magical language bound up with popular religious ceremonies in honour of the Moon-goddess, or Muse, some of them dating from the Old Stone Age. . . .

He goes on:

> The language was tampered with . . . when invaders . . . began to
> substitute patrilinear for matrilinear institutions.[2]

A good many of these concepts of Graves will concern us again
later. Here we are concerned more with the concrete information he
has unearthed in defense of his view of an unbroken tradition of magic
running from the Old Stone Age to the present time—and, in particular,
with his statements concerning the number thirteen.

Straightaway Graves tells us that the theme he is pursuing is "the
antique story which falls into thirteen chapters." Here he is referring
literally to an actual poem or set of poems—as much as to a set of incan-
tations or spells.

There are various descendants of the original actuality. One of these
is the *Song of Amergin,* said to have been chanted by the chief bard of
the Milesian invaders as he set foot upon the soil of Ireland in 1286 BC.
This *Song of Amergin* commences with thirteen statements. Another
descendant is the Beth-Luis-Nion, the most ancient Irish alphabet,
which has thirteen consonants. The consonants of this alphabet in
turn form the basis of a calendar of seasonal tree-magic. In much later
times King Arthur and his knights, of course, also number thirteen in
all, and, Graves tells us, "in Welsh romances the number thirteen is of
constant occurrence."

All these thirteens, and all others, Graves considers to be based on
and to derive from the thirteen-month lunar calendar. He reports that, in
fact, the memory of the thirteen-month year was kept alive in the British
countryside until at least the fourteenth century. The original *Ballad of
Robin Hood and the Curtal Friar* began:

> *But how many monthes be in the yeare?*
> *There are thirteen I say;*

The midsummer moon is the merryest of all,
next to the merry month of May.

The full Robin Hood band itself also numbered thirteen (twelve men and one woman)—but such more widely known matters are reserved for later.

Finally in this section, Graves tells us that the sacrificial stone circles that the Celtic Druids used (but did not build) in the first millennium BC consisted "always" of twelve stones (or "herms"), with a further, thirteenth sacrificial stone at the head or center.

Whether the word "always" is justified or not is perhaps debatable. Graves may only be saying that any purely *sacrificial* circle consisted of thirteen stones, which is a tenable, though possibly in the strictest sense unprovable, claim. For certainly there are many, many circles that consist of more, or fewer, than thirteen stones. These various matters are the subject of a later chapter.

However, on the basis of the evidence I am myself inclined to agree with Graves that sacrificial circles habitually consisted of thirteen stones or herms. And in tangential support of that view, we can note that the Druidic coven itself consisted of twelve priests plus a leader, making thirteen.

Graves believes that Moses in Exodus 24:4–6 was sacrificing at just such a circle; "and Moses rose up early in the morning and builded an altar under the hill, and twelve pillars. . . . "

MARGARET MURRAY AND THE WITCH CULT

In 1921 Margaret Alice Murray, the distinguished Egyptologist and anthropologist, published her book *The Witch Cult in Western Europe*. As in the case of Graves's *White Goddess*, the book created an instant outcry among more narrow and traditional scholars and academics. But *The Witch Cult*, like *The White Goddess*, radically influenced all thinking on these matters from then on.

Murray proposed that witchery in Europe was far from being a matter of the nocturnal cavortings of simple-minded, superstitious peasants, or of bored, lecherous aristocrats, but a survival of a structured religious practice reaching back before man began even to plant crops. (So the *general* parallels with Graves's position are, I think, already clear.)

In his foreword to Murray's book, Sir Steven Runciman wrote as follows:

> A thorough and careful study of the evidence provided by contemporary reports of the witch trials in Britain convinced Murray, as this book shows, that the witch-cult was a survival of a pre-Christian religion in Western Europe . . . which first may have been developed in Egypt. . . . Walter Scott, though he was responsible more than anyone for romanticising the idea of witchcraft, was well aware that witches and fairies, particularly in Western Europe, represented primitive races who were submerged by later invaders.[3]

Again as with Graves, there are many points in Murray's thinking that will stand considerable expansion; but in this chapter it is specifically the number thirteen with which we are concerned.

Murray's claim in this respect is that thirteen was always the membership total of a witches' coven. The coven was composed of twelve individuals plus a leader. Sometimes the leader was another human being. Sometimes he or she (or it) was the evil spirit or familiar that the coven worshipped, and who mediated between them and the actual true Devil himself. ("Devil" is just a convenient word to use here. Later we may write "Goddess" or "God.")

This firm and universal arrangement is, according to Murray, a structural/organizational element deriving directly from the old religion. It is one of the consistencies of witch-group practice in widely separated areas that allow her to claim an ancient and enduring infrastructure—to claim, that is, a long *tradition* for the witch cult. There was no question, therefore, simply of isolated or purely local acts of "daftness."

Another of these enduring and universal elements, incidentally, was the fact that *not one* of the hundreds of convicted witches and wizards of these times in Britain had an Anglo-Saxon Christian name. All were Romance or Celtic names. Clearly, whenever necessary, the witches everywhere abandoned their given Anglo-Saxon names in favor of appropriate others. This taking of another name is, by the way, a process of initiation typical of all mystery societies in all times—also of the early Christian religion itself.

Murray gives the date of the earliest account of a trial involving the number thirteen in England as 1567. This was the trial of one Bessie Dunlop. In France this standard coven was already in existence by 1440 (in the case of Gilles de Rais). And one of Murray's critics, Jeffrey Burton Russell, in his *Witchcraft in the Middle Ages,* while himself emphatically rejecting the thirteen hypothesis, points out that the first trial for sorcery in Ireland *two hundred and fifty years before Bessie Dunlop* (that of Alice Kyteler) involved a coven of thirteen. Russell considers this to be a mere coincidence—although he does have the honesty to admit that the Kyteler case "very curiously" contains elements that would become common from the fifteenth century onward.

Even solely on the basis of the evidence that Murray gathered, I think we have to consider the parallels between Gilles, Bessie, and Alice as no coincidence—and that Russell, like so many, is guilty of a less than reasonable bias against the facts. Our tentative verdict here is, in any case, amply confirmed by the mass of other evidence concerning covens and witchcraft in general that we shall consider. It is odd that Murray herself often chose to ignore this wider frame of reference.

In later books, for example in *The God of the Witches* (1931), Murray did, however, extend her theory of the witch to a rather broader canvas. In so doing she now lost the whole-hearted support even of previously enthusiastic colleagues. One of her claims now was that many monarchs and high statesmen met their deaths in response to the ritualistic demands of the ancient cult.

Some of Murray's material here, nevertheless, compels our attention—

her account, for example, of the significance of the noble Order of the Garter. The story, as given by the history books, is that either the Fair Maid of Kent or the Countess of Salisbury dropped her garter while dancing with Edward III, that she was overcome with confusion, and that the King picked up the garter and fastened it on his own leg, saying *"honi soit qui mal y pense"* (shame be to him who thinks evil of this incident). The King also at once founded the Order of the Garter.

We need to mention in passing that cave paintings already sometimes show the wearing of strings or garters above the knee on the part of shamans or witch doctors, and that in France the head of a witch coven wore a garter as a mark of his or her rank. And the usually purely ornamental garter worn by female strippers today, and thrown by tradition to the audience, seems also to be a descendant of an old folk practice of fighting for the bride's garters at a wedding—for long tradition has it that a garter, especially when worn by a woman, has magical properties.

The order founded by Edward III consisted of twelve knights for the King (12 + 1 = 13) and twelve knights for the Prince of Wales (12 + 1 = 13). In other words, he formed two covens. It is a further most remarkable point that the King's mantle as Chief of the Order was powdered over with 168 garters, which, with his own garter worn on the leg, makes 169, or 13 x 13.

FURTHER CONSIDERATIONS

We can now add much other material more or less without comment, since the previous two sections provide a general background against which the further material at once begins to make sense.

It hardly stretches the imagination to consider that Graves's Celtic and pre-Celtic circles of twelve stones, with a thirteenth serving as the sacrificial altar, have by the Middle Ages become translated into twelve *individuals,* led by a thirteenth possessed of special powers. We do not even need to use our imagination—since Richard Cavendish states firmly that in the earlier Druidic tradition we find covens of thirteen individuals, the leader of which is a high priest or priestess.[4]

Often given by the uninformed as the source of the bad reputation of the number thirteen is the last Supper of our Lord, after which Christ was betrayed by Judas. Even if this *were* the source, we would still be left with the "coincidence" that Christ together with his twelve disciples makes up a coven.

In Eddic or Scandinavian mythology we have the story of a banquet in Valhalla. Here twelve of the gods have been invited to take part, including Balder who is the favorite of all the gods. However, jealous Loki, the Spirit of Strife and Mischief, who has not been invited, nevertheless turns up, making thirteen. He kills Balder.

So obvious are the parallels between this story and that of the Last Supper—both involve a meal, both involve a total of thirteen guests, including a betrayer, and both result in the death of the most beloved—that one is immediately driven to look for explanations. A Christian apologist might well want to consider that a version of the Last Supper story had somehow reached Scandinavia early on (although Scandinavia remained firmly outside the Christian fold until the tenth century). But, in fact, it looks as if the boot is on the other foot—or rather, that both these stories are a confirmation of something much older that goes a good deal further back than either. For there are many other echoes of this story throughout folklore. In the fairy tale *Sleeping Beauty,* for example, twelve wise women or fairies are invited to the princess's birthday or christening and each gives her a blessing. But a thirteenth, who has not been invited, curses her with death when she shall prick herself.

Graves, Murray, and many other commentators insist that the significance of thirteen predates Christianity. We have already seen some of the evidence and we shall see much more.

Turning to the Old Testament, there were it seems (as again Graves and others tell us) originally *thirteen* tribes of Israel, not twelve as is the case today. The "missing" or "censored" tribe is that of Gad. This idea of censorship is, incidentally, an important one. It does, in fact, look as if the Old Testament (as well as other pre-Christian records) has been purged of the number thirteen. This matter deserves special attention. But let us first list in passing a number of well-known thirteens, most, though not all, of which belong to our own times, from the birth of Christ on.

By way of well-known covens, then, we have Jacob and his twelve sons; Roland and the twelve peers of France; Odysseus and his twelve companions; Hrolf and his twelve Berserks; and Romulus and his twelve shepherds. In this list likewise belong King Arthur and his twelve knights; Robin Hood and his band; and, of course, Christ and his disciples.

Aside from these specific items, scattered and obviously significant (i.e., nonchance) references to the number thirteen are found throughout the folklore of many nations and races. In Teutonic mythology we find there are thirteen Valkyries; and Asgard, the seat of the gods, is divided sometimes into twelve and sometimes into thirteen spheres. The *Gulfaginning* also speaks of a golden age when there were twelve seats for the gods and one for the All-Father. In Slavic literature we find the tale of Ivan, who with the aid of twelve smiths subdues a dragon; and the Russian folk-hero Fjodor Tugarin keeps a vigil over twelve mares belonging to an old woman. As far afield as the Indian Pantheon there are thirteen Buddhas, and the mystical discs that surmount Indian and Chinese pagodas are thirteen in number.

The mention of China here already reminds us that there are other worlds beyond Europe and the Middle East—to those we shall come in chapter 3.

THE BIBLE AND THE CENSORED THIRTEEN

The suggestion has been made that the Old Testament and Jewish history may have been purged of their thirteens. The "purged" thirteenth tribe of Israel has already been mentioned, and the fact that in Exodus 24:4–6 Moses appears to be sacrificing at a "Druid" circle of 12 + 1 stones.

We do know for certain, of course, that the original Jewish calendar was lunar, and that the holy days both then and now were set by the movements of the moon, and not by the solar year. This, too, is why some of our own Christian festivals occur on different dates from year to year. It is likely that *all* lunar calendars were originally of the thirteen-month variety. (In historical times, however, the Jews were already using a twelve-month calendar, though still like many other peoples insert-ing a thirteenth month every so often to take up the accumulation of odd days.) Coincidentally or otherwise, the coming-of-age ceremony for Jewish males, as we noted, takes place at thirteen.

Graves cites a passage in Josephus (*Antiquities* vol. 5, 5) that appears to refer to an earlier secret Jewish tradition predating the official Law or Torah. Here thirteen different kinds of spices on the altar are described as one of the three wonders of the Sanctuary. Graves also notes the instruction given in Numbers 29:13 for the sacrifice of thirteen bullocks on the first day of the Feast of Tabernacles. He goes on: "Josephus is hinting that the number thirteen refers to Rahab, the prophetic Goddess of the Sea, guardian of Sheol ('the uninhabitable parts of the world') where God also, however, now claims suzerainty."

I am myself further intrigued by the following passages, which are not mentioned by Graves. They refer to the distribution of lands by Moses to the conquering Jews. Recording this event, Joshua and Chronicles contain endless lists of "cities" distributed to the various "tribes." In those lists the word "cities" at most refers to villages, and the word "tribe" is probably best taken as family. At any rate, the following four references speak of the apportionment of "thirteen cities": Joshua 19:6 and Joshua 21:4, 19, 33.

. . . And Beth-lebaoth, and Sharuhen; thirteen cities and their villages.

. . . and out of the tribe of Benjamin, thirteen cities.

All the cities of the children of Aaron, the priests, were thirteen cities with their suburbs.

All the cities of the Gershonites according to their families were
thirteen cities with their suburbs.

In a list where other numbers also occur, one can certainly argue that
the number thirteen could turn up occasionally by chance. *However*, we
must also not overlook that the *original macrostructure* of Israel itself
consisted of *thirteen tribes*. In the list also it seems to me that the number
thirteen appears almost hypnotically and ritualistically. Moreover, of all
the numbers that repeat, it is the one that repeats most often, except for
the number four. And finally, in a similar account of these events given
in I Chronicles, two of the thirteens are now curiously omitted. Those
remaining are I Chronicles 4, 60, 62.

Meanwhile, references in Genesis 16 and 17 to Ishmael ("and twelve
princes shall he beget") suggest to Graves "a religious confederacy of
thirteen goddess-worshipping tribes of the Southern desert, under the
leadership of a tribe dedicated to Set."

Taking these points together, it seems to me that there are suggestive grounds for supposing that the original social structure of the Isra-
elites (or of their ancestors—and so perhaps of all moon-worshipping
tribes) consisted of ascending hierarchies of thirteens—in other words,
of covens.

We have now exhausted actual references to the number thirteen in
the Old Testament. We have, however, far from exhausted evidence of a
general cover-up.

OTHER PRE-CHRISTIAN THIRTEENS

The cultural or ritual use of the number thirteen predates the rise of
Christianity and the incident of the Last Supper. *The Encyclopedia
of Folklore, Myths and Legends of Great Britain* states bluntly: "the
thirteen superstition is older than Christianity." The thirteen present
at the Supper were not, therefore, the *start* of any kind of tradition,
but a nod *backward* in the direction of something far older, darker,

and yet more powerful (since otherwise it could and would have been ignored).

The *Song of Amergin* alone, with its thirteen statements, is twelve hundred years older than Christianity. The stories of Jacob, Odysseus, and Romulus are pre-Christian. A Graeco-Roman pre-Christian text, moreover, advises us that to get a woman to submit to us we should take a wax doll of the person and pierce it with thirteen needles through brain, eyes (x 2), ears (x 2), mouth, hands (x 2), feet (x 2), belly, anus, and genitals. How strongly this recalls occult practices in medieval England and elsewhere! J. Hastings further assures us, in case we were in doubt, that there are indeed traces of an ancient thirteen worship in Greek literature and mythology. "Plato (Phaedrus 247 A) implies that there are thirteen Greek gods, and Philostrates declares emphatically that 'the Athenians had thirteen gods.'"[5]

Also pre-Christian in origin are the cards of the mystical Tarot pack, from which our modern playing cards derive. Most authorities consider these to have originated in ancient Egypt (though a minority suggests ancient China), and they are emphatically pre-Christian in origin. They seem to have been introduced to Europe in the Middle Ages by the Gypsies, who came from India via Egypt. The purpose of the cards is to obtain divination and to tell fortunes. The medieval pack consisted of twenty-two so-called major arcana (or trump cards) and fifty-six minor arcana, these last being divided into four suits of fourteen cards. Oddly enough, these four suits of fourteen have become four suits of thirteen in our modern pack, but the reason is unclear. We would certainly expect the number thirteen to have been avoided.

What is of considerable importance is that card thirteen, itself of the major arcana, shows the figure of Death, in the form of a skeleton reaping with his scythe. In the grass around him lie the severed heads of a king and a woman, as well as numerous hands and feet. But when we look closely, we see that the hands and feet are, in fact, sprouting from the ground. They are growing again.

The thirteenth Tarot card does indeed convey the idea of death—but only in the sense of regeneration. In the modern western world we have become transfixed philosophically by one element in the equation—that of death—and hence thirteen is unlucky. The ancients better appreciated that only with the death of the old can the new appear. So new plants grow in the decaying debris of the old (and, in fact, grow more vigorously as a direct result), and fresh leaves appear in the spring thanks to the work of the dead leaves shed the previous autumn. The sun himself dies each year and is then reborn. And that momentous death and rebirth occurs during the "thirteenth moon." (Later in the book we shall show that the moon worshippers believed the moon to be directly responsible for the sun's resurrection.) The cycle of death and rebirth was an immensely formative influence on all ancient thought, and the two elements in that equation were considered to be inseparable, simply the two faces of one process. (We also have many links here with such matters as the waxing and waning of the moon, with general duality, and with the two-faced god Janus.) The *positive* view of the thirteenth trump card is certainly the original and correct one—so that thirteen was actually lucky or blessed. More evidence on that score will follow. But for the moment we pause in our study of the number thirteen to look at another important mystical number, the number seven.

2
Seven

I am a stag: *of seven tines*
I am a flood: *across a plain*
I am a wind: *on a deep water*
I am a tear: *the Sun lets fall*
I am a hawk: *above the cliff*
I am a thorn: *beneath the nail*
I am a wonder: *among flowers.*

—ROBERT GRAVES

In his book *The Ancient Wisdom,* Geoffrey Ashe employed a simple device—almost brilliantly simple: he set out to trace the number seven to its source.

In contrast to my own experience with the number thirteen, Ashe must have found his desk groaning under the weight of references to the number seven. For the influence of this mystical number spreads through every facet of our western lives, in both religious and worldly affairs. It is already useful to speculate on the reasons why such very different fates should have befallen these two numbers.

Probably nobody, even if they could overlook the influence of thirteen, could fail to appreciate the hold that seven has on our thinking and institutions. Our week has seven days (a thoroughly un-useful way of dividing up the year, incidentally), apparently in honor of the fact that God created the world in seven days. Most of us are aware that seven is supposed to be a "lucky" number, and almost as many must know that the seventh son of a seventh son is said to have mystical powers. The Bible and the Christian religion are simply littered with sevens: Joshua marches seven times round the city of Jericho with seven priests blowing trumpets; Christ speaks seven times from the Cross; the Pharaoh dreams of seven cows and seven ears of grain, which turn out to foretell seven years of plenty and seven years of famine; we believe there to be seven deadly sins and seven pillars of wisdom; the Jewish sacred candlestick has seven branches; there are seven archangels and seven heavens. So the list continues almost indefinitely.

As already suggested, no less does seven also rule our *secular* lives—and here, really, with no logical justification. There are said objectively to be seven wonders of the world (but their choice is more or less up to you). Likewise there are said to be seven seas (a contorted total only arrived at by omitting the Mediterranean altogether, and dividing the Atlantic and the Pacific into two sections each!). There are said to be seven openings in the human body—ears, eyes, nose, mouth, navel, uretha, and anus—but there are two ears, two eyes, and two nostrils. We divide our harmonic scale into seven notes (but the Chinese divide it into five). We say there are seven colors in the rainbow (but the Chinese, for cultural reasons of their own, again see only five). We claim there are "seven ages of man" and point out that the human body renews itself completely every seven years (but medical science fails to confirm this). It is claimed that, in response to the "cosmic pulse," every seventh wave breaking on a beach is larger than the preceding six. (It isn't.)

There are some problems building up here. Certainly we can already make a rule of thumb and say that whenever seven appears as part of religious ritual or dogma it can stand—as just that. But when the number seven appears *outside* a religious context as an explanation of some real event, there is every chance that the "explanation" is incorrect. In this case, then, what do we make of the alleged seven chakras (or vital centers) of the human body described in yoga? Are they religiously real, but objectively phony?

This constant forcing, not just of religious events into sevens—which can, in a sense, be justified if seven is one of the tenets of your faith—but of logical, objective events into the same framework, is very intriguing. What on earth, or in heaven, is it that could *make* such large sections of mankind follow this ruling? Ashe set out to find the answer.

In his comprehensive research, Ashe extends his inquiry steadily back through history, and finally into prehistory. As he goes, he keeps also a sharp eye on the geographical limits of seven's influence. For he is interested, not only in finding the age when seven began its reign, but also the place. Naturally I cannot do justice to Ashe's work in this brief space. So I now pass over much of his fascinating text and come to his conclusions—which, with one important exception, I find extremely satisfying.

Geographically, Ashe finds that the influence of the magical seven does not extend dramatically beyond India—where, however, it is strong. But the Buddhism of Tibet and Central Asia also shows some influence, notably in supporting the idea that there are seven vital chakras in the human body. A few scattered references to other sevens also occur in the general mythology of these regions. In this respect, at least, seven differs from thirteen, for the influence of thirteen shows no such limits.

At one stage in history, the Middle East was clearly a veritable hotbed of sevens—seen in the number's great influence in the Jewish and Islamic faiths. A fairly strong influence is noted in Sumeria, among those forerunners of Egyptian civilization. And yet "very striking indeed is its near-absence from the religion and mythology of ancient Egypt."

As he journeys further back in time, Ashe's trail gradually leads not East (as one might perhaps have thought) but North. The clues he follows are fascinating in themselves. For example, he notes that our word "arctic" derives from the Greek word for "north"—and it means literally "the bear's place." And that the Latin word for north, *septentriones*, incorporates the number seven, meaning literally "seven oxen."

Journey's end (somewhere prior to 6000 BC) finds Ashe in northern Russia. By now he has produced a mass of evidence to show that the

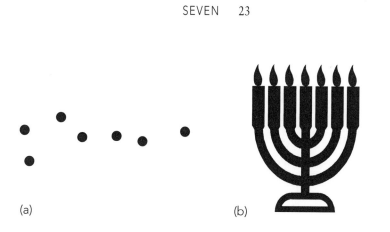

(a)   (b)

Figure 2. (a) The constellation of the Plough, also known as the Great Bear, *Ursa major.* (b) Sacred Jewish seven-branched candlestick (Menorah): a stylized representation of the Plough.

origin of the mystical seven is the seven stars that make up the constellation that we in Britain popularly call the Plough and the Americans the Big Dipper. There seems no doubt at all that the Jewish seven-branched candlestick is a stylized version of that constellation (see figure 2a and b), an interpretation backed up by references to "the seven eyes of God which range through the whole earth," "the seven stars," "the seven heavenly lights," and so on.

This constellation is also widely known as the Great Bear, and on our modern star-maps this is, in fact, its official Latin title, *Ursa Major.* Ashe finds that this name is also the most ancient, and as far as we can tell, the original name given to this constellation by early man.

Why exactly should this constellation have been important to early man? First, it is certainly the most easily identifiable constellation in the sky. Among the Ugi of Melanesia, for instance, it is the only star group recognized and named. Second, it is visible throughout the whole northern hemisphere. In most areas, including Europe, and unlike most constellations, it never dips below the horizon. Instead, through the night it moves in a circle around the sky, orbiting the "still center of the heavens" that is today marked by the Pole Star (though plus 2,000 years ago it was not). This general situation is again echoed in the description "the seven eyes of God which range through the whole earth."

Ancient man, searching for stable reference points and explanations in the bewildering cosmos in which he found himself, raised tentative eyes to the stars and saw *Ursa Major.*

Let us just recap why we can be fairly sure of this. *Ursa Major* is a bright, obvious constellation, floating virtually free of other stars in its own space. It is visible throughout the night, marching majestically around the horizon. Because *it* can be easily identified and followed, one then realizes that all the stars are, in fact, moving or pivoting around a central point—even though some of them occasionally disappear below the horizon and, in some seasons of the year, do not appear at all. Once given a stable reference point, sense can begin to be made of the otherwise confusion of the stars. Archimedes remarked in a different context: "Give me a fulcrum on which to rest and I will move the world." One could say in parallel, give me a fixed reference, and I will map the stars.

Why did early man call this constellation the Great Bear (and another one nearby the Little Bear)? The answer, says Ashe, is because these peoples worshipped the bear here on earth. Since he or it was all-powerful on earth, it followed that he must be all-powerful in the sky. ("As above, so below" is, incidentally, a well-known belief found throughout all primitive magical explanations of the cosmos.)

What grounds are there for assuming that early northern man did indeed worship the bear? Ashe's defense seems entirely adequate here— and, in any case, many other experts agree on this matter of early bear cults. A very important point for my own later theories is that already one hundred thousand years ago Neanderthal man made altars of bear skulls, and laid out bear bones in ritualistic patterns.

In addition Ashe notes that "Ursine" (that is, bear) cults "are spread over a vast region stretching from Scandinavia across northern Asia and far into America." Even the Ainu of Japan have elaborate bear-rituals. Still today many North American Indian and Eskimo tribes hold the bear to be sacred. In some tribes it was forbidden to kill or touch bears at all. In others, the God had to be propitiated whenever a bear was taken for food. We need not outline Ashe's defense any further; but as if to underline its rightness, we find that the early Hindus down in the far south called the Plough "the seven bears."

The wide range of bear worship—far more extensive than the mystical number seven—is important.

Clearly, shamans and witch doctors would have personified or impersonated the bear during holy rituals, probably by wearing the bear's skin and head. No doubt they thought (or their followers did) that they actually became the bear at this point. All these features are well-known in animal worship cults of more recent times. And, as it happens, the leaders of the witches' covens in medieval Britain and Europe also disguised themselves as animals.

We are grateful to Ashe for several reasons. One is for a convincing demonstration that the influence of a number can survive for many thousands of years, even in the absence of any knowledge of writing.

I would myself query Ashe's logic, however, in supposing that the seven magic and the bear worship *began* in Russia at some point between 6000 and 8000 BC. (The tradition could not be *continuously* older in that part of the world, for up to 8000 BC—or 10,000 years Before Present (BP)— that part of the world lay in the grip of an Ice Age, beneath glaciers a mile or more high.) Ashe himself mentions, as noted, that Neanderthal man was making altars of bear skulls 90,000 years BP.

What happens in an Ice Age? In a relatively short period of only a few hundred years (though not quite overnight, therefore), the glaciers march down from the North Pole, driving man and other creatures willy-nilly before them. But where are the displaced men to go? It is not as if the southern lands are unoccupied. The squeezing of large numbers of people into ever smaller space must have certain outcomes. On the one hand, it is likely then that fierce battles for territory occur. Or it may be that peoples merge more or less peacefully, with some kind of tribute being exacted from the newcomers. Whatever way matters go, there are certainly two results. Firstly, cultures perhaps thousands of years old are uprooted. They either smash to pieces in the flight south or, because their bearers are vigorous or numerous, they now swamp other old cultures in other places. But, secondly, virtually never will this process be without *some* two-way countertransference between the cultures involved.

We end up, culturally, with something like the confused mixture of different rocks and strata that are found geologically in most parts of the world, and that are themselves literally due to the movements of glaciers and other similar natural upheavals.

Reverting to Ashe, and to the northern Russia of 10,000 years ago—certainly Europe did then see some kind of new "beginning." For the ice sheets had retreated and man could once more make his way northward. Some northern race, or group of races, could well have come to prominence at this sudden moment of plenty and space on all sides. A "cultural explosion" might well have been the result—the one of which we ourselves, in a sense, are also part.

But as for saying that *everything began* at that point—no that is another matter. I am myself still preoccupied with the Neanderthals of 90,000 years earlier; and also with Cro-Magnon man, who appeared in Europe almost from nowhere 55,000 years later, and a mere 35,000 years ago—once again at a time when an Ice Age had just ended.

I want to say here that the point at which I emphatically part company from Ashe (as well as from the even more brilliant arguments of Robert Temple—see appendix 2) is when he (and Temple) suggest that the knowledge that evolved in prehistory was brought by visitors from outer space. The chances that one set of such visitors (in Ashe's case) just happened to come from the most prominent and permanent constellation in the northern hemisphere, the Plough, instead of from one of the billions upon billions of visible and invisible stars in our skies, are already slim. But when Temple proposes that *another* set of visitors came from Sirius, which just *happens* to be the brightest and most reliable single star of, again, the northern hemisphere, the one by which the Egyptians calculated the dates of the flooding of the Nile, then, I think, we have stretched coincidence too far. No, these constellations and stars are important for very real and practical reasons, but not because they are the home of extraterrestrial intelligence.

Though Ashe himself does not favor this particular connection, I think that seven *was* also originally part of the old moon religion and moon worship. 4 x 7 *is* after all 28, and four weeks do roughly correspond with the four phases of the moon (quarter full, half full, three-quarters full, and full).

But it seems that seven was spared the purging and condemnation that thirteen apparently underwent, and I think for several reasons. One is that newer religions preserve as many features of older religions displaced by them as possible to help followers of the old religion switch their allegiance. (Christianity did a great deal of this, as we shall see later.) Seven did not have the immediately obvious links with moon worship and in particular the menstrual month that thirteen did and so could be preserved. There *are* connections, as I just indicated, but these are at one remove. One can cut those roots without too much difficulty. A further reason for the preservation of seven was in the obviousness and usefulness of the seven stars in the Plough constellation for orientation, or for marking the passing of time through the night. These eminently practical uses of the Plough again could be and, in fact, were divorced from the general context of moon worship.

3

Thirteen and the Horned God

*In France until recently an officially appointed individual
known as the "quattorzième" was available to serve
as a fourteenth guest at any assembly that happened to
number thirteen.*

The firm superstitious hold that the number thirteen has on the public mind is not explained by the history books nor at all satisfactorily by the occult literature. Yet scattered references do enable us to see this influence persisting over many thousands of years and, in fact, still figuring dramatically, not just in recent history, but in our current religious and public life.

The founder of Christianity belonged to a coven of thirteen. In our law courts, the body that sits in judgment on the most serious cases is also a coven—the judge and the twelve jurors.

The French practice mentioned at the head of this chapter undoubtedly dates from medieval times and the hideous witch trials and witch burnings of those days. In order not to risk the slightest suspicion of occult or deviant ceremonies, a public figure was invited to participate in any dinner party or other assembly that numbered thirteen. The witch covens of medieval Europe, however, were themselves no kind of beginning. They continued (in *some* sense of the word "continue") Druidic and Celtic practices long predating the birth of Christ. But the Celtic practices were not the beginning either.

We need to say a little more about the cultural origins of thirteen. Then we can move to some wholly original considerations in the chapter that follows. With these we can begin to make sense out of what is otherwise confusion—and firmly and finally move out of the realm of hearsay evidence, of mere opinion and counteropinion.

CULTURAL ORIGINS

Robert Graves, myself, and others consider that all thirteens derive basically and ultimately from the thirteen months of the moon-calendar. Virtually all experts (and I personally have come across no exceptions) also agree that moon-calendars are older than sun-calendars in all parts of the world. Margaret Murray points out that the dates of the two chief witch festivals (May Eve and November) indicate that they are preagricultural and presolstitial in origin, and on this point most authorities agree with her. This statement alone gives the witch-calendar an age in excess of five thousand years and possibly in excess of ten thousand. There is little difficulty, in any case, in making general links between witches and the moon; but "presolstitial" specifically means "pre-sun-calendar."

According to Graves, the ancient Egyptian legend of Isis, Osiris, and Set was originally a story about the thirteen-month year. In the legend Set kills his brother Osiris and cuts the body into fourteen pieces that he scatters here and there. Thirteen pieces of this are found by Isis, the sister and wife of Osiris, and she puts these together and resurrects her husband. But she cannot find the fourteenth part, the penis. Graves proposes that the thirteen parts are the thirteen months of the year, and the small fourteenth part is the "one day" of "a year and a day" (28 × 13 + 1: see p. 6). As it happens, among his other roles, Osiris *was* considered to be the god of the whole year.

"Small" the penis may be—but, of course, it is a vitally important and magical part. A man without a penis is impotent—so Osiris has been castrated. And as it happens, Set at this time is the god of the sun. So, is the interpretation that the sun (the solar calendar?) has castrated the magical moon-year?

Ancient myths and legends in Egypt, Greece, and Europe are a quagmire of detailed confusion and contradiction. Existing legends are again and again grafted on to new personages, names are swapped around, and new cults and subcults spring into being apparently from nowhere. Such is the confusion that almost any interpretation or "explanation" can be put upon almost any story or event. This situation already poses serious problems for the honest scholar. But worse, it enables irresponsible writers to indulge in orgies of speculation.

So we shall certainly want to produce something better than just another interpretation.

WHY MOON-CALENDARS?

There is really no doubt that the original prehistoric moon-calendar served purely religious purposes. Even in historic times, Jewish and Islamic holy festivals were regulated by the moon—while sun-calendars were employed in respect of purely civic events. There is no *practical* point in having two calendars. No, the position is that an ancient, traditional calendar (serving some nonpractical purpose) has been partly replaced by one of more usefulness for everyday affairs.

The moon-calendar is virtually useless (that is, very, very difficult to use) if you are trying to pin down the equinoxes, or attempting to decide when to plant crops, or to find out when the rains will come, or attempting to nail any kind of date whatsoever. The reason here is that the moon has a variable relation to what we now call the solar year. And this is why religious festivals (like our own Easter) are themselves often variable, shuttling about back and forth in relation to dates of the fixed calendar.

The moon's variability is of course no problem if your sole concern is to worship her. You do whatever you do on the third full moon or the sixth new moon, or whatever the occasion is, and it is of no consequence if this night (or day) is not the same one as last year or is out of phase with the yearly position of the sun above the horizon. *However,* if you should start becoming interested in the best time for planting seeds, or in predicting the end of the dry season, or the migration of game, or any of the regular cyclical events of the year, then you *must* start observing the sun. These events are directly determined by the sun's position in relation to the Earth. Unlike the moon, the sun makes the same movements in relation to the Earth each year, every year. It is at once predictable and reliable.

It is possible at first sight to argue that ancient moon worship (and the lunar calendar) was gradually replaced by sun worship (and the solar calendar) in a wholly conscious way as man became more civilized and practically-minded. However, this is not an explanation that stands up to closer examination. It does not tell us why moon worship should have been *actively* repressed or, in its true essence, have gone underground. It does not consider at all the other *associated variables* that accompany both moon worship and sun worship. And these are very important.

MOON WORSHIP: DECAY OR REPRESSION?

In the writings of Robert Graves, Margaret Murray, and J. G. Frazer—whose magnificent *The Golden Bough* we have so far not mentioned—as well as in the myths and legends of Europe and the Middle East themselves, we find a number of parallel themes. Murray considers that witchcraft was a Dianic cult, an ancient fertility religion based on the worship of Diana (and her male equivalent Dianus or Janus), the goddess of the moon and nature. J. G. Frazer also believes in an ancient fertility religion surviving from the even more distant past into the present. And Graves, as we saw, argues the survival of an antique goddess worship over much the same period. Geoffrey Ashe, Tom Lethbridge, and others sing further variations on these themes.

It is impossible to go into all the detailed pros and cons of the respective positions of these authors—not without writing a book on that subject alone. But in them all we find a number of interwoven threads. Summarizing, on what we might call the "moon" side we have: moon worship, thirteen and the thirteen-month year, a leading role played by women (some sense of matriarchy therefore), secret and often orgiastic ceremonies, and general fertility rites. On the "sun" side we find not only a general absence of all these elements but specifically: sun worship, the twelve-month year, the number twelve held in paramount esteem, and a leading role played by men.

As I was writing the first draft of this section, Colin Wilson's book *Mysteries* was published. The second chapter of that book contains some further very relevant material on these points. For example, Professor Geoffrey Webb, Secretary of the Royal Commission on Historical Monuments, examining an old church badly damaged during the Second World War, discovered a male sexual organ carved in stone inside the altar. He considered this circumstance unlikely to be an isolated case. And in the fourteenth century the Bishop of Exeter found the monks of Frithelstock Priory worshipping a statue of Diana in the woods. Moreover, numerous old churches also bear curious carvings known as *Sheila-na-gigs*. These show a female squatting, with her thighs open, exposing her genitals. This is, of course, the mother-goddess. To this list I would myself add the signs of the labyrinth inlaid centrally, for no apparent reason, on the floors of several medieval cathedrals in France. The original labyrinths, built below ground, played a central role in the rituals of the extremely ancient Mystery religions, led by priestesses, and still practiced in secret in classical Greek times. And finally, in the eighteenth century, a Celtic altar, complete with the names and portraits of Celtic gods, was found built into the choir of the Notre Dame Church in Paris (see p. 115).

These matters (apart from all the other material we have examined) give us a firm answer to the question: did the ancient moon/fertility religion decay or was it actively repressed? Clearly, decay is out of the question. The ancient religion pursues its activities at the very heart of the new!

It is *not* simply a case of humble devotees (but risking their very lives) pursuing forbidden rituals—though it is that also. *It is unquestionably the case that high officials of the new religion were also secretly members of the old.* Even perhaps the *highest* officials. Otherwise the very cathedrals and churches could not have been marked—and, no doubt, actually sanctified—for the continued practice of the old worship. All this, of course, makes Murray's account of the founding of the Order of the Garter in retrospect seem far more plausible.

Before we move on, I do want to stress once again both the *durability* and *universality* of aspects of the ancient moon worship in our everyday life, and in orthodox religion and superstition alike.

The start of the important Muslim festival of Ramadan is, not surprisingly, signaled by the appearance of the current new moon—not surprisingly, because the religious calendar of Islam, like that of Judaism, is lunar. The precise wording of the instruction to worshippers is, however, of great interest. It says that one must see the new moon "with the naked eye" before commencing the festival. Now, this is *not* an instruction to see it *for yourself,* because if three other people tell you they have seen it, you may go ahead.

There is in Britain a common superstition that says it is unlucky to see the new moon through glass. This superstition is related to the Islamic instruction, as I will show. But I do not think we need to imagine the influence of Islam reaching this far! I think we can accept the British superstition as being an independent survival—of what? Of an old and no longer understood belief.

Other considerations first add to the puzzle here but then produce the solution. Glass windows, for example, were unknown until late Roman times (that is, not until well after the birth of Christ), when, in any case, they came into only very occasional use. The Islamic instruction is far older than this. So under what circumstances, apart from through a window (or through spectacles), could one in ancient times possibly see the moon *other* than with the naked eye? Why, by seeing it in reflection of course: either on a surface of water, or in any polished surface.

But yet, what could possibly be wrong with seeing the new moon in reflection? The answer is that when you see it in reflection it is reversed. It is now the other way about. The reversal is quite unmissable. For the new moon is not round but is, of course, the "horned moon." (This, incidentally, is a description often used by poets and as we know from Graves, the poetic tradition is also a descendant of the ancient magical tradition.)

The question of reversal is a very central one indeed, which we shall need to look at carefully. Nor can we pass over the very many other implications of the "horned moon." For the moment, let us just consider two things.

When we ourselves look into a surface of water or a mirror, our own image is reversed, our right hand becomes a left hand and our left hand becomes a right. To test this, stand immediately facing a friend, and both of you then stretch out your hands toward each other. Your left hand will touch his or her right hand, and your right hand his or her left. Now face a mirror and do the same. Your right hand touches the left hand of the other you in the mirror.

We note further, in this connection, a widespread ancient belief that reflecting surfaces show a man's soul, and that they can "catch the soul," especially in times of transition, such as death or marriage. This is why still today orthodox Jews cover up the mirrors in a house when a person dies.

Our mirror-image, then, is left-handed. The left hand itself is considered to be both very unlucky and unclean, and many taboos anciently existed against it and against the left-handed person. In every language in Europe and the Middle East, the word for left-handed is derogatory in the extreme. (In Anglo-Saxon itself *lyft* means "weak, worthless, and womanish.") And one last point here: if a right-handed person is blindfolded and asked to walk straight across a meadow, he or she veers gradually to the right. If a left-handed person is similarly blindfolded, he or she veers gradually to the left. So the right-handed or clockwise circling movement comes *naturally* to right-handers; but the natural movement for left-handers is that of anticlockwise, or "widdershins."

Witches and other mystical groups (like the Whirling Dervishes) danced widdershins. In the Black Mass all rituals are also reversed—the candles are black, the prayers are said backward, the cross is hung upside down, the congregants present their buttocks to the altar. Margaret Murray herself makes the suggestion, however, that it is not so much the pagans who reversed the rituals of the Christian Church, but that the Church reversed the rituals of the witches! I emphatically agree with her. The reversed or "left-handed" way of going about things is actually far older.

The matters we have been considering are one kind of evidence. But already we have begun to touch on other evidence produced by internal dynamics—what we might call the politics of takeover.

We have many examples in history of one religion supplanting another by force. This very often happens when a country is defeated in war and the conqueror takes over. In primitive societies especially, where "church" and "state" are much more one than in the modern world, you *must* break the religion along with the government of the conquered people. To allow the old religion to continue is to give them a focus and a rallying point. And, in any case, their religion is blasphemous. *Yours* is the true religion.

The (hypothetical) handbook for these occasions indicates two strategies:

1. "As far as possible adopt current religious practice to your own, especially where feeling is strong. If a particular date is important, place one of your own religious festivals on that day."

This strategy was adopted by those in charge of converting pagan Europe to Christianity. The most popular feast in the pagan calendar was the Saturnalia, celebrated from 17 December to 24 December. This is a winter solstice festival, the shortest day of the year actually being 21 December. In deference to it, Christmas, celebrating the birth of Christ, was fixed for 25 December—needless to say, not the day Christ was born. The Christmas tree and mistletoe are likewise of pagan origin.

2. "Where it is impossible to incorporate any major feature of the deposed religion, and this applies especially to its chief god, that practice or deity must be stigmatized as evil, devilish, and immoral."

This was the fate of the "horned God" at the hands of Christianity. (The horned God is a complex, composite figure, represented at one extreme by cave paintings of actual stags and bulls, and of shamans wearing horns, and at the other by figures such as the mighty Osiris. Pan is another horned deity—and, incidentally, Isis, too, has horns like her brother Osiris.) This once God then became the Devil—in which guise he has, of course, been relentlessly persecuted by Christianity for the last two thousand years.

The forced overlaying of pagan beliefs and practices by Christianity goes a good way to explaining the "underground" nature of ancient religion during the last two millennia.

But we have not unraveled all the mysteries by any means. The horned God, after all, is very much a masculine figure. We cannot equate him, just like that, with the mother-goddess, if at all. To be precise, Osiris is not the moon. And Diana, a woman, is the goddess of hunting—which is very odd, because whatever else women may have done in prehistory, they did *not* hunt. Diana (though here we are really talking about the composite Diana-Artemis-Luna-Hecate at the very least) *is* also the moon; yet we do not *hunt* by night. It does very much seem then, even at first glance, as if we have more than one compacted layer here.

We have dealt with Christianity superimposing itself on paganism. *What we still have to deal with, I propose, is sun worship imposing itself upon moon worship.*

All writers place the origin of the "ancient religion" in the Stone Age, which *must* mean before 6000 BC at the very least. Murray's acute observation that the witch festivals are preagricultural could take us back to something like 10,000 BC. There, however, the matter is left. As with all academics, none of these writers mentioned seem to think of enlisting the help of other far-removed disciplines—of biology, physiology, or even of anatomy. Yet in the belief that the witches and followers of the ancient religion are in origin the "Little People," the fairies and goblins of folklore and legend, I think Murray was very much on the right lines. She does actually speak of a "diminutive" race of Neolithic peoples (presumably she is thinking of the Picts or even the Celts), who might have given rise to the legends of fairies. But the events she has in mind belong to the last few thousand years or so. So I personally find them not of much help.

If only Murray had cast her thoughts a couple of tens of thousands of years further back.

Let *us* try tackling the whole question from the other end.

4
Moon River

The magical connection of the moon with menstruation
is strong and widespread. The baleful moon-dew used by
the witches of Thessaly was a girl's first menstrual blood,
taken during an eclipse of the moon.

— ROBERT GRAVES

This chapter begins with a discovery that I hope will astonish the scientific community as much as it has astonished me. It is "my" discovery only in the sense that I put together data already lying around in full view in the biology textbooks, and in whose collection many individual scientists have shared. In fact, I did even less than I have said. I did not really even put the data together. I simply drew from it an inference that is wholly obvious, but that has shattering implications for present orthodox views of the evolution of man.

The inference is that the apes—of which we are one—evolved as a group because its females abandoned the normal mammalian estrus cycle and developed instead a menstrual cycle governed and regulated directly by the action of the moon.

Having announced the conclusions, I shall now present the evidence. But, in addition, the pattern has now in a sense been set for the rest of this book. We shall never again find ourselves very far from matters of sex. Sex is the very heart and center of the old moon religion. As Peter Redgrove calmly and bluntly puts it: all magic is sex magic.

In chapter 1 we saw that menstruation in modern women takes place on average every twenty-eight days, or thirteen times a year; and that the ancients, despite the fact that the full cycle of the moon lasts twenty-nine-and-a-half-days, based their lunar calendar on thirteen twenty-eight-day months.

It was this hint of the importance of menstruation that, for the wrong reason as we shall see, put me on the right track. Searching for clues, I now began studying the information on menstruation in primates, that is, in monkeys and apes.

Biologists divide monkeys into two large groups, New World monkeys and Old World monkeys. New World monkeys are those found in South and North America. All the rest, from China to Britain, are Old World monkeys. Clear differences between these two very large groups show that they have been separated geographically and genetically for a very long time. One of the key differences between them is that Old World monkeys menstruate, but New World monkeys do not. Or to be absolutely precise, the New World monkeys menstruate only microscopically, with no visible external signs; but Old World monkeys menstruate copiously and visibly.

Apes, our closest relatives, are not found anywhere in the New World, only in the Old World. Apes, like Old World monkeys, also menstruate copiously and visibly.

It is when we take the trouble to compare the menstruation patterns of the Old World monkey and the Old World ape that the shocks begin. *All apes menstruate at intervals approximating to the full cycle of the moon, while in monkeys there is no relation to the cycle of the moon whatsoever.* Tables 1 and 2 illustrate this circumstance dramatically.

TABLE 1. AVERAGE DURATION OF MENSTRUAL CYCLE IN SOME TYPICAL OLD WORLD MONKEYS (Based on data from E. S. E. Hafez, ed., *Comparative Reproduction of Non-Human Primates*).

	SAIMIRI	CAPUCHIN	HOWLER
Duration in days	10	18	23

	CHIMPANZEE	GORILLA	ORANGUTAN	GIBBON	MAN
TABLE 2. AVERAGE DURATION OF MENSTRUAL CYCLE IN APES (Based on data from Vernon Reynolds, *The Apes*).					
Duration in days	36.5	30.5	30.5	30	28

The implications of these tables, as I have said, are remarkable and very far-reaching. It seems undeniable that one of the major features that led, about thirty million years ago, to the separate evolution of apes from the common ape/monkey ancestor was the development of a physiological response to the cycles of the moon.

A shock for anthropologists is that the chimpanzee is least close to the cycle of the moon, and furthest away from man. But I myself am delighted at this circumstance.

In an earlier book, *The Neanderthal Question*, I argued that from a large number of psychological and physiological points of view, modern western man seems closer to the gibbon and the orangutan than he does to the chimpanzee and the gorilla. Orthodox theory, however, currently places the chimpanzee and the gorilla closest to all varieties of man. The items I listed in support of my own view include pair-bonding (that is, the tendency to take one sexual partner for life), the habit of defending a specified territory, the fact that at puberty gibbon youngsters leave home and set up on their own account, the gibbon's flexible spine, its athleticism, and its two-footed, fully upright walk. To that already lengthy list must now be added the menstrual cycle. The gibbon (at thirty days) is actually closest of all apes to the true length of the lunar cycle (at 29.53 days).

It is clear, nevertheless, that in all cases some drifting away from the exact lunar cycle seems to have occurred. One factor that may well be spuriously affecting the issue here will be mentioned in a moment. But just in case there is anyone who still feels that the approximate agreement between the menstrual cycle and the lunar cycle in apes is "just a coincidence," let me point out that the average duration of normal pregnancy in human females is itself almost to the minute 9×29.53 days.

But more importantly still, let us again refer to the work reported by Louise Lacey and others (see p. 7) showing that the human female menstrual cycle can be regularized by sleeping with the light on during certain nights of the month. What is meant, among other things, by "regularized" is that the cycle *now* runs very close to twenty-nine-and-a-half days. So the currently accepted estimate of a twenty-eight-day cycle for women is incorrect—or, at least, indicates a distorted cycle. More of this later.

It seems certain that the bedroom light is functioning as the moon. This being the case, incidentally, means that the origin of the effect must date from an evolutionary time when man's ancestors did not even sleep in caves, but slept in the open, in a climate where clear skies were the firm rule.

The shocks for orthodoxy are not over yet. First, the suggestion is actually made by many biologists that ape menstruation has some connection with lunar cycles—and it is the *gibbon* who is put forward as the prime candidate for demonstrating this. But more importantly still, it is held to be the *new moon* that triggers the cycle.

We recall that the new moon is the "horned moon." We recall, too, that the festival of Ramadan is started by the new moon. But there is more. C. A. Ronan *(Britannica)* not only remarks that the Jewish calendar was certainly determined by the observation of the crescent moon but also points out that the word for "month" in Hebrew, *chodesh*, literally means "the newness of the crescent moon"! Could we continue to doubt at this point a connection between moon worship and menstruation?

An important question is why has the menstrual cycle in apes and man apparently tended to drift away from the lunar cycle?

The situation is that much, though not all, of the data on menstruation in apes has been gathered from animals in captivity. It is well-known that captivity and/or domestication often has marked effects on the physiological responses of animals. Modern man is himself "domesticated" and "in captivity" in this sense—and the often wildly irregular menstruation of modern civilized woman is certainly one result. (She can be put right in this respect by reverting to the natural conditions of moon stimulation.) What we need in respect of apes, then, is large-scale surveys of the creature in the wild to confirm the data given in table 2. It may be that "natural" apes as well as "natural" women are really still more closely under the moon's influence.

Was this in fact why witches danced in the moonlight—as did also the Faerie Queen and her fairy people?

OTHER FACTORS

Among a very large majority of mammals the female only permits copulation when she is in heat or, as we say more technically, when she is in estrus. During estrus, or heat, the female is secreting a live egg or eggs. Intercourse with her at this time is, therefore, most likely to lead to a pregnancy.

Some mammals, like deer or sheep, only come into heat once a year and then only for a spell of a few weeks. As a result, one set of offspring are produced every year, usually in the spring. Some mammals, however, like mice and rats, breed throughout the year.

Most primates (monkeys and apes) are capable of producing offspring throughout the whole year and under compatible conditions (in the tropics, for instance) will do so. Even then, peaks of births are observed at particular seasons; and where environmental conditions are unfavorable, births tend to occur only at these times.

But even in mammals that breed all year round, the requirement is still that the female be in heat, otherwise intercourse does not and cannot occur. For unless the female is in heat, she will not permit intercourse; and without the signals that normally accompany estrus, the male will not be motivated to attempt it.

Female monkeys come into heat on a cyclical basis many times a year, in principle throughout the whole year. But these cycles in monkeys have nothing to do with the action of the moon.

But in female apes an amazing thing has happened. The sex cycle is now linked to and dictated by the action of the moon. Therefore the female now comes into heat once every lunar month. It is the new moon that triggers the cycle, so that in alternate calendar years she ovulates twelve times and thirteen times respectively.

So far so good, in the sense that everything we have said about apes thus far basically applies also to the human female. But human beings now go on to write a new scenario on top of this basic ape script.

First, a few more details. Though the female ape goes through a continuous yearly sex-cycle, this only leads to intercourse in the days of the actual estrus itself (when the female is maximally fertile). In the chimpanzee, estrus lasts for a maximum of ten days a month. (And when a female is pregnant or when breast feeding a baby, she does not go into estrus *at all,* a situation that can last as long as *five years.*) In gorillas, orangs, and others the estrus period is even shorter—lasting as little as three or four days.

And what of actual intercourse? Well, in chimpanzees the male normally remains mounted on the female for only ten to fifteen seconds! During this "quickie," the male may meanwhile nonchalantly munch on a banana; the female meanwhile experiences no orgasm whatsoever; and there is also no foreplay and no after-play. Gorillas and orangs take somewhat longer over the actual intercourse, and occasional rudimentary foreplay is observed. On the other hand, these two apes make love far less *frequently* than the chimp.

Given that actual intercourse is such a perfunctory affair in chimpanzees, it is surprising that nature goes to such lengths in this animal to advertise the estrus period. During it, the female genitals become monstrously swollen and turn bright pink in color. They can be clearly seen at distances of hundreds of yards. The same effect occurs in the baboon. But in gorillas and orangs no such swelling occurs. Still, although we lack precise information on these points, no doubt the estrus female does release a sexually attractive scent (and produce the rise in body temperature that is the origin of the phrase "in heat"); and she will, of course, at this time actively solicit the male's attention with a view to intercourse.

All this is a very far cry indeed from the sex-mad human being. So casual and relatively infrequent is *ape* sex that it is only a minor contender as a "bonding agent"—meaning an activity or satisfaction or appearance that causes animals (in principle male and female) to stay together. But in human beings sex has become *the* bonding mechanism *par excellence*.

Interestingly enough, there is one other ape that is in many ways just like us—the gibbon. Gibbons, like us, also make love all month long and all year long. The male has intercourse with the female not just during estrus, but during menstruation and pregnancy as well! And, as it happens, the male and female gibbon remain together for life, living alone on one patch of land, and producing a series of children that really are a family. Presumably sexual bonding, as with ourselves, is the main cohesive agent in the adults' relationship—but we lack precise information on this point.

But now, what about ourselves? And what are the precise details and points of interest for this book?

I mentioned earlier that in the human female the estrus cycle has become a menstrual cycle. Actually it is more accurate to say that the estrus cycle has been overlaid and augmented by a menstrual cycle. (Estrus is the time when the fertile egg is produced; menstruation is the time when the unused and infertile egg is destroyed.)

Modern woman has a menstrual cycle in this sense—that the most marked changes in her emotional behavior are observed at menstruation. She has an estrus cycle in the sense that sexual intercourse still takes place most frequently around the time of estrus; there is, however, *also* a sharp secondary peak of intercourse just before menstruation, which almost matches that of the estrus period. (This data concerning the sex lives of women was, incidentally, gathered from two large samples of white and African-American women.[1])

What are the changes in emotional behavior in women at menstruation? As is well-known, there is typically a marked increase in irritability, in feelings of tension, in outright aggression (toward husband, children, and society at large, see chapter 9) and in depression (which actually leads to a rise in female suicide at this time). There *are* also positive aspects to the time of menstruation, and we come to these again in chapter 9.

An increase in aggression toward males and offspring during menstruation has also been observed in other primates, including baboons and chimpanzees. This observation assures us that the menstrual behavior of women is not purely social, but is rather the outcome of hormonal changes taking place within the body. (Virtually all human emotional behavior is, incidentally, hormonally-based.) *However,* in baboons increased social stress has also been observed to lead, for example, to a lengthening of the period of menstruation. So social factors are also very much involved.

The "bad" behavior of the menstruating woman in our society is disapprovingly noted by males. The "good wife" temporarily vanishes. She is replaced by a harpie and a harridan, whose aggressive behavior is suddenly more masculine. At the same time her sexual desires are running unusually high. But this is not the aroused, though yielding and receptive female of the estrus period. This is a demanding, punitive, castrating, and sexually-male female. (There is also the matter of woman's increased powers of dreaming and clairvoyant vision at this time, another topic for later discussion.)

But, all in all, we can well understand why Penelope Shuttle and Peter Redgrove argue that the witch burnings of the Middle Ages and earlier were "menstrual murders." Such persecution is a punitive reaction to those aspects of the female that are most in evidence during menstruation.

Turning back to more clearly positive aspects of female sex-life, one of the very great changes that distinguishes woman from her primate relatives (except the gibbon?—we are ignorant on this point) is the female orgasm.

In order for sex to become the prime bonding agent in human social affairs, it was necessary (a) for the male to achieve something rather better than fifteen-second satisfaction, but (b) more importantly, for the female to acquire a satisfying orgasm of her own. This is the reward, inducement, or productivity payment that nature has given the human female—an excellent early example of successful industrial relations. The female from now on has her own independent interest in promoting sexual intercourse, quite divorced from the instinctive desire to produce babies.

HOMOSEXUALITY, LESBIANISM, AND ANDROGYNY

One final group of important features of human sex-life also breaks entirely new ground. It is the rise of homosexuality, lesbianism, androgyny, bisexuality, and asexuality.

These last are aspects of human sexual life that are virtually undetectable among animals living in the wild. What *has* been observed, both in animal husbandry and in the experimental laboratory—and this point is of great interest—is that forms of homosexuality arise when animals are drastically overcrowded. The word "drastically" is important here. I think myself it is possible that some of our own homosexual behavior arises from this source (as Jung dryly remarked, nature has many ways of dealing with excess populations), but I do not think it is sufficient explanation for all aspects of homosexuality.

In nature there is no obvious way that homosexuality can reproduce itself. The condition leads precisely to no offspring. It breeds itself out of any population in which it arises, simply by definition. But this condition has emphatically not bred itself out of the human population.

My own opinion as a psychologist is, first, that homosexuality, lesbianism, and androgyny are not in the main sick or pathological conditions. I think them to be perfectly "natural." It is occasionally the case that some early trauma turns a would-be heterosexual to a lifetime association with his or her own sex. But I believe this condition to be rare and exceptional.

A reasonably typical example of the natural homosexual, or "gay," is Don Smith. In his pamphlet *Why Are There Gays At All?* he writes as follows:

My name is Don Smith. It is my real name, not a pseudonym. I am forty-one years old. I have been aware of my gayness since about the age of ten. Like most of us, I tried to ignore it for a while, hoping it would go away. In due course I even got married and fathered two sons, now in their teens. I didn't feel and still don't feel any bitterness about my marriage but in time the moment came when I felt I had to call it a day. Although the two were not directly connected, my decision to end my marriage ripened into action soon after the law concerning gays was changed.[2]

What about the number of gays in the general population? Don Smith, drawing on Kinsey's two famous surveys of sexual behavior, proposes the statistics that follow. These, of course, are likely to be an underestimate. Many of those, like Smith, sufficiently in control of their impulses, hid and hide under a guise of normality. The changing law has allowed some to come forward. But social stigma still attaches to being gay, and so an unknown proportion still avoids public view. Here are Smith and Kinsey's figures:

According to Kinsey, something approaching twenty per cent of the population throughout their lives or for some periods in their adult lives are exclusively or primarily homosexual. Another seventeen per cent will dabble in occasional homosexual contacts throughout their lives or at least at some periods in their lives. A further thirteen per cent admitted homosexual impulses without actually entering into such contracts. This adds up to fifty per cent.[3]

How does homosexuality perpetuate itself biologically? One possibly minor contributant has already been mentioned, the overcrowding that is part of civilized life. A stronger possibility, which we have become more aware of since Richard Dawkins's *The Selfish Gene*, is that there are behaviors genetically related to homosexuality, which are beneficial to the survival of the heterosexual *relatives* of the gay, who also carry some of his or her genes. Characteristics like gentleness and insight might well be examples of such behaviors (and there is no doubt that gays are above average in intelligence, creativity, and understanding). Yet another point is that many gays, even if mainly homosexual rather than heterosexual, do also have occasional heterosexual relationships and even marriages that produce children.

In fact, a better term for many homosexuals and lesbians is the word androgynous—the person who to an extent plays aspects of both the social and biological roles, and who, in fact, to an extent possesses both sexual endowments simultaneously.

I do not want to seem to skate glibly over what is actually a very complex situation. There are many different kinds of both homosexuality and androgyny. There are also behaviors and lifestyles that are asexual, but that outwardly resemble homosexuality, and sometimes even produce similar ways of life.

As both a professional psychologist and a freelance lecturer I have visited institutions that house closed orders of nuns and priests respectively. I have even stayed in the latter. These orders have, of course, entirely given up sex as an aspect of their lives—or so they say. Undoubtedly some of them have *not* done so, despite their claims, and it would be interesting to be a fly on the wall of the individual devotee's room. Still, I think many have genuinely given up sex—or perhaps, rather, never had very much interest in it in the first place.

I have been struck in the institutions mentioned by the generally boyish behavior and attitudes of the men and the girlish behavior of the women. On the basis of such observation, I would think that many of these people are cases of unfulfilled or arrested sexual development. In that general emotional area, then, they are not so much asexual as pre-pubertal.

Well, no doubt that comment has offended some religious readers of this book, but I am afraid my next suggestion will offend them still further. I am going to suggest that the priesthood has always been a refuge for types of homosexual and lesbian, as also for other kinds of sexual "deviance"—i.e., sexual, presexual, or asexual behaviors whose goal is not the production of children. I am going to go even as far as to suggest that the homosexual/lesbian and androgynous human being has made a significant contribution to the evolution of religion. Perhaps by the end of this book that statement will not sound as wild as it may now.

I must emphasize that I am in no sense here trying to trivialize or show contempt for the religious process or, as it were, to mock evolution with itself. I think we are dealing with a vital and integral part of evolution. Other serious writers like June Singer[4] and Charlotte Wolfe[5] clearly believe the same. And the cosmologist Charlotte Bach, in particular, bases her whole theory on evolution on the importance of homosexuality, androgyny, and bisexuality.[6]

As a broad generalization (and while agreeing that, in fact, many subtly differing qualities of behavior are involved here), I would myself say that we as a species appear at least emotionally to be taking up the two hitherto empty poles or axes (shown in figure 3b) of the basic biological male–female compass (shown in figure 3a).

Well, I did say this book would not again ever be very far from sex.

To bring us back to base, let me just say why I titled this chapter "Moon River." It is because I always think of evolution as a river flowing through time, occasionally meandering and hesitating, but ultimately

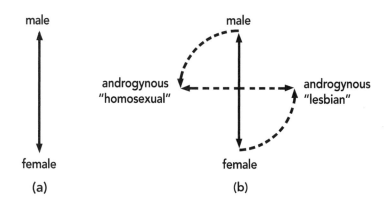

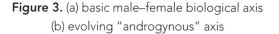

Figure 3. (a) basic male–female biological axis
(b) evolving "androgynous" axis

always growing broader and stronger. At a very late stage, in ourselves and our closest relatives—and, to extend the metaphor, like every large body of water—this river has come under the influence of the moon. In very recent times, as geology goes, the moon began playing a crucial role in human affairs. It still does.

5
Two of a Kind

The movement of yang is thought of as being toward the right and that of yin toward the left.

—I CHING

The exercise we are engaged in at this moment is that of approaching the question of religion in modern historical times—and all the many related aspects of culture, social practice, and thought that tie in with it—from the far end. We are trying to find the basic roots, biological rather than cultural (though these are but two aspects of each other), from which the complex and luxuriant growths of present times have flowered. We are trying to stand in the very distant past, looking forward—instead of standing here, looking back.

Religion initially grows out of what is, biologically. *Every* aspect of mind grows out of what is, biologically. How on earth could matters be otherwise? Our mistake—the mistake of modern thinkers, that is—has been to imagine that mind is not biology and that biology is not mind.

Jane Goodall has observed chimpanzees in the wild, shaking young trees and performing a rain-dance at the beginning of a storm. *That* is where it begins. In your relationship to "it." But the point is that your *relationship* is *you*. (And in any case you are also "it.")

In moon religion, the moon is "it" and menstruation is the relationship. In time moon/menstruation comes to symbolize and stand for all aspects of fertility, sexuality, death, and rebirth. In further time fertility means also the fertility of wild crops, and so sustenance; and death and birth mean also the death and birth of the year; and then more abstractly and mystically, the death and rebirth of the entire universe; and so finally, the motivation and meaning of that universe.

Let us look for a moment also at a hypothetical example that I have used in earlier books. Let us imagine that the mole has moved up the evolutionary ladder and developed consciousness and culture as we understand those terms.

Now, as a species the mole (the real mole, that is) is going blind. Many varieties already have their eyes permanently sealed up. For the mole has abandoned the surface of the ground, and the daylight, and has begun to live completely underground. Yet it possesses in its genes, and its history, the memory of daylight and of surface life.

The religion and philosophy of my imaginary mole tells, in hushed whispers, of the awful light and surface whence they came, how after long travail they were delivered out of the daylight and the openness and emerged at last into the darkness and the clinging, surrounding mud. Mole mothers discipline their disobedient children with threats that the daylight will come. The surface of the earth is where all rubbish is thrown and old unwanted packing cases stored. Mole psychiatrists evolve a theory and model of the mind, in which unwanted mental contents and traumas are thought of as being expressed into daylight.

Well, that is probably enough of that. But keep the hypothetical mole in mind as we go along.

Therefore, when I hear that in the old religion dancers circled to the left (anticlockwise) and were keen on reversals, my first thought is that these people were left-handed; for anticlockwise movement is natural for a lefthander. Or, in the event that these people were right-handed like ourselves, I start looking at ancient evolutionary aspects of the nervous system, to see whether reversals once formed any part of its function. (That particular line of thought leads to a consideration of our "other brain," the cerebellum.[1])

When I find evidence of *two* old religions (apparently originally separated, though now somehow amalgamated), one concerned mainly with the moon and the other concerned mainly with the sun, why, then I start thinking in terms of two different—biologically different—varieties of man.

To press the point a little, I start assuming the possibility of two quite separate evolutionary strains in our prehistory. I assume the one type of man came out of a biological situation in which his attention was naturally (and compellingly) drawn to the moon; and that another type of man came from a biological situation where his attention naturally focused on the sun.

As it happens, we do have two quite distinct types of early man available in the last hundred thousand years, who might be the two bearers of the two suggested cultural traditions. These are Neanderthal man and Cro-Magnon man, respectively.

I have already written a book about these two varieties of man *(The Neanderthal Question),* in which I proposed that we, modern man, are a biological, hybrid cross between Neanderthal and Cro-Magnon. Such a genetic mixing would almost certainly involve some cultural mixing also, and I attempted to pinpoint aspects of our present-day culture that each of our two ancestors might individually have contributed. In particular, I was led to consider that Neanderthal would have been the moon worshipper, and Cro-Magnon the sun lover.

I do not intend to cover again ground I have already covered, but a few points do need summarizing for the purposes of this book. The biological aspect of my theory is briefly this. Between twenty and fifteen million years ago (and, therefore, about ten million years *after* the moon had taken charge of the female menstrual cycle), one of the many apes then in existence was destined to become the ancestor of all subsequently emerging forms of man. As far as we are concerned, this creature was the last of the apes in that particular line. For all its subsequent descendants were not apes, but types of man.

The actual children of this ape, I propose, had sparse white or blonde fur, white skin, and blue eyes. But at puberty or slightly before, the fur became a full, thick coat and turned dark brown or black as did the skin and the eyes.

This is a perfectly reasonable scenario. The young chimpanzee has white skin on its face and a white spot of fur on its rump. As an adult, the facial skin turns black and the white spot disappears. The pink skin of the baboon youngster also later turns black. The young of gibbons have sparse, pale hair and skin. As adults they too have a thick, all-over, dark coat.

So the only point I have "invented" is that of the blue eyes. But the young of many mammals, such as kittens, do have blue eyes. It is quite clear that the white and pale aspects of all baby primates are inhibitors in the ethological sense, and prevent adult males from attacking them. They are probably also releasers of maternal affection. So right away we see there are "attitudes" to blackness and whiteness (and blondeness) in all apes, and in our own ancestors.

About fourteen million years ago nature contrived to bottle up the then widespread apes into three separate containers: Africa, India, and the Malay/Borneo peninsular.

While the particular ape we are observing had more or less the run of Africa and Malay/Borneo, in India it was confined to the extreme north. During the period of many millions of years that we are now discussing, north India was frequently cool and overcast and food was in short supply. Under these conditions of food shortage, the Indian representative of our ape ancestor developed pair-bonding. We observe precisely this behavior in the baboon when food is in short supply. When it is plentiful, baboons then form multi-individual groups like those of the chimpanzee. Gibbons have also evolved pair-bonding, again probably for the same reason of food shortage. At the same time, they have developed the habit of living in and defending a specified individual slice of territory. I think our north-Indian ape did the same.

But more important still was a further aspect of the situation. For reasons mainly connected with the diffuse and intermittent sunlight, the fair coloring and hair of the infant, along with the blue eyes, was preserved later and later into adult life. Ultimately this change was complete. Only light-skinned and fair-haired individuals of all ages were left.

In Africa, especially on the equator itself, a quite opposite situation prevailed. Perhaps, because of competition from other apes, our ancestral ape there moved out from the jungle into the scrubland. Here he was subjected to the pitiless tropical sun. The pale infants were now at a disadvantage. There was a strong selective pressure in favor of early darkening of the skin. Ultimately this process was also carried to its logical conclusion. Only fully dark infants were left. At the equator itself the skin was extremely dark. Away from the central tropics simple swarthiness, or a yellow-brown skin, was adequate protection.

In Africa and Malay/Borneo food was not in short supply so the multi-male/female troop structure was preserved as the basic social unit. All males mated with all females. But though not threatened by food shortage, I believe these African and Asian apes faced another threat (and the suggestion comes from Carl Sagan[2]), namely that of large, carnivorous reptiles. Reptiles require a high temperature at which to operate (and, for this reason were either not present in northern India or were sluggish), and the *tropical day* provides their ideal environment. So probably the apes in Africa we are discussing became, as a defense, seminocturnal in their habits. The tropical moon is, of course, very bright. . . . Sagan suggests that the apes eventually wiped out the reptiles by feeding on their eggs at night, for eggs are among the primates' favorite delicacies.

Some other points arising from these situations are these. In a pair-bonded situation you know who your father is, as well as your mother, and he is always in charge of the family unit. (Perhaps also pair-bonding in some way produces a reduction in the flow of menstrual blood, because in the gibbon the discharge is said to be "sparse.") In a troop situation, however, you only know who your mother is. You do not know your father—and for that reason alone he is not in charge of you. (We do know that gibbon fathers take an active interest in their offspring. Chimpanzee fathers, however, have no special relation to offspring at all.)

It will probably be clear by now that I believe the African and Asian apes we have just been discussing ultimately, over millions of years, evolved into varieties of Neanderthal man; while the Indian ape discussed earlier evolved into Cro-Magnon.

Before I summarize the respective legacies that we look out for in the behavior of Neanderthal and Cro-Magnon in the last 100,000 years or so, let me take one step forward into the themes of the next chapter.

Writing about the Red Indians of America (whom I myself list as a "Neanderthal" people), W. N. Stephens tells us that one tribe in the Pacific Northwest was said formerly to have practiced true promiscuity. A man would visit a woman's house, bringing presents for her, and then make love to her. But no individual man had any rights over any woman, nor over her subsequent children.[3]

We shall come back to this report. Hopefully it assures the reader, even at this stage, that my theoretical projections are well supported by modern observation.

I believe the actuality of Neanderthal man—of whom archaeologists find only a handful of skeletons, a few altars, traces of ritualized burial, a range of flint tools, and an apparent knowledge of herbal remedies—was this: his was a moon-goddess-worshipping, matriarchal, food-gathering society, where women governed all matters. The only tasks delegated specifically to men were those where muscle power was directly and literally required, as in fighting, for example.

The structure and nature of Cro-Magnon life was diametrically opposite. This was a patriarchal, hunter-warrior society, of which men governed all aspects, including religious life. Women were mere adjuncts in all things, whose main purpose was to bear sons and to comfort and care for the male. The supreme deity worshipped was the sun god.

The models of these two societies enable us to explain a good deal.

6
The Not So Little People

The Australian Aborigine has a story telling
how the white swan became black. But
there are no white swans in Australia.

—ABORIGINE LEGEND

The official identi-kit descriptions of Neanderthal and Cro-Magnon man are as follows:

NEANDERTHAL: OFFICIAL

Neanderthal was a very successful and widespread type, the only type of man found simultaneously in Europe, Africa, and the Far East in the last 100,000 years, prior to the sudden appearance of Cro-Magnon.

The generalized Neanderthal type is short (males average 5'4", females 4'10"), heavily-bodied, and thickset, with dense, strong bones and a thick skull. The head is large in relation to the body. The forehead recedes quite sharply from the brows, and, as if in compensation, the skull juts out markedly in the rear. The brows themselves are heavily armored and protrude in a prominent shelf of bone, divided between the eyes. The jaws are massive, though the chin itself is recessive. The mouth and teeth are large and prognathous (muzzlelike). Eye sockets and ear apertures are also large. The nose is broad and probably flat. The short stature and the barrel body suggest adaptation for living in scrub or undergrowth.

Neanderthal man produced a fair range of adequate flint and bone tools.

A specialized subdivision of Neanderthal is so-called classic Neanderthal (see p. 60). In him, all the features of the generalized Neanderthal type are exaggerated still further.

CRO-MAGNON: OFFICIAL

Cro-Magnon man was another very successful type, who rapidly displaced Neanderthal in Europe.

This type is extremely tall (males average 6'0"; females six or nine inches shorter), well-muscled, and athletic. He has a high, straight forehead, a strong chin, and a narrow, probably high nose. Mouth, teeth, ears, and eyes are regular. His general physique suggests that he evolved on the open plains as a hunter of game animals. He appears abruptly, more or less out of thin air, in the Europe of 30,000 years ago. No trace of his original homesite has yet been found; but a few skeletons with strangely mixed Cro-Magnon and Neanderthal features are found from around 35,000 years ago in the Middle East.

He made a very wide range of almost exquisite flint and bone tools.

NEANDERTHAL: UNOFFICIAL

The following are my own unofficial (but not unfounded) speculations concerning Neanderthal man.

Naturally, he had ancestors. A prime candidate for one of these is *homo erectus,* who was found both in Africa and China around 500,000 years ago. *Erectus* possessed fire, cooked his food, and lived in cooperative groups.

For present purposes we take 500,000 BP as our starting point. Throughout this half-million-year span (as also during the previous 1,500,000 years), a rapid succession of Ice Ages of differing lengths come and go. Officially, some now think there may have been as many as twenty Ice Ages. Such periods, by their quality of desperation, are believed to lead to very rapid evolution.

In Africa, then, in 500,000 BP, we have an evolving type of man whom I shall refer to as Neanderthal 1. In the Far East (Malay/Borneo and China), we have at the same period Neanderthal 2. These two related types are already diverging slightly from each other.

Now, especially during the warmer spells in between the actual Ice Ages, African Neanderthal (Neanderthal 1) can and does move up into Europe, via what is now Egypt and Israel. The climate of these times is, though, very complicated. But what generally occurred was this: Whenever Europe was warm, the Sahara became a desert—an uncrossable one. Some types of Neanderthal 1 would be cut off south of it, isolating them for the time being from their relatives in Europe and the Middle East. When Europe was *cold*, the Sahara was a grassy plain covered with rivers and occasional trees. It was crossable once more. But, on the other hand, after the very first colonization of Europe, some Neanderthals found themselves stuck in southern Greece, southern Italy, and southern Spain when the ice returned. They never got back to Africa. (In Asia, where Neanderthal 2 was evolving, no such geographical problems of free movement north and south arose.)

In short, the Neanderthals of Europe/Africa became in time the Neanderthals of Europe *and* Africa. They became separate subvarieties with only occasional mingling in the Middle East and North Africa at certain times. We can refer to them as Neanderthal 1a and 1b respectively.

But here is a most crucial point. Because of his continual flirting with the cold of the actual ice, European Neanderthal—Neanderthal 1a—did *not* lose the body hair that all his relatives had by this time typically, wholly or partly, evolved away.

So around 500,000 years BP and after, we have something like this situation:

Europe	—	Neanderthal 1a
Africa	—	Neanderthal 1b
Asia	—	Neanderthal 2

Even this is not quite the end of it. During the last 100,000 years, yet a new subvariety of man evolved. Some Neanderthals of the 1a variety were then trapped in central and western Europe during an Ice Age. Fortunately they had fire and there were deep caves, but even so the odds were against them. Incredibly, they survived. They evolved into the so-called classic Neanderthal. This type is, in many ways, the least human of all types—at any rate from our modern, chauvinist standpoint. He was more stunted and powerful than any other Neanderthal, probably entirely covered with thick hair.

So, finally, for Europe we have to read:

Europe — Neanderthal 1a ⟨ "classic" variety / regular variety

Throughout all this time and all these movements, Cro-Magnon, of course, continues to evolve in northern India, minding his own business, and for the time being unknown.

THE HYBRID

My basic view is—and it is supported by the mixed skeletons found in Israel dated 35,000–25,000 years BP—that with weather conditions once again improving, Cro-Magnon decided to leave India for the first time in 35,000 BP, heading west. Perhaps he was following the sun. He then met and interbred with Neanderthal man, initially in the Middle East.

Sometimes when I am lecturing on these matters I present my audience with the following list of questions—to which there is, of course, no single answer: Do elephants have large ears or small ears? Do camels have one hump or two? Do male sheep have horns or not? Do shrimp live in salt water or fresh water? Do members of the cat family live alone or in groups?

There is no single answer to any of these questions because, in every case, we are talking about more than one species.

Here are some more questions: Do human males go bald in later life or not? Do they have straight hair or curly hair? Do they have fair hair or dark hair? Do they have fair skin or dark skin? Do they have hair on their chests or not? Do they have canine teeth or not? Do they mate with one woman for life, or do they take several wives simultaneously?

We are, surely, talking about more than one species of man. The odd thing, though, is that certainly in Europe, the Middle East, and India the two species (for it is two) live all mixed up together. There is actually an endless list of the questions I have just asked about man; and the answers to all of them lead us to the conclusion that we are talking about more than one species.

It is also possible to show, for instance, that vegetarianism is much more popular in some countries and in some subcultures than in others, where instead meat-eating is preferred. In the south of India, for example, vegetables are preferred, in the north meat. The reasons are by no means always economic. Or rather, the "economic reasons"—that is, the lifestyle—and the other reasons are aspects of each other, aspects of an attitude to life. It is, again, possible to show that the instinctive gesture of submission in some peoples is that of lowering the head, while in others it consists of presenting the buttocks.[1]

What is most interesting of all—and the final word in this form of argument—is that these various pairs of opposite psychological and biological possibilities tend to cluster together. The possession of so-called canine teeth, for example, is associated with tallness, and large, flat teeth with shortness; while tallness and fair skin, and shortness and dark skin, are in general similarly associated.

These are, of course, *very* broad generalizations that, in any case, do not apply equally or regardless in all parts of the world. Africa, perhaps, deviates most from these guidelines. (Yet, while Africans, with dark skins, produce some of the tallest people in the world, they also produce the shortest, the Pygmies.) The uneven mixing of the various subvarieties—Neanderthals 1a, 1b, and 2—with Cro-Magnon does not result in as neat a final design as one could wish. But the main general outlines of the picture, though they waver, I believe stand.

The Neanderthal element in our makeup is universal. I have to emphasize that. It is found in *all* peoples of the world; and it is always everywhere in a sense, the minority element. As a whole, modern man more resembles Cro-Magnon than he does Neanderthal. But some present-day ethnic groups do have a slightly *greater* admixture of the Neanderthal strain than others. This is true of all Asiatics and Africans. In "Europe" it is truest of Jews, Gypsies, and most Mediterranean peoples (including here the Celts), and least true of north and west Europeans (excepting the Celts).

This hybrid ancestry is, on the one hand, our great strength. From it we derive our great vigor and inventiveness, and to it we owe the release of the great potential man has always possessed. But our hybrid nature is also our weakness, our Achilles' heel, and one of the main sources of the "divided self." Individual members of our society feel torn within themselves, while modern society as a whole continually seeks to tear itself apart—into religion and science, socialism and conservatism, communism and fascism, peaceable farmers and aggressive hunters, the male society and the female society. This continuing struggle has taken many different forms in past and present, but underneath it is always the same struggle.

The version of the struggle that concerns us in this book is that of the moon goddess and the sun god.

MOON GODDESS VERSUS SUN GOD

If we avoid particulars, my position in this field is the same as that of the already mentioned Robert Graves, Margaret Murray, J. G. Frazer, Tom Lethbridge, and many others. This position is that there exists throughout recorded and legendary history, right up to the present, traces of an ancient religion. This was principally a goddess worship (moon goddess,

earth goddess, all mother), involving fertility rites and probably orgiastic rituals. For some reason or reasons, it fell from official grace in late
prehistoric times and was driven underground. There, nonetheless, it
remained both vigorous and widespread, claiming many followers and
leaving clear marks of its presence even on the rituals and places of worship of orthodox religion.

What I feel that other writers have failed to appreciate, even though
they are aware that the ancient religion is somehow more about goddesses than gods, is that the ancient religion itself consists of a *very*
ancient level, overlaid with something else less ancient that came after.
There are actually plenty of hints toward this position in the specialist
literature. The *New Larousse Encyclopedia of Mythology,* for example,
talking of the days before classical Greece, states: "The chief deity of the
Aegeans was—like that of many Asiatic cults—feminine. She was the
Great Goddess, the *Universal Mother.*"[2]

We do not know the actual name the Aegeans gave her, but in Crete
she was called Rhea. In that mythology Zeus (later the chief god of the
Greeks) was the son of Rhea. Similarly, as we shall see in a moment,
Osiris was originally the son of Isis, not her brother and husband. In
symbolic form both these accounts are telling us that an original goddess worship was replaced by a (later) god worship. (Hesiod, the ancient
Greek poet, citing Gaea as the original goddess, calls her "deep-breasted
Gaea, universal mother, firmly founded, the oldest of divinities." The
precise links here with the figurines on pp. 68–69 are obvious.)

Further afield in China, we find a very complex official worship and
pantheon (resembling very much a kind of bureaucratic civil service promoted to heaven), which incorporates homage to both sun and moon.
But this complex superstructure is overlaid on what is called the religion of the people. There is nothing forbidden about this other religion,
however, it is a public phenomenon. In the people's religion, the moon
receives more sacrifices than the sun, and the Festival of the Moon is one
of the three great annual Chinese feasts. It takes place at the full moon
nearest the autumn equinox. *Larousse* tells us: "It is especially a festival

for women and children. . . . *Men never take part in this ceremony*" [my italics].

The Chinese calendar is a moon-sun calendar known as the *yin-yang li.* C. A. Ronan states, however, that this was probably originally purely a moon-calendar, and that in any case the lunar details of it are more important than the solar. I have myself suggested (p. 5) that the yin yang symbol itself is a stylized moon.

As I remarked earlier, religious mythology and history are so complex a confusion that almost any interpretation of events can be made by careful selection of examples. ("Indian mythology is an inextricable jungle of luxuriant growths . . . in Mexico the innumerable crowd of deities"—*Larousse.)* And, certainly, one does find both moon *gods* and sun *goddesses.* Yet the following generalizations hold. There are more moon goddesses than moon gods, and there are many more sun gods than sun goddesses. Also, goddess worship is universally older than god worship—and its ancient preeminence can still be glimpsed under the more modern and masculine structures.

The other writers I named earlier believe that what *they* call the ancient religion was brought into Europe (from the east) by the people known as the Indo-Europeans, sometime before 6000 BP. They do not speculate what the existing religion of Europe might have been at that point.

Yet Graves does argue that Isis, "the horned moon-goddess," only "subsequently" became the sister and wife of Osiris; and that originally she was his mother. Also, Ashe's bear-cult of the far north is fairly obviously a night-religion in view of its allegiance to the Plough or Great Bear constellation (to say nothing of its links with actual Neanderthal some tens of thousands of years earlier). This particular religion seems very much at variance with the daylight worship of the stag. Do there not seem to be somewhat different tendencies or traditions here?

I myself have no doubt that there are, indeed, two very different kinds of tradition involved. But first a word about dates.

Orthodox theory (and here we must include Robert Graves and others as orthodox) believes that the Indo-Europeans came to Europe from the east, between six and ten thousand years ago. Apparently they took over the whole of Europe from eastern Russia to western Ireland, and from the tip of Italy to Norway, Iceland, and Greenland. Quite a take-over! And yet in folklore and legend we have no whisper of any such alleged takeover. Surely if the influence of the number seven or the number thirteen, as well as actual religious practices, can come down to us over the same time span, then so could tales of the entry into and over-running of Europe?

Moreover, when a new, powerful race of people comes and takes over a whole continent, we expect to find what the archaeologists call a "cultural horizon." When one nation takes over from another, one type of pottery, weaponry, style of house, and so on is then suddenly replaced by another—or at least is suddenly mixed with another. And much later as we dig down through the layers of old buildings and refuse, there it suddenly is—the horizon, the point where culture X met culture Y.

But in the Europe of six to ten thousand BC, despite the alleged massive takeover, we find no trace of any cultural horizon whatsoever. Pots and weapons evolve slowly and continuously on, without a break.

Can we find the massive kind of cultural horizon we are looking for at any earlier point? Yes, we can. It is when the Mousterian culture is suddenly (in archaeological terms) replaced by the Aurignacian culture, in a spreading wave from East to West across Europe. This is *also* the point at which Cro-Magnon appears and pure Neanderthal vanishes. The date is 30,000 BP.

"Mousterian" is the name given to the culture of Neanderthal, found prior to the events we are discussing all over Europe. There are slight variations of style in different localities, but these are far outweighed by the similarities of the, although effective, rather inelegant flint tools. The tools of the Aurignacian culture, the culture of Cro-Magnon, are immediately different. These are lighter and more elegant, to the point of being exquisite; and are yet more diversified than the already appreciable range of Neanderthal tools.

I suggest that the Mousterian tools are those of the general purpose man, the odd-job killer and hunter; while the Aurignacian tools are those of the specialist, the professional warrior and hunter. It seems no coincidence that the superb cave paintings Cro-Magnon has left us not only show the same degree of skill as the tools but are almost without exception those of *antlered* and *horned* game animals. Cro-Magnon, it seems, was a dedicated hunter and these, in particular, are the animals he worshipped along with the sun, and the ones he preferred to hunt and eat.

Do we have anywhere at all any suggestion of a protracted battle between two totally different types of man (such as the takeover of Europe demanded), and especially of the battle with the stunted, deformed classic Neanderthal? Yes, again I think we do. It is in the oldest of fairy tales, which tell us that the woods and mountains of Europe were once haunted by fearsome trolls and goblins. That is, by the Little People.

My proposal is very simple and is a very elegant solution to the theoretical problems mentioned a little earlier. It does, though, involve a small time-shift of some 20,000 years. My proposal is that Cro-Magnon and the Indo-Europeans (the ancestors of the modern inhabitants of Europe) are one and the same people.

Harold Wilson said that in politics a week is a long time. In the history of man, however, 20,000 years is not such a long time. Already 500,000 years ago, for example, *homo erectus* had fire, cooked his food, and lived in permanent cave sites. Moreover, throughout the present century the time-space allotted to the existence of man, unmistakably as man, has steadily been extended, until we now believe that man as man has been in existence for four million years. We can certainly afford to stretch our recent time scales by a mere 20,000 of those years.

NEANDERTHAL MOON CULTURE (AS I SEE IT)

Though men did the heavy work, the fighting and killing when necessary, and made most of the tools, the religious and economic life of the people was run by women. Their religious influence, moreover, extended into all aspects of life. No doubt there were days when tool-making was forbidden, for example. That which was worshipped was "the female principle." In its unearthly form this was the Goddess—the Moon Goddess and the All Mother combined. Perhaps there were minor goddesses also, and perhaps all of them, including the supreme deity, had husbands; but these played no major role.

On earth, woman was the incarnation of the divine principle, and as such she was sacred, as were all her womanly attributes. Menstruation, governed by the moon, was the continual sign of the presence of the Goddess and her continuous power. All the women of the tribe menstruated together, and these were the holiest of holy days, the time of the new moon. Pregnant women did not menstruate, and these were, therefore, the especially favored of the Goddess, temporarily relieved of the warning sign of mankind's subservience to the Goddess. So it was clear, therefore, that the Goddess loved children and that these were her special property. But also all nature and all fecundity were hers and the cycle of the seasons and the wheeling of the stars, and the movement of the sea.

At night the Goddess reigned in all her changing, moody glory among her myriad circling courtiers. By day she allowed her unvarying, shackled consort to run his monotonous, and always prescribed, path across the sky. He first rose to glory but then bowed in submission to her throughout the year.

But the moon was always new.

DEFENSE

Here, first, are some of the prehistoric "Venus" figurines (see figure 4) found all over Europe. These appear from around 30,000 BP onward.

As is clear, these are fertility figures. Breasts, buttocks, thighs, genitals, and pregnancy are glorified. Head and feet are diminutive and stylized, and facial features are unimportant. Though the figures are certainly exaggerated, we have good reason to believe that they are not *too* far

Figure 4. (a) Front, side, and back views of figurine from Kostienki.

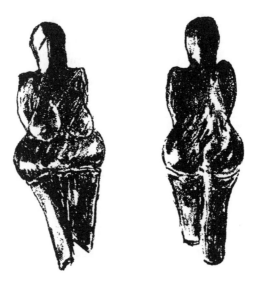

(b) Front and back views of figurine from Monrovia.

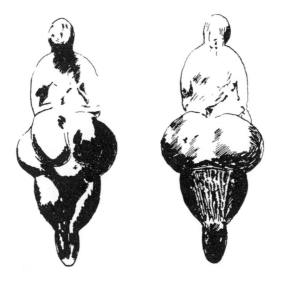

(c) Front and back views of figurine from France.

from life—for they resemble the women of some present-day African tribes, notably the Bushmen and Hottentots. Incidentally, while Neanderthal anatomy with its heavy bones and barrel body could support such a physique, Cro-Magnon anatomy could not. There is one further thing we can say with absolute certainty about such a woman: a huntress she wasn't.

Another figure (figure 5), a relief carving from France, shows another "Venus" balancing a horn on her raised hand.

This figure is important for many reasons. It unquestionably allows us to associate the horn with the mother-goddess independently of any connection with hunting. This horn is a symbol of fertility, as all commentators agree. It is also, I suggest, unmistakably the horned, crescent moon.

Here we have to note, too, that the "horn" and "horny" are slang terms for the male organ in erection and sexual excitement, and that, in Shakespeare's day, the phrase "wearing the horns" meant that a husband

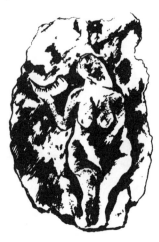

Figure 5. Venus figure and horn from France (relief carving).

was being cuckolded by his wife. This is the origin of our horned V sign of two raised fingers, which we use as an insult today.

Yet there is, perhaps, a more crucial point still. I have said I believe that Cro-Magnon worshipped the horned stag and bull, and many cave paintings support this view. At the point when he came around to conceptualizing his god, he made him a male god and gave him horns. He was also a daylight god, identified with the sun. (The eclipsed sun reveals the horns of solar flares.) In the course of time, Cro-Magnon more and more vigorously promoted this form of religion (which, of course, went on evolving and becoming more and more complex) against the older, "womanized," moon worship. And if you, as a Neanderthal or part-Neanderthal were wise, you went along with this forced conversion—for otherwise you died. But it is more than possible that many reluctant converts went along with the conversion only outwardly and with this secret proviso: "We will outwardly worship the horned god of the hunters; but inwardly we will be worshipping the horned moon of our own faith."

Fortunately we have many precedents of just such subterfuge. In the eighteenth century, there were many nobles loyal to the Catholic would-be King James III of England in exile in France. When asked to drink the loyal toast to the Protestant monarchy, they first passed their glasses over the finger-bowls. This meant "we are drinking to the king across the water." Similarly again, when the Marrano Jews of Spain and Portugal were forcibly converted to Christianity by the Inquisition, they introduced elements of Jewish ritual into the Christian service. This meant that their descendants were still practicing the Jewish faith (though in this case they did not know it). These Jewish rituals are still in use among these "Catholic" families to the present day. And Marranos still marry Marranos.

In the context of the coalescing of (secret) moon worship with (public) stag/sun worship, we can understand anomalies like Diana the moon-goddess becoming a huntress (see p. 36) and the fact that Pan becomes associated with orgiastic fertility ceremonies. The Roman *cornucopia* or "horn of plenty" (i.e., fertility) is probably also linked to these matters.

Now to yet other evidence. I have suggested that both the menstruating woman and the pregnant woman were sacred. Among Jews, a "Neanderthal" people, we find very severe prohibitions indeed (accompanied by flogging and the curse of an early death) against a man having sexual relations with a menstruating woman. After menstruation also, the woman must attend a ritual bath (the *Mikveh*) to be ceremonially purified.

What we see here, of course, and will see much more of below, is the commonplace circumstance of that which was sacred becoming that which is accursed. As we well know, what an existing religion holds sacred is often stigmatized as unholy by the new religion that supplants it. Graves comments: "Demons and bogeys are invariably the reduced gods or priests of a superseded religion." Murray notes: "When invasion is warlike the conquering deity is invested with all good attributes, while the god of the vanquished takes a lower place and is regarded by the conquerors as the producer of evil, and is consequently often more feared than their own legitimate deity."

We can turn these statements around and restate them. *Whenever we find rigorous repression or avoidance of any practice or condition, we can with fair assurance assume that the practice or condition was once holy.* This could even apply to a practice such as incest. We also note that among the Pharaohs, for instance, brother married sister.

It is ultimately in what I term the "Neanderthal" races today that we look to find the strongest taboos, for here the residue of Neanderthal ways and attitudes is strongest.

Among Gypsies, another "Neanderthal" group, we find an even stronger version of the menstruation (or perhaps fertility) taboo. Women must wash their hands after touching any part of the lower body *below* the waist, even when fully clothed, before touching any part of the body *above* the waist, even when fully clothed. They may not even wear a full or continuous dress. They must wear one garment above the waist and another below—a blouse and skirt, for example. Any crockery or plates that a woman accidentally touches with her skirt must be destroyed, particularly if the woman has recently given birth to a child.

Among Australian Aborigines a menstruating woman is forbidden to touch anything a man uses, under pain of death. She may not even walk on a path used by males. During childbirth women are held in seclusion and all vessels used by them are subsequently burned. Precisely the same rules apply in Uganda. In Tahiti women are secluded from all contact with other human beings for two to three weeks after childbirth. The same holds in Alaska, where a special hovel is even built for the woman. Food is reached to her on sticks.

What a reversal from the figurines of figure 4. For surely these are beloved objects. (And yet "sacred" and "accursed," as Freud noted, have always been particularly close opposites.)

In Europe proper we find a similar kind, though a lesser degree, of such fears. These are found more in country districts than in towns (the "Neanderthal" element being stronger there, see p. 80). There it is said that the touch or presence of a menstruating woman kills bees, kills seeds, makes beer, wine, and milk go bad, dims mirrors, corrodes metal, and causes animals to miscarry. Some sources say that these effects are more marked "at the waning of the moon."

Gypsies, incidentally, are still self-professed moon worshippers, as were once, in all probability, the Jews. So here are links enough for our general purpose. It is again, I suggest, precisely because of the moon and other "Neanderthal" links of these two peoples that they have been so persecuted throughout historical times.

Another strong "Neanderthal" connection among Jews and Gypsies is the tendency to allow women (despite the menstrual and pregnancy taboos) an equal or more than equal say, especially in matters pertaining to the general welfare of the tribe. This is a separate issue from that of matrilineal descent, which we nevertheless find with Australian Aborigines, the Pharaohs, and again the Jews, and which is also a "Neanderthal" feature. So we find that while Gypsy tribes have a male chieftain and a council of male elders, this council also consults the Tribal Mother. Her power is separate from theirs and her views carry great weight. In this connection, too, we can note the apocryphal authority of the "Jewish mother."

But a more significant link is with the "wise woman" of former times. Though only found active today in gypsy tribes and in occasional voodoo centers like Haiti, she was clearly once a general and revered figure. Prehistoric burials often show evidence of this position. One such burial is that of the "Fox Lady" of Dolni Vestonice in Czechoslovakia, 23,000 years BP.

> The skeleton is that of a small and elegantly built woman, five foot three inches, and about forty years old, which is very old for those days. She had been given an elaborate burial inside one of the huts, laid in a prepared hollow on the left side in a contracted position, facing west. Body and head were covered with red ochre and protected by two shoulder-blades of mammoth, one of which had a network of irregular lines incised on its surface. With the woman were placed her stone tools, and close to her left hand the paws and tail

of an arctic fox, with the teeth in her other hand. The ceremonial of crouched burial and the westward facing position of the body were already part of the rite of Neanderthal burial during the Ice Age. . . . Great spiritual or intellectual power must have belonged to the slight old woman who had been singled out for such careful burial.[3]

The oldest sculpture ever found (dated between 30,000 and 25,000 BP) not far away in Brno belonged to a man of "rather primitive physical type: robust with unusually heavy brow ridges very slightly hollowed between the eyes."

Notice the strong Neanderthal connections in both these cases. I have not dragged them in. These are the words of N. K. Sandars, one of the foremost living authorities on prehistoric art.

Without much of a stretch of the imagination, the Fox Lady can link us both with the priestesses of the ancient Mysteries and the wise woman of folk tales. While Murray also remarks that in fairy stories the Little People appear to be ruled by the Elfin or Faerie Queen, rather than by any king.

This, too, is possibly the best moment to mention the figure of the Virgin Mary in the Catholic pantheon. Her importance to the average Catholic in some ways actually exceeds that of Christ, and it is probable that more prayers are offered to her than to her son. The parallels between Rhea and Mary cannot be overlooked (both gave birth to the All Father, for example). But I am not this time arguing so much a historical connection as an independent development arising out of a deep psychological need. Later we shall see that the All Mother is in no way simply a historical or sociological phenomenon, but a permanent feature of the human psyche.

Two more "Neanderthal" behaviors are (1) a high, general level of superstition, and (2) a doting love for children. These I will be considering also along with the psychological nature of the All Mother. But the relevance of these two behaviors for the purposes of this chapter is noted and emphasized. These are two more of the elements that bind (or bound) Neanderthal society together and distinguish it from that of Cro-Magnon.

What can be looked at in a little more detail is the knowledge of, and skill in, administering herbal and nature remedies. This tradition, found again in Gypsies, has a long Neanderthal history. In 1951 Professor Ralph Solecki began a lengthy series of excavations in a cave at Shanidar in Iraq. This cave was occupied in all for a period of tens of thousands of years by Neanderthal man, and several burials had taken place here. One of these dates from 60,000 years BP. This dead man was ceremonially buried in a huge mass of flowers and a great feast was held upon the grave. But this is the more important point. The majority of the plants used in the burial are known for their medicinal properties. The people who live in the Shanidar region today use these same plants for medication. (So here we have a tradition apparently unbroken for 60,000 years.) On this evidence alone we need not doubt Neanderthal's knowledge of natural medicine.

To me it seems more likely that a browser-gatherer would have discovered the properties of plants than a hunter.

CRO-MAGNON SUN CULTURE

Cro-Magnon loved and feared the sun. He loved it because, in the summer, when it reached its high point above the horizon, the game grew fat. Then came the hunting, which he loved best of all (better even than fighting and sporting), and the great feasts. Meanwhile the children grew straight and tall. But in the winter, and in the years when the Sun-God hid his angry face even in summer, the children grew sickly, with bent limbs, and the game vanished. (The children of Neanderthal in Europe also sometimes grew bent from lack of vitamin D: but Neanderthal never learned that this was a gift the sun gave and took away.)

When the last of the dried meat was gone, there was only fish, and the fish also became few. Sometimes then the people ate mud.

Cro-Magnon saw that the sun gave and took all life, and that though

He withdrew, He always came again. And He always would come, as long as man worshipped Him and gave the human sacrifices He wanted. It was the iron law of life and it was just. One expected no less of an all-powerful god.

Best of all was when the sun shone.

DEFENSE

Sun worship is such a well-known phenomenon of historical times that it needs little describing or defense. Many of the great gods of antiquity are sun-gods: Ra of the Egyptians, Helios and Apollo in Greece, Sol of the Romans, Shamash of the Assyrians and Babylonians. Christianity is also a sun religion (Christ is the light of the world and the glorious radiance). Nazism, too, is basically a sun religion.*

The festival of the winter solstice (found among virtually all peoples) is the festival of the birthday of the sun, for from then on he is reborn, growing stronger daily. The Saturnalia (see p. 35) is a sun festival and so is Christmas, which replaced it after the conversion of Europe. Midsummer Day is the festival when the sun is strongest, and at the equinoxes are the Spring and Harvest festivals.

However, these last matters are of prime concern to farmers and agriculturalists and so cannot have originated earlier than ten thousand years ago. Most certainly the development of agriculture did give a major fillip to sun worship. But I myself consider that the essential masculinity of sun worship is of far older origin. This is a psychological matter requiring a psychological explanation as will become clear.

A POSSIBLE VIEW OF EVENTS

My own view, as I have said, is that when Cro-Magnon entered Europe (from the East), he was already well on the path toward full-fledged

---

*For further discussion of these matters see *The Neanderthal Question*.

sun worship. (Perhaps in traveling west he was following the sun.) In the Middle East and Europe, however, he found a type of human very different from himself—Neanderthal—who was well on the way to full-fledged moon worship.

The exact state of complexity or self-consciousness that these two respective religions had reached by then is actually not too important. For what we are really discussing is the worship of the *female principle* and the worship of the *male principle.* These are among the enduring motivations of human kind, built into the very fabric of his being, as, in fact, they are into the very fabric of the universe.[4] Moon worship and sun worship are only two fairly recent expressions of these two eternal principles.

It is not the case that Cro-Magnon entirely lacked any sense of the "female principle" or that Neanderthal lacked any sense of the "male principle." That would be impossible. Both principles were present in both by basic construction. But what is nevertheless true is that Cro-Magnon had capitalized on his "male" endowment and was to do so further; while Neanderthal had capitalized on his "female" endowment and was about to do so further, or rather *would try* to do so further, he would meet in Cro-Magnon a (temporarily) stronger force that would oppose that development.

I have described in my earlier book on this subject what I believe took place in the Middle East 35,000 years ago, when these two varieties of man came into contact for the first time. Briefly, it was this.

Cro-Magnon, a superior fighter, overran the Neanderthals of the Middle and Near East in short order. In any case, they made little attempt at resistance. The Cro-Magnon males took the usual conqueror's advantage of Neanderthal woman. Some of Cro-Magnon's number perhaps also stayed and "went native." A hybrid population now arose in this part of the world. Meanwhile, the main body of the Cro-Magnon peoples marched on into Europe, *taking no Neanderthals with them* at this time.

In Europe Cro-Magnon discovered classic Neanderthal (see p. 70), a total affront to his humanity. This variety of man he simply erases from the planet—a kind of "final solution" of that problem. The event is recorded in our "fairytales" of misshapen dwarfs, who among other things kidnap and eat human children, work magic, and live and move by night.

But fairly soon after these happenings—at least, fairly soon as far as nature is concerned—a new Ice Age begins. Cro-Magnon, the conqueror of Europe, is driven down into the southern extremities of that continent. Here, during the next ten thousand years, he survives with difficulty and with reduced numbers. Gradually, too, his ranks are infiltrated with mixed types from the Near East. Pure Cro-Magnon now virtually ceases to exist, but traces of his physical type are still found today in the western and northern fringes of Europe. Pure Neanderthal has also ceased to exist, but traces of his physical type can be seen to this day, especially in Asia and Africa, in the southern Mediterranean and the Middle East, and perhaps most notably of all among the Jews.

So much for biological events. But what has been happening sociologically and psychologically?

The "half-breeds" of the Middle and Near East behaved as do such people to the present day. They tried to be as much like the "superior" parent race as possible, so they endorsed that race's social and religious customs and attitudes. Such dispossessed peoples often go further even than necessary. They "lean over forward," so to speak, in order to distinguish themselves from the "natives" (whom, of course, they nevertheless somewhat resemble).

The purer varieties of Cro-Magnon in Europe, over the millennia, behaved much like the South Africans and Rhodesians of today. They did everything in their power to remain separate and on top (as in ancient Greece). But slowly, slowly, their position and their absolute monopoly of events was eroded. As in present-day South Africa, it became harder and harder to see just who was a half-breed (or a quarter, or an eighth breed, or whatever). There was, too, another kind of pressure, and this was simply numerical.

For "Neanderthal" is more fruitful in terms of number of live babies produced, and in terms also of general survival stamina. He is simply hardier, and better at staying the course when the course is bad. So over the millennia—and, in fact, right from the first days of the first mingling 25,000 years ago—the proportion of "Neanderthals" in the world in relation to the "Cro-Magnons" has steadily increased.

These various events, one way and another and sometimes paradoxically, cause the social and religious structures of "Cro-Magnon" to become ever more rigid and repressive in respect of "Neanderthal" and *his* social and religious leanings. Less and less as time goes on can "Cro-Magnon" afford to tolerate the presence and influence of "Neanderthal." (One specific outcome—one direct action—is that all thirteens of the old moon-calendar are changed to the twelves of the new, and thirteen itself is stigmatized as evil and ungodly.)

This repressive/destructive "Cro-Magnon" movement eventually reaches its insane peak in the behavior of Nazi Germany, and to a milder extent in the McCarthyism of America and the fascism of Spain.

However, partly in reaction to the ever-increasing repression inflicted upon it, the "Neanderthal" element in turn becomes counterrepressive and, in fact, revolutionary. This countermovement reaches its also insane peak in Communist Russia, in the horrors of the French Revolution, and to a milder extent, in the activity of left-wing groups throughout the world. These various movements, apparently antiracist, are themselves entirely racist in origin, as I am trying to show.

THIRTEEN AGAIN

Modern man is not simply a hybrid. He is unfortunately what the biologists call an unstable hybrid. His two ancestries cohabit only uneasily in the one body, the one skull, and the one society. The "Cro-Magnon" and "Neanderthal" mix behaves like an unstable emulsion of oil and water. The oil constantly seeks to rise and the water constantly seeks to sink—both to realize their separate potential and their unique being. The respective ethics involved here at the social level are (as generalizations) those of "the aristocracy" versus "the people." Each, of course, thinks of itself as the only thing that matters. Further forms of the same attempt at separation are "town" and "country"; and "bosses" and "workers." There are many others besides.

With what justification do I speak of the Neanderthal and Cro-Magnon elements in our ancestry as being an unstable emulsion of oil and water that does not gel? Where does this happen in nature?

The answer is that it does not happen in nature. Like homosexuality and asexuality (see chapter 4), the nonmix is a condition that continually puts paid to itself. It breeds itself out by definition and from the first moment of its own existence. But we *can* readily produce incompatible instinctive tendencies in a single animal in the laboratory. The example of the hybrid cross between the Peach-Faced Lovebird and Fischer's Lovebird is instructive. These two species have different, wholly instinctive ways of carrying nest material. The former carries the leaves and bark tucked into its rump feathers, and the latter carries them in its beak. The hybrid offspring is found to possess *both* instinctive behaviors of both parents.

So the unfortunate offspring tears itself off a strip of bark. This its Peach-Faced ancestry instructs it to push into its rump feathers, which the bird does. However, the bird's Fischer instincts refuse to let it release the material from its beak—for it is not yet at the nest. So the bird resumes the ready-to-fly position with the material still in its mouth. The Peach-Faced instinct, noting that nest material is in the beak, again instructs the bird to place this in its rump feathers. And so the cycle repeats itself without conclusion. It would mean certain death for this bird in nature.

What is a laboratory freak as far as animals are concerned is an everyday fact of life for us (Faustian man), with our "two souls in one breast." We each of us bear two sets of incompatible instincts, in greater or lesser measure. The evidence can be found in every human activity.

Take the romantic European love story, for example, the standard basis for an endless flood of paperback novels and stories in women's magazines. In the large majority of these stories, the hero is torn between two girls. One is a straightforward, decent, honest, moral, loyal, home loving, *fair-haired, blue-eyed* girl, who really loves him. The other is a shameless, sexy, greedy, immoral, passionate, *dark-haired, brown-eyed* hussy. (She may well even be a Gypsy!) The first girl wants to marry the man, bear his children, and help him in his career. The second girl is only out to catch and ensnare him, to spend his money, to bend him to her wild will, and make him leave his family and his job, and follow her into disgrace. Then she will leave him for another man, because her depraved sexual appetite is insatiable.

Another version of the same story is where a girl is torn between two men. One is reliable, dependable, loyal, predictable, genuinely loves her, wants to marry her, buy a house, and have children, etc., who has *fair hair and blue eyes.* The other is a handsome, dark-haired, incredibly attractive and sensual, animalistic rotter, who is only after *one thing,* and when he's had that he'll be off. All he can do is to ruin a girl's happiness—but he is so sexy and attractive, that when she's with him all her common sense and moral values and her love for what's-his-name fly out the window.

But this is all true, you see. It has been an enduring theme of west European literature since literature was invented.

Basically involved here are, in general terms, the two general Neanderthal and Cro-Magnon endowments. What is involved, in particular, is pair-bonding on the one hand and promiscuity on the other.

In this connection, let us remember W. N. Stephens's report on the promiscuous Indian tribe (p. 56). There, as we saw, the father of a child could not be known, and no male had any claim on any woman or any child. It is clear that in any such social set-up a bloodline can only be traced through the woman, through the mother. Many "Neanderthal" peoples have the remains of a system of tracing bloodlines and of conveying property and civic and religious titles through the female—the Australian Aborigines, the Jews, the ancient Egyptians, and (as we shall see) the Celts. *The very existence of such a system of tracing descent argues for an original culture in which male-female sex was wholly promiscuous.*

As I have said, such a state of affairs—such a clash of opposite instincts—is not and could not be found in the animal kingdom. Only in a self-conscious and, to an extent, self-governing entity such as ourselves can such conflicts, up to a point, be tolerated and dealt with. Even so, a partial solution is only possible in the last analysis because the general instinctive basis of our lives is weaker. We are in the process of evolving-out what used to be nature's only means of regulating life—the absolute rule of inherited instinct. We, the first creature to do so on this planet, have changed the rules—or had them changed for us. In us, nature is in the process of designing a truly self-governing organism—but, unfortunately for us, the project has only just left the drawing-board. The prototype is not very good—and there are still far too many clashes in us between our instinctive desires and our conscious decisions; as well, of course, as between our opposing instincts, the point here.

Reverting to our general theme, some of the original mixed types of the Middle East, instead of following Cro-Magnon into Europe, turned eastward. They went back through India and into China. Not too long after, mixed types also pushed across the Russian-Alaskan land bridge and colonized North and South America.

In China and the rest of the eastern world, we have a situation where genuine Neanderthals (Neanderthal 2) are overrun by a mixed Cro-Magnon/Neanderthal type. In all senses of the terms there is here, in the end (despite the pretensions of the newcomers), much less of a cultural and psychological shock. The newcomers are absorbed or, as we say today, integrated. Again we have hybridization, but all-in-all we have a much more balanced position.

It leads, really, to the yin-yang philosophy of ancient China, in which both "male" and "female" principles are given equal weight. Yet even so, this statement of the position is still much more intuitive than scientifically rational. The whole question of "intuitive thought" is a major issue.

But, perhaps, the real evidence for an integration as opposed to a repression hypothesis in the East is the attitude outside Europe to the number thirteen.

We have already seen that the Chinese basically favored the moon over the sun, so we would already, perhaps, expect to find thirteen not stigmatized as unlucky. And, in fact, we do find traces of this number embedded in religious ritual in Asia. Thirteen "mystical discs" surmount Chinese (and Indian) pagodas. Enshrined in the temple of Atsura in Japan is a sacred sword with "thirteen objects of mystery" forming its hilt. But it is in central and South America (furthest away from the main "Cro-Magnon" influence and thirteen repression of Europe) that we find absolutely clear proof that thirteen was once a fortunate, favorable, and most sacred number.

First we should mention just once again that the native North American and South American Indians are migrated Asiatic stock coming mainly from China, who passed into North America via the Bering Strait and the Aleutian Islands. These migrations began about 20 or 25,000 years ago—*after* the admixture of the "Cro-Magnon" element.

(Because of that migration the Mayas in South America call the constellation we know as Scorpio by the same name. Our Orion the Hunter, Aries the Ram, and Taurus the Bull also have their equivalents in China. Then, the Chinese speak of the years of the Dragon, the Snake, the Rabbit, the Dog, and the Monkey, while the Aztec calendar has the days of the Alligator, Snake, Rabbit, Dog, and Monkey. "[The names] were repeated without question substantially the same from Mexico to Africa and Polynesia—and have remained with us to this day.")

Throughout the religion and culture of the Mayan, Aztec, Inca, and Mexican civilizations, thirteen is a "very significant number" and an integral component of the calendar. Thirteen is the "most sacred number" of the Mexicans. Tonacatecotle presides over the "thirteen causes." Among Aztecs the thirteen-day period defined by the day numerals was of prime importance, and the list of deities designated as Lords of the Day numbers thirteen. H. B. Alexander tells us: "The Hopi Indians—a fact of especial interest—make use of thirteen points on the horizon for the determination of ceremonial dates." Presumably the interest lies in the fact that these are the Pueblo Indians of Northern Arizona. But thirteen also figures centrally in the rites of the Osage tribes of Missouri and Kansas. The Toltec of Central America describe the universe as composed of "twelve heavens and the Earth"—which is, incidentally, another coven. H. B. Alexander comments that "the origin of the peculiar uses of the number thirteen in Central and South America is a puzzle without satisfactory solution." But he should have said: "and North America."

Perhaps now we have the answer to this riddle. It is that a very ancient variety of early man once worshipped the moon and the moon alone. All her attributes were sacred, including the thirteen new or full moons seen each year. Later, partly by reason of what I term "Cro-Magnon" influence, and also ultimately for practical reasons connected with the planting of crops and similar matters, sun worship is added to the cultures of all nations and peoples. But, especially among those who reached Central and South America, the sun religion did not swamp or entirely replace the old moon religion. The two there integrated (much as they did in China, in fact, though there the official sun influence was more marked). *There was no repression, no purging of the moon elements.*

In England there is just one single, solitary hint of the status thirteen once enjoyed. Folklore tells us that a person born on the thirteenth of the month will have success in all ventures begun on that day in later life. One faint echo of the glorious thirteen of South America, across tens of thousands of miles (by land) and twenty thousand years.

Or perhaps across thirty million years.

7

Wisdom and Know-How

A theatre critic is like a eunuch. He watches it all day long, knows everything there is to know about it, but when he comes to do it himself he's absolutely useless.

—BRENDAN BEHAN

For this chapter to make sense, we need to set up a distinction that is at least a cousin to the distinction between wisdom and know-how. This will help us to establish which mental products of early man can legitimately, accurately, and necessarily be assigned to a container labeled "ancient wisdom," and which ought rather to go in a box called "early modern know-how."

The distinction I am after is not quite the one that Brendan Behan was making, though that is a good starting point. And it enables me to say in passing, though it is not being entirely fair, that there is a sense in which we can think of a scientist as a "life critic." We can say that he knows all there is to know about life, but when it comes to doing it. . . . But this is unfair, of course, in the sense that much of what the scientist achieves is (unlike the activity of the theater critic) directly relevant to the living of our lives. Where the scientist deserves the snub is in respect of his arrogant belief that science and the scientific method are the only way of going about things—that only by the use of these can we ever understand anything—and in the end will understand everything. That is complete rubbish. This is the "male principle" talking out of the front of its neck.

For there remains, you see, the matter of talking out of the back of your neck. And the comments of Swedenborg here are relevant and important:

> And the influx of the celestial angels is into that part of the head which covers the cerebellum, and is called the occiput, extending from the ears in all directions even to the back of the neck; for that region corresponds to wisdom.[1]

Prior to this remark Swedenborg has been talking about intelligence, which he assigns to the regions of the top, sides, and front of the head.

We are beginning to get together a number of pairs here: creativity and criticism; wisdom and knowledge (or wisdom and know-how); wisdom and intelligence. And then Peter Redgrove, effectively echoing Robert Graves, calls them poetry and science. I myself also call the two pairs experience and information, as well as sometimes intuition and cognition.

I am going to stick, finally, with the last pair: intuition and cognition. I will define these simply as "direct perceiving" and "indirect perceiving." In direct perceiving (intuition), you get things right straightaway—"just like that"—and usually without any real idea of how you did it. In indirect perception (cognition), one arrives at the correct answer by trying out various conscious strategies, discarding each one that doesn't work as one goes along. Eventually, you get the right answer—and you also know exactly *why* it is right.

With intuition, as I said, you do not, as a rule, know why you are right. In fact, the explanation you devise, usually afterward, is always much more of a metaphor than an explanation. It will not usually, for instance, help anyone else to do what you did. But the explanation of the scientist, by contrast, always entirely helps someone else to do the same.

I do not want to wade any deeper into these waters here: they deserve a whole book to themselves. We would really have to examine the notions and functions of subjectivity and objectivity from the first principles. But one passing example of the intuitive "explanation" of an event, which is no obvious use at all in explaining *how,* is dreaming the winners of future horse races. One such dream I had myself involved seeing, twice, in the dream, a very interesting film, the second time in color. The title of the film was "Showman's Fair," the name of a horse I didn't even know existed at the time—although it was drawn to my attention the day after the dream. There are many such dreams on record. Each one is wholly personal and peculiar to the individual having the dream.[2]

It seems to me that the ancients, in particular, of course, Neanderthal and then those who came after who were close to him, did gain real understanding intuitively, a real knowledge of aspects of human life and human biology, of some of the functions of this planet's geology, and perhaps some knowledge even of atomic and molecular structure. They did this—how? By dreams perhaps, by forms of clairvoyant scrying, or simply by looking and saying "this is so." And—this is the point—they were right.

In this chapter we shall be looking at some "nuggets" of knowledge (or wisdom, if we judge it by its source), which the ancients had no business at all to have—if they were the primitive, untutored cavemen that orthodox history claims, and given that they lacked both our scientific tools and our scientific approach.

Where there are nuggets, of course, there will usually also be a mother lode, from which the nuggets have been washed down.

Aside from what I think are incontestable examples of ancient wisdom, that is, of ancient intuitive thought that produced hard, accurate results, we also come across items that are far better labeled examples of early modern know-how—items that surprise us, but that seem on close examination to be products of the last few thousand years only (like the electrical batteries of historical India and the Middle East), and the brain-children, apparently, of brilliant early scientists working alone, along a particular line. These, however, are not what this chapter is about (see appendix 2).

NUGGETS

Various individuals have unearthed some fairly impressive nuggets of wisdom, but I want to begin with some finds of my own. Rather unusually, these are psychological nuggets. Exactly what I mean by that will become clear.

In Greek legend one of the stories about Hercules concerns his fight with Antaeus, the son of the Earth Goddess. Hercules discovered that every time he dashed Antaeus to the ground, his opponent sprang up with renewed vigor. He realized that every contact with his mother (the Earth) gave Antaeus fresh strength. On this realization, Hercules lifted his adversary clear of the ground and was then able to crush the rapidly-weakening giant to death.

In the 1950s, H. F. Harlow, in the course of investigating the relationship of infant monkeys to their environment, made the following discovery. As long as the young monkey could touch its mother, normal psychological development proceeded. But when prevented from touching the mother, even when they could see her, the development of the young monkeys underwent complete and permanent breakdown. The really astonishing finding, however, was this: the possibility of touching a crude wire model of the mother covered with *rough cloth* resulted in entirely normal development. This model was much preferred to another wire model *not* covered with cloth, which as an additional inducement gave milk through a nipple. If a threatening object, like a moving doll, was introduced into the cage of a young monkey alone, the monkey went into a fit of abject terror. But in the presence of the wire-and-cloth mother, the same young monkey, confronted with the same doll, first ran and hugged the totally inert mother. Then, without fear, he ran forward to explore the threatening doll.[3]

The question is—and for me the answer is yes—did the ancients understand the central importance of physical touch between mother and offspring as a vital formative influence, which is totally instinctive and *totally independent* of such apparently related variables as feeding, and caring for, and loving? And if the answer *is* yes, how could they have known it? For certainly they performed no experiments, and any human child that was not in touch with its mother in any chance situation would also be a child that was not being fed and not being protected. It would be dead within a day or so.

Are these circumstances, perhaps, also the origin of the superstition of "touching wood"—the rough bark, like the rough cloth of the wire model, representing the fur coat of the primate mother we also had when this response was first planted in us? And does the tree therefore symbolize "Mother" in much the same way as for us the Cross represents Christ? I think it does.

The story of Adam and Eve provides more food for thought. It should be noted, by the way, that this story predates its inclusion in the Old Testament, and elements of it are also found in the folklore of many other ancient peoples. In this story it is Eve who first eats the apple and discovers sex. One of the items of information contained in this symbolism, I suggest, is that girls on average reach puberty before boys. This may seem an undramatic piece of information—but I venture to say that, if you stopped a hundred people in the street and asked which sex reached puberty first, you would get neither a hundred confident nor a hundred correct answers. But there is more.

The apple is a symbol of the roundness of the adult, sexually-attractive female. It is not merely the breasts, buttocks, and hips that are round and full, but the stomach also ("thy belly is like an heap of wheat"—Song of Solomon), the lips, the thighs, and the totality. For women possess a layer of subcutaneous fat that softens and rounds all the outlines—shoulders, chin, calves, and whatever. Roundness is the major characteristic of the female, just as angularity, its opposite, is that of the male.

I am suggesting here that the apple in the Adam and Eve story is telling us more than that round women are sexy. I suggest it is conveying an understanding that roundness is a releaser (as that term is used in modern ethology) of a specific behavior, in this case male sexual behavior. This tentative idea gains support not only from the Venus figurines

Figure 6. Stylized "ethological" figurine from
Czechoslovakia (Dolni Vestonice).

of figures 4 and 5 (pp. 68–70), but from yet others still more stylized in which all form has been omitted except the roundness—as in figure 6.

There was also, as we shall see in chapter 10, the further association of the roundness of woman with the roundness of the full moon.

There are still many other points of interest in the Adam and Eve tale. In a lecture given at the European Conference for Humanistic Psychology (Geneva, 1978), R. D. Laing proposed that the tree and the serpent are a highly stylized rendering of the umbilical cord of the newborn child. In support of this claim, he showed slides of "tree and serpent" designs from many cultures and ages. Often the serpent, and sometimes two serpents, are twined about the tree.

The actual umbilical cord consists, in fact, of three cords—a central vein with two arteries twining about it. These convey used and unused blood to and from the placenta to the embryo. At the two junctions of placenta and embryo, the cords connect in a manner strongly recalling the roots and branches of a tree.

The symbolism of the tree is very widespread. Significantly enough, it is often referred to as the Tree of Life (notably, of course, in the Jewish Kabbalah). A well-known reference work states: "A common theme in mythology is a tree of mystic significance connected with the fount of life." Trees are also frequently said to connect the earth with the sky; while in Scandinavia the world tree, Yggdrasil, was said to be the core of the universe. Graves's tree alphabet and the tree magic of the Celts are also undoubtedly linked here.

We now begin to perceive a very interesting position indeed and some very significant associational links. The umbilical cord is the "tree-of-life" and we "touch wood" for luck. Unless a child can continually touch the mother, normal development cannot occur. In the tree of life grow the round fruits (Eve's apple), which are the roundness of woman and the roundness that governs fertility. The (universal) tree connects earth with heaven. In heaven grows the round moon fruit. And the moon, of course, directly governs both menstruation and pregnancy.

This associational picture, fascinating though its details are in themselves, is not the central point here. As just a picture it contains no threat to science and to orthodoxy. As a picture it is only the elaborate superstition of a perhaps imaginative, but otherwise ignorant, people. The point to emphasize, however, is that *in* this picture, as we have seen, are contained fragments of what looks very much like a hard knowledge of biology.

Reverting to Greek mythology, here is one for the medical profession to ponder. Prometheus, one of the Titans, stole the secret of fire from the Olympic gods. As a punishment, Zeus condemned the chained Prometheus to have his liver pecked out and eaten by an eagle for eternity. After each of the eagle's meals the liver grew again.

On closer reflection the story is already a little strange. Why the liver exactly? The eyes or the heart might seem a more obvious choice. The plot quickens dramatically, however, when we appreciate that the liver is the only human organ capable of regeneration after loss. A standard medical text tells us: "The liver has great power of recovery. If the disease is neither progressive nor so severe that it overwhelms the patient, lost or damaged cells regenerate."

It looks very much as if the ancient Greeks, or more likely still their forebears, knew this. (The legend, incidentally, is at least three thousand years old.) The question is how did they know?

It is true that surgery was known and practiced in prehistoric times but it was seldom successful in all but superficial cases. Among the reasons for the almost invariably fatal results of major surgery in prehistoric societies are: their inability to control hemorrhage; the failure to appreciate anatomical interconnectedness; ignorance of the nature and control of infection; and postoperative trauma arising from lack of anaesthesia.

What then are the chances of a prehistoric surgeon opening a man with major surgery, so that the liver is exposed for examination, successfully closing the wound, and then at some later date once again opening the man and noting whatever it exactly is one notes that indicates that regeneration has taken place? I think doctors today would be the first to reject the possibility of such major and detailed surgery. Yet I think we *cannot* reject the knowledge shown by the legend.

So the question is, did the ancients, at least sometimes, know what they were talking about? That is, were they stating *hard facts* in the only language available to them—that of symbolism and association? I think that they were. And I think that they obtained their knowledge not logically and scientifically but intuitively. Now a different kind of still impressive behavior on the part of the "lunatic" people.

THE MOON DANCE

The experimental work on menstruation already discussed showed that the regularization of the menstrual period resulted specifically from the woman in question sleeping with the bedroom light on during the fourteenth to the seventeenth nights after her period.

The period actually *occurs* at the time of the new moon. But it is clear that the new moon does not *trigger* it, as some biologists observing primates have incorrectly supposed. The period is *triggered* by the influence of the moon shining fourteen to seventeen nights *after* the new moon. This is actually a more reasonable position, for the moon at that time is more than half full and so is producing an appreciable amount of light. The new moon, with its minimal disc, though of course visible, gives out much less light.

What seems clear is that the moon worshippers themselves were aware of the effect and importance of the moon during the fourteenth to the seventeenth nights of its cycle—for otherwise the menstruation of their women would not have been regular and specifically would not then have occurred at the new moon. By the time of which we are talking, the last hundred thousand years or so, mankind had long been living in caves or man-made structures. These people would, therefore, effectively have removed themselves from the moon's natural influence and so blocked the physiological response that had been established when their distant ancestors lived and slept continuously in the open.

My proposal is that the moon peoples observed night festivals on the fourteenth to the seventeenth nights of the moon cycle. On those nights they danced for the moon.

These monthly festivals would have been among the most sacred of the moon religion. I suggest that they were attended only by women and children—children being defined as those who had not yet reached their thirteenth year (i.e., 13 x 13 menstrual months). We recall that at the great Festival of the Moon in modern China only women and children took part. I suggest that men were forbidden even to observe these prehistoric ceremonies, on pain of death.

My further feeling is that these midmonth ceremonies were orgiastic in character, though probably not in the usual heterosexual sense. They were probably lesbian (and here we have a link with the poetess Sappho and her followers on the island of Lesbos, whom Graves refers to, in context, as "a white-gowned moon"). There was very possibly a child sacrifice, whose blood the women then drank. Or possibly the participants ritually cut themselves and licked each other's wounds. (Support for this view is found in the secret Dyonisian and Bacchic orgies of much later Europe, where human beings were sometimes torn to pieces and eaten.) Wine, or more likely some other intoxicant (I suggest the "sacred mushroom"), would be consumed in quantity, so that in the end the congregants would sleep. This last circumstance is important.

The scenario just described accounts satisfactorily for all kinds of garbled odds and ends that come down to us at the present day. It explains why fairies are said to dance by moonlight and why observing them results in death. It is also why the medieval witches of Europe danced by moonlight (though I do not think they understood why they did it or what nights were important). The scenario accounts also for tales of werewolves—human beings who change into animals at full moon and drink blood. (The moon was not actually full during Neanderthal ceremonies, though it was more than half full, so there is not too much slippage there.) It accounts also for the (of course totally untrue) story that medieval Jews used the blood of Christian babies to make their Passover bread.

It is, on the contrary, the case that Jews are not allowed to consume blood at all. All meat must be bled absolutely dry, under the supervision of a priest. However, this practice does look like one of the reversals we spoke of earlier—where a once very holy practice is subsequently made very unholy. The extensive taboos against blood in Judaism, including the blood of menstruation, do necessarily suggest a very different distant past. Catholicism, on the other hand, as in so many ways, has managed to preserve symbolically many Neanderthal features intact—including the role of blood. Thus the blood of Christ is terribly important and is said to wash the world clean of sin. This blood is also drunk, symbolically, during the sacrament. Here I think we have a very clear echo indeed of those far-off ceremonies under the moon.

I believe that the Neanderthal moon worshippers understood the importance of *sleeping* under the midterm moon (the "Cro-Magnon" folk superstition that warns against sleeping in the moonlight alone argues for this), but they may have done so for the wrong reasons. They may have thought it important to let the goddess "send them a dream," which would then be examined for meaning the next day.

It would be nice, from the thrilling point of view, if we could argue that the moon must emit some kind of mysterious magnetism, or even that its light is special in some way. Alas, neither of these statements can be true—for if they were, the bedroom light could not perform the triggering function, which it does. So what is involved is the simple action of a source of light on the *sleeping* organism. My own opinion is that this light reaches and activates the pineal gland that, despite its being buried deep in the human brain, is still light-sensitive.* For it to perform its function, however, probably requires the usual light receptors (the eyes) to be out of action, as they are precisely when we sleep.

In this connection we can move to India and beyond.

INDIA

In the context of ancient wisdom, I myself award Hindu and Tibetan yoga only one scoring point, but it is a very good one.

As early as three thousand years ago, and in all likelihood long before, the Hindus were referring to the pineal gland as the "third eye" and claiming that it played a central role in mystical life. As it happens, the pineal gland *was* once an extra *pair* of eyes placed on top of the head of our distant reptile ancestors. As stated, it is still light-sensitive in us to this day and is probably centrally concerned in mediating the effect of the moon in menstruation.

Louise Lacey also reports a most interesting saying of the Hopi people of North America—a very far cry from the Indian subcontinent. It is: "Keep the hole on the top of your head open." (And as we saw in the last chapter, the Hopi also treat the number thirteen as sacred.)

This particular piece of both Hindu and Hopi wisdom seems to be a once again fragmentary but genuine Neanderthal memory, this time of the function of the pineal gland. As such it adds further considerable

---

*See references in Louise Lacey's *Lunaception,* and my own books.

support to the claim that Neanderthal possessed a hard knowledge of human biology, which, however, it seems he proceeded to wrap up in all kinds of "unnecessary" religious rituals and dogmas. (Were these *really* unnecessary? Or, was the wrapping done by later peoples acting in ignorance? These are not questions that we can answer easily.)

I wish it were possible to endorse without further ado the chakras of Hindu and Tiberan yogic mysticism. These alleged chakras, allegedly seven in number, are said to be points of connection between the so-called etheric or spiritual body and the physical body. They are said to be centered along the spine, from the base up to the top of the skull.

Modern defenders of yogic philosophy claim that the chakras correspond with the position of the endocrine or ductless glands of the nervous system. The endocrine glands are extremely important producers and regulators of hormones vital for the function and well-being of body, mind, and nervous system. Unfortunately for yoga, there happens to be nine of these: the hypothalamus, pineal, thyroid, parathyroid, thymus, adrenal, pancreas, kidney, and female/male sex endocrine glands. And, in addition, many of these glands are in themselves complex, sometimes having lobes with different functions that secrete different hormones. Sometimes there are two of each gland, as with the kidneys and the testes, and sometimes only one, as with the pineal.

All in all, the alleged chakras are only a poor approximation to the reality. It looks very much like another case of forcing the mystical number seven on to a framework that will not support it, which we saw so much of in chapter 2. But there is, perhaps, this time a glimmer of hope, a glimmer, that is, of a more genuine memory. For some sources speak of eight or nine chakras.

Naturally, I am not at all saying here that it is not possible for man to have some direct or intuitive perception or experience of the functions of his nervous system. On the contrary, I am arguing *for* just that. The understanding of the pineal gland alone gives major support to the idea. It is not *a priori* out of the question that the alleged chakras have some kind of existence. But there is no objective support at all for there being *seven* of them. To stick stubbornly to that particular claim can only damage the case for the existence of intuitive perception.

Generally speaking, Hindu mysticism as a whole is not an especially inspiring source of reassurance about the intuitive powers of the mind. There is in India no great tradition of healing or clairvoyance as we find in China (see below). Instead, on the Indian subcontinent we find a great deal of talk—a very great deal of talk, it is their specialty—but not very much in the way of hard facts.

As to the main body of yoga itself, the long-drawn-out and said-to-be indispensable apprenticeship leading to "enlightenment," which (aside from all the words) consists (a) of "seeing things," and (b) of controlling the functions of the autonomic nervous system, can be short-circuited with no apparent loss of performance.

For it is the case that anyone can have mystic visions simply by starving himself for a few weeks, or by taking a small amount of any psychedelic drug. The sometimes quite dramatic control of the autonomic nervous system—whereby knives can be driven through the flesh without pain, the heart rate or breathing rate very significantly reduced, and so on—has been duplicated by westerners without any recourse to yogic disciples or beliefs. One living instance is Jan Merta, who can hold red-hot irons in his hand and stub cigarettes out on his tongue, and an earlier one was Jerome Cardan.[4]

The practice of yoga is, I suggest, a closed circuit. It does not lead anywhere apart from itself. It never turns outward from itself to the objective world, where nevertheless we all live and need to live. It *can* (sometimes) produce "inner peace," which is certainly a very valuable commodity—but so can all manner of other paths and self-regulating practices that make no claims to spiritual transcendence. By and large, the Hindu "achievement" is a series of dramatic party-tricks.

These hard words can be justified—and I hope understood—by a look at China.

CHINA

It is in China that we find firm and incontrovertible evidence that a nonscientific, intuitive approach to phenomena really can produce hard facts—facts just as valid as those produced by science itself. The facts produced by the intuitive method do seem, however, almost without exception, to be in the area of biology—as long as we include as branches of biology both psychology and religion.

The basis of Chinese philosophy/religion is, as has already been mentioned, the notion that there are two interacting processes or principles in the universe, which in that interaction produce all phenomena. These two principles are named *yin* and *yang*. They appear in many guises, or, if you prefer, have many attributes. *Always* paired together, they appear as dark–light, female–male, moon–sun, mother–father, and so on.*

A westerner coming across these ideas might feel them to be charming, poetic, romantic, artistic—whatever you will, in that line of country—but certainly not scientific or logical. Therefore not justified, and in the last analysis (and objectively) worthless.

It is true to say, strictly, that as expressed these ideas are neither scientifically nor objectively valid. They are, however, I insist, wholly justified, accurate, and meaningful. They are *intuitively* valid. The ancient Chinese yin-yang philosophy leads to major achievements that, individually, match anything achieved by western science. These are (1) acupuncture, and (2) the I Ching, the Book of Changes.

Acupuncture, as most people know today, is a method of treating illness and of anaesthetizing without drugs. Bitterly resisted by western doctors for many generations as quackery, acupuncture is today accepted as valid. The treatment consists, briefly, of inserting small silver needles in the skin at various points of the body, the so-called meridian points. Other types of needles, including bone or wooden needles, can work just

---

*Once again I must stress here that the insistence that neither of the paired attributes can exist in isolation without the other is staggeringly accurate.[5]

as well, and simple pressure also. There are hundreds of these points, and they are sited in all kinds of unlikely places—the earlobes, the toes, and so on. The effects are usually far removed from the sites of stimulation. Needles inserted at the wrist affect the ovaries, and the chest is governed by the right forearm, for example.

Acupuncture is used in the treatment of a vast variety of malignant diseases and pathological conditions—malaria, pneumonia, sciatica, arthritis, rheumatism, fractures, wounds, epilepsy, insomnia, deafness, dumbness. These examples give some idea of the range.

The *anaesthetizing* powers of acupuncture were only discovered—or perhaps *re*discovered—by Chinese surgeons in 1966. Since then, however, many thousands of operations have been performed with acupuncture as the sole anaesthetizing agent.

In the 1970s a report in the *Sunday Times* described the removal of a tubercular lung from a fully-conscious man having only one needle inserted in his right forearm. The man was awake and aware through the whole operation. After the wound was closed and the needle removed, he sat up and gave a press conference. A film of such an operation (perhaps the same one) was shown recently on British television. Again the man was fully conscious throughout, smiling and talking with the camera crew.

No pain is felt during surgery or other treatment, yet the rest of the nervous system remains fully normal. Among other major benefits of acupuncture over conventional anaesthesia is that there is little bleeding and almost no postoperative shock. Blood loss and postoperative shock are among the major hazards of western surgery.

It is in one sense immaterial whether one accepts the Chinese *explanation* of acupuncture. The fact remains that it works. *Maybe* also Neanderthal man used acupuncture as an anaesthetizing agent? And so did perform operations?

Also based on the yin-yang philosophy is a still more major achievement—that of the I Ching or Book of Changes. In the I Ching, we meet with the fact that intuitive perception reaches into the realm also of paranormal phenomena, an area where this time science cannot follow. The situation that the paranormal, while readily accessible to the advanced intuitive mind, is a no-go area for science is probably the main reason for the implacable hatred of most scientists for the paranormal.

The I Ching is an oracle. You consult it by a prescribed ritual, putting to it a precise question about whatever it is that is troubling you. The I Ching replies not in vague generalizations, but in terms that impress *you personally* as showing a precise, detailed understanding of the situation in which you find yourself. This is certainly already a striking enough achievement. The still more daunting fact of the matter is that the I Ching can be consulted with equal accuracy about the future, about events that have not yet occurred.

These are claims that cannot be wholly proved simply by writing about them. But any interested person can make his or her own acquaintance and experience of the I Ching, and this is what I urge you most strongly to do. Here I will just repeat what I said in an earlier book, in which I also quote many instances of what the I Ching has achieved:

> I believe anyone can convince himself of the efficacy of the *I Ching*, providing he obeys the rules and approaches the book in the right spirit. The rules are these. You can only ask the oracle the same question once. The answer you get is *the* answer. The rule of one question, one answer has applied in the magical world down through the ages. . . . There can be no testing of the *I Ching* as science understands testing, because you can never seek to get the same result twice. . . . I can promise you, however, that this book will startle you with a sense of a presence in the universe beyond space and time.[6]

OTHER NUGGETS

The discoveries of intuitive ancient knowledge are confined mainly to biology. But there are notable exceptions. One such apparent discovery comes from alchemy.

Alchemy, as practiced in medieval times, sat uneasily in the area somewhere between pure magic and modern chemistry. I say uneasily, because virtually nothing of any practical value, either way, came out of it. By this I mean that none of its central tenets or central quests—the search for the elixir of youth and the philosopher's stone, for example— were ever fulfilled. Really, alchemy seems to have been a vast collection of *psychological* statements about *physical matter*. And, as such, these simply have no *literal* meaning. Physical matter is governed by the laws of physical matter, not by the laws of human psychology.

Alchemy does not seem to have very much to tell us about the nature of physical matter. (Occasionally, of course, the alchemists did stumble across some chemical truth, but that is a different and minor issue.) Alchemy *does,* however, tell us a good deal about the human psyche—as Jung realized—especially about the workings of the unconscious mind, and functions as a kind of projection technique. But that was not what it was supposed to be doing. In terms of its avowed purpose it was a large-scale failure—with, perhaps, one notable exception.

Alchemists believed in the "transmutation of metals." That is, they believed it was possible to turn so-called "base" metals into so-called "noble" metals—say, lead into gold. They spent a great deal of time trying to do just this. (A singularly worldly pursuit, more motivated apparently by a desire for money than by a search for higher truth: for it would have been just as marvelous to have transmuted granite into flint, or iron into tin—or even gold into tin!)

However, among the most popular proposals of which metals would change into which, we find it suggested that lead and mercury are most suitable for conversion to gold.

In the mid-nineteenth century the scientist, Mendeleyev, noticed that there was a recurring pattern in the properties of elements when arranged in the order of their increasing atomic number. The atomic number is the number of protons found in the nucleus of the atom in question. In Mendeleyev's "periodic table of elements" the atomic number of gold is 79, that of mercury 80, and that of lead 82. To better appreciate the implications of this position, the atomic number of iron is 26, of copper 29, of silver 47, and of tin 50.

Did the alchemists, therefore, have any kind of intuitive grasp of atomic number? It is impossible to say for sure on the basis of such slender evidence, but the "coincidence" here is certainly most interesting.

The concept of the atom itself was widespread in ancient Greece and India. Lucretius said that "atoms rush everlastingly through all space," and that it was impossible to see them because they were so small. The *Yoga Vashishta* remarks: "There are vast worlds within the hollows of each atom, multifarious as the specks in a sunbeam." This can, certainly, be interpreted as a reference to subatomic particles. Yet, perhaps, any thoughtful, imaginative person might suppose that particles too small for the eye to see could exist. And given that "as above, so below," the notion of moons circling a planet, or planets a sun, might provide the model for the infinitely small "planetary system."

It seems quite clear, in any case, that such thoughts were by no means uncommon in ancient Greece and ancient India, well before the birth of Christ. The ancient peoples of India actually went further in these respects than the ancient Greeks. According to Andrew Tomas's sources:

> The original time measurement of the Brahmins was sexagismal. . . .
> In ancient times the day was divided into 60 kala, each equal to 24 minutes, subdivided into 60 vikala, each equivalent to 24 seconds. Then followed a further sixty-fold subdivision of time into para, tatpara, vitatpara, ima and finally kashta—or 1/300 millionth of a second.

The question is, did the Hindus really realize what they were doing? That is, were they simply playing around with mystical or metaphysical ideas—or were they trying to describe the length of the life span of subatomic particles, which are close to that figure? It is the only practical use which measurements of that shortness could have.

Another ancient text quoted by Tomas appears to state the size of a hydrogen atom—the hydrogen atom, incidentally, being one of the two basic building blocks of the entire universe.

This line of inquiry is fascinating and becomes still more so when Tomas cites parts of ancient Indian texts (the *Mausola Parva* and the *Drona Parva*), which appear to describe atomic war—a "gigantic messenger of death," which reduced whole armies to ashes and caused the hair and nails of the survivors to fall out. Or again: "A blazing missile possessed of the radiance of smokeless fire was discharged . . . clouds roared into the higher air, showering blood. The world, scorched by the heat of that weapon, seemed to be in a fever." The same detonation is also later compared to the flare-up of "ten thousand suns."[7]

I am not inclined to dismiss these descriptions out of hand as simply the work of overactive imaginations—any more than I dismiss out of hand the vision of Ezekiel (of which Däniken and others have made so much), or the theories of Sassoon and Dale in *The Manna Machine,* or the prophecies of Nostradamus.

Ezekiel's vision of the wheels turning in the sky is well enough known and is found in the Book of Ezekiel 1. Sassoon and Dale's book is a recent publication (1978). This is an attempt to see the Jewish, mystical, kabbalistic text, the *Zohar,* as a description, by a nontechnical, primitive, nomadic people, of an atomic machine! It is an insidiously persuasive account, which certainly makes a kind of sense ("a mad Velikovskian plausibility," as a critic once said of a book of mine) of what is otherwise a rambling, pre-Freudian, sexual nightmare, making no sense at all. (What Sassoon and Dale's book urgently requires in the way of proof, of course, are some ancient radioactive skeletons from the Middle East.) Nostradamus's prophecies are also rather well-known. Nostradamus was a medieval doctor and mystic, who believed he saw genuine visions of the future, which he wrote down. Some of these, again one relating specifically to an apparent atomic explosion, seem uncomfortably accurate.[8]

Having mentioned Velikovsky in passing, I will also say that his views can in no way be left out of account when debating the validity of unorthodox or apparently meaningless material found in ancient texts. His latest book, *The Peoples of the Sea,* is another valuable attempt to organize adequately the true chronology of ancient events.

But it is with Nostradamus that, if I am forced to give one, I find a possible answer to these "atomic" mysteries. It is for me possible that gifted individual psychics in ancient times did have fragmentary visions of the real future of mankind. When I say "for me," I mean that as a psychic myself, with a reasonable amount of experience in these matters, I can accept the possibility of precognitive clairvoyance whereas a hard-line scientist could not. For him, that explanation is no better than that of visitors from outer space; but it is a far better one for me personally.

Reviewing the "ancient wisdom," I ask myself the question, did early man once possess a comprehensive body of knowledge (especially concerning human biology) now lost to us, apart from a few fragments— or were these only ever small fragments of something that began to be understood but never really got off the ground? I am not quite sure what to answer. But I think we can certainly say that the volume of ancient wisdom was once larger than what we possess of it now. The final chapter will return to this point.

The material we have been looking at is certainly very ancient. Acupuncture is at least 4500 years old, and similarly the I Ching existed as a verbal tradition long before writing. Already three thousand years ago, the Hindus were calling the pineal gland the third eye. Nor had this apparently purely intuitive approach been extended *since.* It is, therefore, more reasonable to regard it as an end of something rather than a beginning. From that time on increasingly, of course, our modern logico-rational method takes over.

My position is, I suppose, a middle one. I am not arguing at all for any kind of full-scale "golden age" from which we have since fallen away. But I do believe, it is clear, that Neanderthal man had, from certain points of view, an advanced culture, one far more advanced than he is currently given credit for. Although his central frame of reference was religion, and though his terminology was that of symbolism, I think he nevertheless did have a fair grasp of many hard biological and psychological facts, and to some extent the facts of geology and physics (see here also chapters 8 and 12). It is occasional items of this understanding that come down to us in historical times.

Neanderthal's worldview was, perhaps, rather like a cake with a lot of currants in it. The cake was the "unnecessary" religious superstructure, the currants were the real facts. Objectively speaking (in terms of know-how), I think this must have been the case. For when we look at the *explanations* offered for, say, acupuncture, we find these things to be vintage Heath Robinson models. And yet acupuncture works. It seems, therefore, that Neanderthal had a persistent ability to get things right for the "wrong" reasons. Hence, in attempting to say how he succeeded, we fall back on the concept of intuition—with which faculty, as I say, you first get things right without any conscious understanding of how you do so and then invent an explanation. The explanation often doesn't actually matter.

I must emphasize again here that, in my opinion, Neanderthal certainly possessed abilities in respect of the purely paranormal that far exceeded our own.

Neanderthal botany-biology-psychology-philosophy (whose finest flowering I think to be the I Ching) was a considerable achievement. It was not backed up by, nor set in, what we today would call hard or objective technology. For whereas modern man builds cities of stone, it appears Neanderthal was content to build cities of dreams.

A REPRIEVE FOR SEVEN?

There is a last item concerning intuition, but this is more the intuition of a modern, living scientist, Arthur M. Young, who, I believe, has hit upon a profound truth, though again perhaps for the wrong reasons.[9] Young was forcibly impressed with the influence of the number seven in the mystical lore of Europe and the Middle East. Like Geoffrey Ashe, he asked himself why this should be so.

Among mathematicians it is well-known that if you draw a normal two-dimensional map on which there are several countries with adjacent borders, you will need to use four colors to be certain that no color is directly adjacent to itself. But on a *torus*—which, for the nonscientist, is simply the shape of the normal doughnut with a hole in the middle—you need to have seven colors to make sure that the same color does not occur twice in immediate succession. And, as it happens, seven was said to be the number of colors in the rainbow. Were these events connected? And was there a reason here somewhere for the mystical influence of seven?

A vortex is also a torus and an extremely common shape in nature. It is the shape of a tornado and of eddies in water, for example. In fact, it is, Young tells us, "the only manner by which self-sustained motion can exist in a given medium."[10]

A bipolar magnetic field (and *all* magnetic fields are bipolar) is also a vortex. What, asked Young, if the universe itself were shaped like a torus?

I believe this intuitive view to be absolutely correct. And it has received significant scientific support since he published it.*

Either we can say, and this for me is the more reasonable position, that Young came to his conclusion for the wrong reasons—that is, because he wrongly assumed sevens to be genuinely important. Or, if we so wish, we can reverse the arguments of chapter 2. In that case, the "seven lights in the sky" would not after all be the *cause* of seven worship, but themselves merely another expression of it, a memory of a memory.

Perhaps, on this new point, we should keep our options open.

---

*See *New Scientist*, 25 May 1978, and my book *The Double Helix of the Mind*.

8
Standing Stones

*Further research led Graves to the conclusion that
the moon goddess is central to a whole range of pre-
Christian cultures and mythologies: that it is, in fact,
the fundamental Ur-religion of the whole world. The
moon goddess was the goddess of poetry and magic and
the irrational; and she was gradually supplanted by the
sun god, the god of light and rationality. As the mystical
Druidic alphabet gave way to the commercial Phoenician
alphabet, the age of magic gave way to the age of science,
with its emphasis on the physical world and "daylight"
knowledge.*

—COLIN WILSON

Over nine hundred, man-made, stone circles are known to exist in the British Isles. Perhaps twice as many again have been destroyed. Without doubt others remain still to be discovered. Some of those that we now know were found under peat and even under the sea. Most of the circles were built between 2500–1000 BC (or 4500–3000 BP). The oldest so far reliably dated goes back to 3300 BC; that is, 5300 years BP.*

Without doubt the best factual guide to these megaliths is Aubrey Burl's *The Stone Circles of the British Isles*. This is itself a massive

---

*It is, perhaps, an interesting coincidence that the Jewish calendar began 5739 years ago.

bedrock of a book that no ancient mysteries' enthusiast should be without. It is precisely the solid base that anyone intending to pursue far-reaching speculations must have for his launch pad.

A good deal of my own interest here centers on the use of the number thirteen in megaliths—a subject that, as far as I know, nobody but Robert Graves has considered at all. I hope to show once again that the influence of the number thirteen, and all that goes along with it, is a matter that overrides the boundaries of what are far too often considered to be separate ages—and successfully ignores apparently unbridgeable gaps between widely different cultures.

What we must first indicate with absolute finality is that neither the British Celts nor any of their European cousins were responsible for the erection of the stone circles. The Celts as a people first come to the attention of the historian around 1000 BC. Their origins (as far as the historical record can show) were in the neighborhood of the Balkans in Eastern Europe. They reached the peak of their geographical and cultural powers by 500 BC—and arrived in Britain around 600 BC.

The heyday of stone-circle building, however, was already over by 1000 BC.

To repeat, then, the Celts and their religious leaders, the Druids, did not erect the stone megaliths. They did, however, take them over.

We have already seen that the number thirteen had a very strong significance for the Celts (chapters 1 and 3), and there is more to say about such matters in any case. If we can show that the megalith builders had a similar interest in that particular number, we will already have gone some way to demonstrating a *religious* continuity between the megalith builders and the Celts, despite otherwise perhaps large cultural gaps. (The megalith builders may not even have spoken Indo-European.) And we would also have the beginnings of an explanation why the Celts adopted the stone circles with such enthusiasm.

In considering the number of stones that make up a circle or complex, a good deal of caution must be exercised. Burl tells us that, because of collapse and destruction, a "reasonable estimate" of the original number of stones can be made only for about a third of the sites. In the case of the remainder any estimate has to be guesswork.

Examining a total of 316 reliable sites, Burl produces a table of the number of stones in each. We find that fourteen of these sites are made up of thirteen stones (some of which are diagrammed in figure 7). This may not at first seem a high percentage. But the *most* frequent number found, which is twelve, occurs only thirty-two times. So there are only just over twice as many sites with the most frequent number (twelve) as there are with the number thirteen. (The numbers four, six, eight, nine, ten, and eleven, however, all exceed thirteen.)

We can say immediately that thirteen was certainly not a number that the megalith builders tried to avoid in any way. But we can improve further on this position with some reasonable speculation. Incidentally, it is clear from the detailed breakdown of his table that Burl omits the complexes shown in figures 7c, 7d, and 7e, presumably because they fall into his category "unreliable." Although we must welcome such strictness, 7c, for example, looks a pretty safe thirteen.

Now, on Burl's own admission, it turns out that "many of the thirteen-stone circles are twelve-stone circles with an extra recumbent stone." It may be the case, therefore, that many (or perhaps all) of the circles described as twelve-stone are really thirteen-stone circles, from which the center stone has been removed. We will consider why this event might have occurred in a moment.

First, a remark by Burl himself from his introduction:

> . . . in the silence of the circle of stones, the visitor receives no answers to his questions. There are, perhaps, twelve stones around him, some erect or leaning, some fallen and three-quarters covered with peat and turf. Worn, deep patches show where sheep have grazed or cattle have come to rub themselves against the uprights. There may be something of a hollow within the circle.[1]

It is the last sentence that is important. These "hollows," when examined, often contain the burnt remains of human beings—sometimes of many human beings.

Sometimes again, in slightly different circumstances, we have at the center of the twelve stones a cairn of stones. Below this cairn, once again in a hollow or pit, are the burnt remains of a human being. (So it is the tomb, possibly, of some great king or priest.) Figure 7h shows one such circle. It is possible to consider the twelve stones plus the cairn as making up a thirteen or "coven." On the other hand, we do find such cairns

(a) A thirteen-stone circle in Wicklow, Ireland.

(b) A thirteen-stone circle, with three of the stones placed centrally on a cairn (Low Longrigg, Cumberland).

Thirteen stones enclosing a burial cairn (Dartmoor, Devon).

(d) A thirteen-stone complex in Brecknock, Wales.

Figure 7. Thirteen and the stone megaliths of the British Isles.

Note: These and the following diagrams are not to scale, and no account has been taken of the size or shape of individual stones, nor whether these are upright or fallen. This kind of detail can be found in Aubrey Burl's diagrams in *The Stone Circles of the British Isles.*[2]

(e) A thirteen-stone circle
or complex at
Avebury, Wiltshire.

(f) A thirteen-stone circle
or complex in
Perthshire, Scotland.

(g) Ring of thirteen stones
surrounding a fourteenth
(Cork, Ireland).

(h) Ring of twelve stones
with center cairn—making
a possible "coven"
of thirteen
(White Moss, Cumberland).

(i) Twelve stones surrounding
a central cairn—again making
a possible "coven" of thirteen.
Alternatively, the gap in the
circumference may originally
have been filled by a thirteenth
stone (Inverness, Scotland).

(j) Circle of twelve stones
(Stanton Drew, Somerset).

that are surrounded by, or are otherwise composed of, thirteen actual stones (see 7b and 7c). We are now, of course, talking about the whole of the British isles, where regional variations among tribes and tribal practice both occur and are to be expected. These do not cancel each other out—rather they are variations on a theme.

Reverting to the hollows in the circles of twelve stones, which also, as we noted, sometimes contain a recumbent thirteenth stone, it does not stretch the imagination too much to imagine this thirteenth stone as an altar, or perhaps even a sacrificial stone. This is the view that Robert Graves takes.

Once Christianity reached Britain (around AD 600), the era of the stone circles (taken over by the Celtic tribes, who had put paid to the original owners) was at an end. The circles did not simply fall into disuse but were now often actually destroyed. Sometimes churches were built on the sites. In other cases, the circles were merely scattered or broken. We have church documents specifically urging parishioners to undertake the destruction of these "devil's circles."

Yet superstition (or, more accurately in some cases, secretly continued respect) often prevented their total destruction. Naturally, in the course of moving such gigantic stones people were occasionally maimed or crushed to death. These, no doubt, accidents were ascribed to the powers latent in the circles. So a frequent compromise solution was to *partly* destroy the circle.

What better way of doing this than by removing the central altar stone—perhaps also at the same time excavating the hollow and filling it with fresh soil? Thereby one had at the same time also destroyed the coming-to-be-hated and feared thirteen and replaced it with the acceptable twelve. As we saw in earlier chapters, *that* process had already been going on sporadically all over Europe and the Middle East for some time in respect of all kinds of subject matter, prior even to the advent of Christianity. Christianity merely gave the process another nudge.

So, the *possibility* is that all twelve-stone sites can be counted also as thirteens. Added together with the extant (reliable) thirteens, we then have a total of sites for this number far exceeding that of any other.

THE BUILDERS OF THE STONE CIRCLES

What do we know about the peoples and tribes who built the megaliths? Not very much.

Robert Graves and his sources report as follows: Various non-Indo-European, seafaring peoples in Greece and Asia Minor were displaced by Indo-European peoples moving down from northern positions. Some of these displaced peoples, over the course of generations, made their way ultimately to Ireland and Britain, in some cases by way of a stay in Spain, and in others without apparently settling anywhere *en route.*

Irish history (or legend) names these as Danaans who came from the Aegean, and first invaded Ireland around the year 2000 BC, then in a fresh wave (perhaps this time from Britain) again two hundred and fifty years later. Also involved during the period in question are the Milesians, a people coming similarly from Greece and Crete, who reached Ireland some time after 2000 BC.

Of interest to us is that the Danaans were specifically goddess-worshippers (the goddess Danaë) and that both they and the Milesians were matrilinear—meaning variously that the title of king passed down to the children of the king's sister, or that the husband of the king's daughter became king, or whatever.*

Such historical accounts necessarily involve speculation, and there is much disagreement about them among individual scholars. And as regards the stone circle, with the recent backward revision of the age of the megaliths, both the Danaans and the Milesians were rather latecomers—and so would not have been the first to build circles in these

---

*Let us remember that the descent of the pharaohs of Egypt was traced through the female line; and that among the Aborigines of Australia, one's totem group consists of blood relatives on one's mother's side.

islands. Such difficulties need not delay us here, because my own speculations are amply supported in the first instance by reference to the Celts, a people about whom we have a good deal of reliable information.

THE CELTS

The following facts about the Celts are of importance to the theories of this book.

It will be recalled that the Celts flourished in the thousand years preceding the birth of Christ, and that their empire at one time extended from the Balkans in eastern Europe to the British isles in the west. The Gauls, about whom Caesar wrote so much and who lived principally in the area that is now France, were also Celts. Switzerland was another Celtic stronghold.

Among these Celtish tribes, *Larousse* tells us, goddesses often enjoyed a wider distribution than gods. Moreover, the goddesses appear to date from an earlier period. The most important goddess of all is the Mother Goddess. The royal line of descent among Celts is originally matrilinear, as we know from Celtish folklore.

As to where exactly the Celts originated, most authorities favor eastern Europe. However, all we are saying here is that the earliest historical references to the Celts by name are in that geographical area. Their cultural origins are clearly far older. This we see in the fact that the Celtic culture has definite links with India. For example, the Celtic horned god Cernunnos is shown on the famous Gundestrup cauldron (from Denmark) seated in the lotus posture. He wears the horns of a stag and is surrounded by animals, including a serpent with a ram's head. He is also shown in the lotus posture on important finds in France and Scotland, once again flanked by animals. In these portraits, and in his function of "Lord of the Animals," Cernunnos strongly resembles the Indian deity Siva Pasupati. The Celts also sacrificed a mare at the inauguration of a king, and the same ceremony was performed in India. Aside from such cultural/religious connections, there are also clear linguistic affinities between the Celtic and Indian tongues.*

Of great interest is the fact that the Celts practiced a cult of the bear. So they did of other animals also, but the bear veneration is a major, if not indeed *the* major, cult. In the stone carving of Cernunnos found built into the choir alongside the altar in the Notre Dame church in Paris, the god is flanked by a bear, as he is also in the Perthshire find. Stone carvings and cameo brooches of bears are of frequent occurrence. An important object is the so-called Monster of Noves (France). This object is a mythical amalgamation of a man and a bear. From the jaws protrudes a human arm, and under the two forepaws are the severed heads of two men. Very common in Celtic Wales and Ireland are two names that both mean "son of a bear." And, perhaps most interesting of all, is that in Berne, Switzerland, we find the worship of a bear goddess. Her name, Andarta, means "powerful bear."

I believe we have good grounds for considering that this bear worship, in particular, traces an unbroken line of descent from the altars of bear skulls, which Neanderthal man built a hundred thousand years earlier.

The religious practices of the Celts also involved, among other things, the worship of wells, rivers, and sacred trees. The word "Druid" actually means "he who knows the oak," and ceremonies were often conducted in forest sanctuaries. These details are important for reasons we shall consider later, but for the moment we note that these practices constitute forms of "earth magic."

The Celts were firm believers in life after death and so buried their dead with food, weapons, and ornaments. Much is often made of the sun-worshipping practices of the British Celts. But it is clear that many megalithic sites, which they took over and did not change, are constructed equally and sometimes more especially for the worship/observation of the moon. The original megalith builders "were even able to detect the

---

*We might again remember in passing that the Gypsies of Europe also came from India.

Moon's 'minor standstill,' a phenomenon caused by its elliptical orbit that has a cycle of 18.6 years; discovering this tiny 9 degree irregularity in the moon's orbit must have taken many generations of scientific study."[3] Moreover, the aligning of some sites only begins to make sense when we consider the point on the horizon where the sun sets (not where it rises). The reason for the alignment here would seem to be to signal the commencement of night ceremonies, which would naturally involve the moon.

In physical type the Celts are often described in ancient times as being fair, tall, and blue-eyed. This statement can be taken with a pinch of salt, however, for two very good reasons. First, some Greek and Roman writers confused the Celts with the Germans. Second, examination of the actual skeletons of former Celts shows a very wide variation in body size and head type. It was specifically the warrior class who were tall (and perhaps also fair-skinned and blue-eyed). The description does not hold for other occupational groups in Celtic society.

For the solution to the "riddle" we can turn to India, whose people share a common cultural ancestry with the Celts. Here, to this day, we find a caste system in operation, with relatively impermeable barriers between the castes. It happens to be the case that the higher castes (like the Brahmins) both have fairer skin and are taller than the lower castes (like the Untouchables). What I believe we see in modern India is one attempt to come to terms with the fact of our own duality, with the fact that we are a hybrid species. This answer is "to live together while apart." Our personally differing inclinations and natures—the "Cro-Magnon" or "Neanderthal" preponderance that we each personally have and that tend to correlate regularly with certain physical attributes like height, skin color, and hair color—are "dealt with" by appropriate role assignments. It is logical that the "Cro-Magnon" type should perform the functions of the warrior and of leadership generally (in the authoritarian sense of that term). This "solution" was evidently practiced by the Celts also. But the majority physical type found among the Celts approximates to the short, dark types we associate with Wales,

Ireland, Cornwall, and France at the present day. What happened to the tall, fair, blue-eyed minority? Well, warrior classes do, of course, have a habit of wiping themselves out in protracted warfare against superior opposition. (However, against myself, it must be agreed that present-day Celts also do not lack aggressive qualities.)

AN INTERPRETATION

These scattered observations, along with others yet to come, seem to me to make best sense in terms of my own central hypothesis—and in so doing in turn offer support for the hypothesis.

To recap briefly, my basic scenario is as follows:

1. Cro-Magnon man evolves in northern India during millions of years of isolation from other forms of men. He develops and practices sun worship and hunting magic. His culture is patriarchal.

2. In the remainder of the world during the same period different forms of Neanderthal evolve. We are concerned here with Neanderthal 1 (see p. 59)—the Neanderthal of Europe and the Middle East. He develops and practices moon worship and earth magic. His culture is matriarchal.

3. Around 35,000 years BP, Cro-Magnon abandons India and heads west through the Middle East into Europe, overrunning Neanderthal. By 25,000 BP the predominant type in Europe proper is Cro-Magnon.

4. In the Middle East a hybrid population, that is a cross between the Cro-Magnon and Neanderthal types, emerges. Pure Neanderthal has largely ceased to exist either here or in Europe (but see chapter 13).

5. By 15,000 BP, pure Cro-Magnon man has also ceased to exist. He has meantime been driven out of north and west Europe by renewed glaciation, into southern Europe. Here he has been gradually infiltrated and absorbed by the mixed types (that is, ourselves).

Meanwhile mixed types have also penetrated Africa—for during glaciation in Europe the Sahara becomes a well watered, grassy plain—and back into India, and then on to China. In these places, the mixed types further mingle with the local Neanderthal types. In Africa, China, and ultimately in North and South America, "Neanderthal" influence is, therefore, generally stronger than it is in Europe and the Middle East.

Now, even during glacial times, the inhabitable part of Europe is not small (comprising southern France, Spain, Italy, Greece, and so on). Once the glaciers retreat again in 10,000 BP, the territories of Britain, Germany, Scandinavia, Poland, Russia, and so on are also, once again, at man's disposal. There are no roads and no maps in this vast area, just tens upon tens of thousands of square miles of territory, mostly virgin forest. It is not difficult, for the time being, for tribe to remain separate from tribe.

The main point here is this. The mixture of Cro-Magnon and Neanderthal genes is appreciably different in various modern peoples (both in and outside Europe). The mingling of cultures is similarly uneven. Some pursue very much the path of earth magic and moon worship, others that of hunting magic and sun worship. Some for a time maintain a fairly even balance between the two; but this arrangement creaks more and more as mankind evolves (and essentially because in the human psychological landscape *objectivity* increasingly dissociates itself from *subjectivity*). Nowhere, in any case, is there any longer either moon worship or sun worship as they once separately existed before the great mingling.

The increasingly complex events that take place in historic Europe in the last ten thousand years (since the last Ice Age) are well understood, culturally, in terms of the varying fortunes of later moon religion and later sun religion. They can be equally well understood sociobiologically in terms of the clash of our two natures, the "Neanderthal" and the "Cro-Magnon." In this context these two terms should always be written in quotes, because as parts of our own make-up they have only a tangential relation to the original Neanderthal and Cro-Magnon natures.

I also believe that the so-called Indo-Europeans and Cro-Magnon are one and the same, and that the so-called non-Indo-Europeans and Neanderthal are one and the same (and I have given my detailed reasons for so believing in *The Neanderthal Question*). Whether my reasons are acceptable or not, what is interesting is that other writers and thinkers, quite independently, make the same statements about the last ten thousand years as I do—except that they use the words "Indo-Europeans" and "non-Indo-Europeans" where I use "Cro-Magnon" and "Neanderthal," respectively.

Robert Graves, for instance, writing about the perennial tendency of goddess worship to revive itself among certain peoples despite fifteen hundred years of repression by Christianity, has the following to say. He is referring specifically to the present-day Celts of the British Isles:

> . . . the popular appeal of modern Catholicism is, despite the patriarchal trinity and the all-male priesthood, based rather on the Aegean Mother-and-Son religious tradition to which it has slowly reverted, than on its . . . Indo-European warrior-god elements.[4]

We have already noted the dominant position that Mary has for many Catholics over her son Jesus. The point I want to make here is an additional one. It is that I would be perfectly happy to have written exactly the same sentence as Graves myself, but putting "Neanderthal" where Graves has written Aegean, and "Cro-Magnon" where he has written Indo-European. Our *thinking* on these matters is identical. Only our terminology separates us.

Graves is also, without knowing it and perhaps without agreeing with it, foreshadowing the increasingly respectable science of sociobiology. (It is nice for those of us who have been arguing sociobiology for years to be now given a respectable label for our arguments.) Sociobiology states that culture is an expression of our nature, which is in turn an expression of our biology (both past and present). An ethnic group will produce the culture that suits or fits that group "naturally." If another unfitting culture is forced upon it by warfare or conquest, that other culture will *never* be accepted in the longer term, the appearances of the current short term notwithstanding. Using my terms, the "Cro-Magnon"

German/Scandinavian/Anglo-Saxons ultimately threw off Catholicism because it was too "Neanderthal" for their nature and replaced it with forms of Protestantism. But for the "Neanderthal" peoples of Ireland, Italy, Spain, and so on, Catholicism is not "Neanderthal" enough! Consequently they have been steadily augmenting the "goddess" and "female" elements within it.

For some, even that augmentation will not do and never has done. They have always longed for the true "Neanderthal" religion of moon worship, earth magic, and goddess worship—for the priestess, the witch, and the wise woman. These were the individuals who concealed fertility symbols in the altars of churches, who inlaid labyrinths on the floors of cathedrals, and saw to it that a Celtic altar bearing the names and portraits of Eseus and Cernunnos formed part of the fabric of the choir in Notre Dame. Ultimately these same instincts give rise to spiritism, spiritualism, and the occult revival of the present day.

MEGALITHS, CELTS, AND WITCHERY

A lively and widespread association between the megaliths and magical practice has persisted in the public mind for the last fifteen hundred years since the demise of the Druids. But we can produce evidence to show that this traditional association is far older.

Geoffrey of Monmouth, writing in AD 1136, spoke of Merlin causing the stones of Stonehenge to be brought from Ireland to Salisbury Plain. As Aubrey Burl notes, this is an extremely interesting remark, in that the stones *were,* in fact, transported along the then Ireland-Wessex trade route. Majority opinion today, however, believes that these stones were only transported a mere two hundred miles from southwest Wales. Nevertheless, Monmouth does have Merlin specifically saying "send for the Giant's Ring which is on Mount Killaurus in Ireland," an emphatically precise statement. Burl's sources point out that Killaurus may be a medieval name for mountains around Kildare and Wicklow, which have several stone circles related in form to those in Wessex.

The points for us here are these. First, Monmouth's writing shows that in the twelfth century AD interest in Stonehenge was lively, and its origins by no means wholly misunderstood. Second, granting that Monmouth was reporting a Druidic/Celtic legend dating, therefore, only from the first millennium BC, that legend nevertheless shows that the Druids themselves had some knowledge of events that took place a thousand years before their own coming—for the Giant's Ring dates from 1500 BC (while the very first work on the site was performed in 2700 BC). So, to come back to Monmouth, legendary/historical material is available in the twelfth century AD that arose in the fifteenth century BC, and that therefore has in a sense leapfrogged the Druidic/Celtic civilization.

The interest in no way dies at this point. In AD 1560, the Synod of Argyll finds it necessary to destroy a stone circle on Iona (under whose ring of twelve stones men had been buried alive), because of its continued use as a place of worship. And then again far earlier still, on the continent of Europe, a council in AD 658 at Nantes ordered the destruction of stone circles "at which people often worship . . . and present oblations," while the Lateran Council forbade the worship of stones in AD 452.

Here we see some of the many links between the stone circles as such and the eventual medieval cult of witchcraft. Two very solid links between witchcraft and the Celts are the fact that the witch's coven consisted of thirteen, just as did the Druidic coven of the first millennium BC; and the fact that the leaders of the medieval covens without exception adopted Romance, i.e., Gallic/Celtic names (see p. 12). But more interesting still is the proposition that both the Druids and the witches were continuing a tradition far older than the Celtic civilization.

The Merry Maidens, the Trippet Stones, and other Cornish circles are said to be human beings who were turned to stone for dancing on the sabbath. The Pipers in Wicklow, Ireland, are said to be another group of dancers and their piper who similarly offended. Interestingly, one such group is actually called the Witch and her Daughters. The Hurlers, again in Cornwall, are said to be a group of men who were playing ball on the sabbath.

The many references to dancing are of the greatest interest in connection with moon dancing, already discussed in earlier chapters (and see also the reference to mazes on p. 126). Of course, while in Christian terms the dancers were desecrating the sabbath, in terms of the Old Religion they would have been celebrating the sabbath.

What exactly *is* the sabbath?

Penelope Shuttle and Peter Redgrove[5] report that the word sabbath (which Christianity takes from the Hebrew word *shabbat*) comes originally from the Akkadian *shabattu* (or *shappatu*), which is a feast held in honor of the full moon. These authors further tell us that Ishtar, the moon goddess of Babylon, was thought to menstruate at the full moon; They and their sources, in fact, consider that *shabattu* was actually the feast that celebrated the menstruation of the goddess.

Before we look at further direct support for this idea, we find tangential support for it in the concepts attending Jewish sabbath observance. In Judaism the apparently once monthly festival has become a weekly festival (not an unreasonable step, because as we know 4 x 7 does make 28, seven is a powerful mystical number, and the moon does pass through four identifiable phases each month). The point of interest is that the Jewish sabbath is considered to be a woman, and the religious ceremony that takes place on Friday evening at dusk in Jewish homes (Saturday, of course, being the Jewish sabbath) is to welcome "the sabbath bride."

In India, at the present day, the Mother Goddess is believed to menstruate. At such regular intervals when she does so, bloodstained cloths are displayed as evidence that she has had her sickness (the cloths themselves are much valued for their healing powers). Meanwhile the statues of the goddess are kept secluded.

Shuttle and Redgrove tell us further that the ancient Greeks also observed the festival of the menstruation of Athene. Her "laundry" was initially washed monthly, but with time this became a yearly ceremony.

On the basis of these items of information, I now myself consider that the English phrase "don't wash your dirty linen in public" is actually a very dim echo of these same ceremonies—an idea that also gains support from the fact that in Japan today one of the gravest causes of loss of social face is to be seen doing or carrying laundry.

In all the outright religious festivals associated with these beliefs and practices, all work is forbidden on the day of the festival. (Shuttle and Redgrove consider that the prohibition applied originally only to "male" or "business" work.) In our own religion (and in modern Judaism), the prohibition covers not just work, but travel and merrymaking also. Hence "dancing" (= merry making) is not allowed: but in terms of the Old Religion the "dancing" that celebrated the religious rite would, of course, very much be allowed. It was the whole point!

The "harmless" Maypole dancing at village fairs and in schools today, which in origin consists of dancing round a tree, is clearly an actual remnant of the dancing of the Old Religion.

So the witch and her daughters, and the merry maidens, and the piper and his troupe were quite in order to be dancing on the sabbath as far as the Old Religion was concerned. They were only "desecrating" the Christian idea of the sabbath.

Again, perhaps the main point in all this is that we have leapfrogged the Druids back into a past that precedes the Celts (as such). The mention of Babylon alone takes us back to 3000 BC. But, no doubt at all, the actual predecessors of the later Celts are very much involved in all this—for they do, of course, have ancient links with India, as we have seen. And talking of links with the very ancient and the very modern, let us not overlook some of our opening material—that fact, for example, that an instruction to devout Muslims concerning the new moon, which is several thousand years old, is found existing as a current, independent superstition in modern England (see p. 33).

One way and another we have already produced a fair amount of evidence to show a continuous set of traditions running from pre-Celtic times, through actual Celtic civilization, to the witches of medieval Europe. But there is more evidence to come.

BEFORE THE STONE CIRCLES

Not only in Britain, but in many parts of Europe, we find circles predating the building of the first stone megaliths. These are, variously, circles of pits dug in the earth (often filled with items of religious significance, such as the remains of sacrifices) and of circles of pits in which wooden posts were also erected. It is likely that there were also circles composed of wooden posts alone, but without accompanying pits these would leave little or no trace after destruction or collapse.

Here, then, we seem to have the prototypes of the later stone circles, which, unlike the early stone circles, are found in many parts of Europe. The suggestion gains support from still other considerations.

The Celts were tree worshippers—so much so that the word Druid means "he who knows the oak." Tree worship was practiced virtually everywhere in ancient times, in fact, and certainly all around Greece (where the Danaans and the Milesians came from). The Scandinavians had the World Tree, Yggdrasil. Christianity, Judaism, and many other religions have the Tree of Life, of Knowledge, or whatever.

May it not be, therefore, that the first circle was a circle of *actual* trees, no doubt twelve in number, with a thirteenth at the center? (And are Yggdrasil and the Tree of Life the descendants of that central tree?) The task would have been either to clear an area of forest to leave the required trees standing, or to plant saplings in a cleared area. (One would need to dig a pit to plant a sapling. . . .) The fact that such planted trees would take many human generations to reach maturity poses no problem. We have ample evidence of that degree of continuity. Support for this idea can be found, too, in the circumstance that the Druids actually performed some of their ceremonies in "forest sanctuaries," while in Greece and elsewhere we have the concept of the "sacred grove" (of trees) dedicated to particular goddesses and gods.

Later, actual trees might be replaced by poles of prepared tree trunks. Such measured and trimmed poles would actually be of much greater use in the astrological tasks of aligning and observing the heavenly bodies. Aubrey Burl is not against this particular idea and, in fact, suggests it himself.

In Crete, Greece, and the eastern Mediterranean in general, sacred trees became formalized as stone pillars! These frequently had spiral or vertical flutings—so here, perhaps, is a link with and a stylized descendant of the twining umbilical cord/serpent around the tree (see pp. 90–91). Or possibly, in the case of vertical flutings, we are seeing stylized bark. The bark of many trees is striated or channelled vertically to facilitate water runoff. A Greek temple, then, is a stylized forest grove.

Several thousand miles further west the tribes of the British Isles hit upon substantially the same idea—that of replacing wooden pillars with stone pillars. Stones, of course, were far more permanent and reliable. (As far as the builders were concerned, they were eternal!) The British stone used could not be as readily worked as the softer stone that the Greeks chose—and the Greek columns are, in any case, of later date and workmanship.

Here, perhaps, is the moment to draw attention to the prodigious amounts of effort and investment involved in the British enterprises in terms of early man's resources. And to the fact that, in some cases, the stones were apparently granted *safe* conduct over considerable distances. Both these circumstances point to the enormous power of the priesthood and the religion itself: and to the probability that there was *one common religion* among all these differing (and remember, pre-Celtic tribes) over this very large area. There was certainly warfare between them. Yet, as far as we can judge, they never damaged each other's shrines and, it seems, exempted religious affairs from their quarrels.

That religion was a version of what is referred to in folklore and ancient writings as the "old religion." At a later point we shall summarize the contents and practices of the old religion. For the moment we simply state that it always contained a mixture of moon/earth and sun/sky elements. The Celtic religion was also a version of the old religion. Thus it resembled the religion that the Celtic invaders found in pre-Celtic Britain, perhaps as closely as Protestantism resembles Catholicism, or perhaps as distantly as Christianity resembles Islam. But either way, the case was that the Celts easily recognized the religious practices of the pre-Celts, and were able to adopt their shrines and their uses without any hesitation or change. One imagines them saying: "*Stone* circles. What a marvelous idea!" Unlike the later Christians, they did not at all feel that they had to destroy the circles.

Two points connected with these matters. The first offers yet further support for the enormous geographical distribution of the ideas we are considering. Figure 8 shows four representations of a maze from Cornwall (England), Crete, India, and North America. Their similarities as such require no comment. But regarding the origin of such mazes, it is thought they arise from the increasingly complex movements of ritual dancers—probably of a "womb dance" that leads symbolically to the origin of life and out again. The mazes/labyrinths used in the Mystery ceremonies were actually built below ground, and the origin of the word "labyrinth" is pre-Greek.

sacred symbol,
Hopi Indians

Halebid temple,
Mysore, India

coin design,
Knossos

rock carving,
Tintagel

Figure 8. Maze drawings from different parts of the ancient world.

The second point is an extension of one already noted. The Greek column appears to be a stylized tree and the Greek temple, therefore, may be a stylized grove of trees built in stone—*as perhaps are also the stone megaliths of Britain.*

There is one very important difference, however, between these two versions of the sacred grove. The Greek version is often rectangular, with sides at right angles to each other. The British version is almost without exception a circle or oval. The reason, I suggest, is that the curve, the spiral, and the rounded shape are the cultural hallmarks of Neanderthal; while the straight line is the cultural hallmark of the Cro-Magnon personality. These cultural manifestations are, in turn, the sociobiological expression of psychological difference. The straight line is the natural expression of the conscious, rational, and logical mind. The circle and the spiral are the natural expression of the unconscious.

WHAT WERE THE STONE CIRCLES FOR?

A strange question to ask, in a way, since this chapter has already done little else but try to answer it. But we need still to spell out some specifics.

The first circles, which long preceded the actual stone megaliths, were certainly purely magical/religious in intention. They marked a spot at which, and in which, you gathered to worship your deity and to make sacrifice. The moment of sacrifice might be when the moon (say) was directly in line with a particular tree and/or the altar tree, or when the shadow of one of the surrounding trees touched the center tree, or whatever. Perhaps, as a result only of such simple maneuvers or "observations," it was then realized that this circle of objects could actually be *used* to record and study (and eventually predict) the movements of the celestial body. So, in time, a tradition of moon, sun, and star knowledge began to be assembled—passed on from generation to generation of priests by rote learning. (Druids, Caesar tells us, took twenty years to learn by heart the Druid "laws.")

These astrological/astronomical functions of the more complex stone circles are what so many books have recently been written about. But we are more concerned with the magical/psychological aspects. Incidentally, my view here of the gradual or accidental genesis of the astronomical functions of the circles gains support from Burl's comment that a circle is not the ideal form for such observations. A line of stones or a horseshoe shape, he says, would be more appropriate.

In any case, for a wide variety of reasons, many of the circles, stone and otherwise, can never have functioned as observation points. (They might be slap bang against a mountain, for instance.) In a study of fifteen sites in Cumbria, for example, Professor Thom himself only proposed five as possible for astronomical use. The part purpose of all circles was magical; and, in many cases, that was the sole purpose. What "magic" are we talking about?

Well, a good first point to consider is why a circle is where it is. What persuaded the circle builders to put it here instead of there? Approaching the possible answer obliquely, we note that circles and other standing stones are said still today to have curative and restorative healing powers. Touching the stones is said to make a barren woman fertile, for example. In far away North America, Red Indian medicine men will rest with their backs against a standing stone. They claim this restores their own healing powers. Then, in ancient Greece (and presumably elsewhere), a custom was to spend the night sleeping at a shrine or in a sacred grove. In the course of the night one would have a dream, sent by the deity, that would solve one's problem.

All these various beliefs (if true) are capable of explanation in terms of "vibrations"—some kind of radiation produced by the stones, or by the ground in which they rest. It has been theorized that a stone (or a tree?) placed in the soil above a running underground stream will generate an electromagnetic charge. Some psychics (mainly dowsers) claim that they can sense such actual charges in some stones, and Professor John Taylor is currently investigating this particular possibility with sensitive electronic equipment. (Or maybe, after all, the legends derive from "touching wood" see chapter 7.)

A similar kind of theorizing suggests that, since the earth is a giant electromagnet, which it is, composed of a great variety of materials, certain "forces" may be concentrated at particular points on the earth's surface. While as yet no real proof exists for this particular hypothesis—apart from the megaliths themselves, that is—it is not in itself an unreasonable one. We shall take it up again. At any rate, the Christian Church did not hesitate to build its own churches and cathedrals on the selfsame spots.

If ancient peoples, who were undoubtedly better psychics than we are, prove to have been right in "diagnosing" certain areas to be especially healthful—or, at any rate, to be emitting unusual types of radiation—we should have to list the megaliths and the ancient shrines as genuine components of, and contributions from, "ancient wisdom." The astronomical functions of the megaliths, however, about which there is no doubt in principle, really form part of "early modern know-how" as defined in chapter 7 and so are not of central relevance to the main thrust of this book.

9
The Holy Grail

As for Robyn, she liked the opposite technique. Gregory loved to bring the dream into waking life. She loved to use objects and actions of waking life to bring herself closer to the dream. She loved magic. . . . She would burn candles, and she would bring the darkened moon down into her house.

—*The Terrors of Dr. Treviles*

Penelope Shuttle and Peter Redgrove's fine book, *The Wise Wound,* came into my hands in late 1977. I had by then clarified my own thoughts on menstruation and already drafted the sections of this present book that deal specifically with that topic.

I was absolutely delighted with *The Wise Wound,* not least because it confirmed my own conclusions from new directions. The question was how best to integrate this new material with my own? I decided basically to present these authors' case in a chapter of its own (this one), adding my own comments, reactions, and amplifications as I went along. Shuttle and Redgrove believe that the story of the Holy Grail, told in Celtic myth, is in origin an account of menstruation worship that formed part of a fertility religion—in fact, of the Old Religion of the Moon Goddess.

As with many ancient legends, there are several versions of the Grail story, each differing in detail. The story has been heavily Christianized to disguise its true significance—a fact that attests to the great importance of this legend. For, as we know, when establishing a new religion the takeover handbook instructs: destroy as much of the previous religion as you can, but what you cannot destroy adapt to fit your own. Another interesting feature of the Grail legend is that it was not written down till quite late on. This suggests either that Christianity was hoping that, if ignored, it would go away; or that it formed part of the more central message of the Old Religion, and so was disclosed by its later keepers only reluctantly.

The first written version of the Grail story comes to us from Chrétien de Troyes, who in the twelfth century AD wrote his *Le Conte del Graal* or *Roman de Perceval*. He never finished his version of the story, and the manuscript ends with Perceval waking in a deserted place having failed in his task (see below). There seems little doubt that Chrétien intended to write the further adventures of Perceval comprising a later and successful quest. Other writers then variously undertook this sequel after Chrétien's death.

As far as the Christian elements in the tale are concerned, the Holy Grail is the cup or bowl that Christ used at the last Supper. At the Savior's crucifixion, Joseph of Arimathea caught some of Christ's blood in this bowl and then brought it to England. Here the Grail disappeared.

Alternative stories tell how Perceval/Parsifal (or another knight) comes one day to a castle by the sea. He is received into the castle and there sees a procession of maidens and knights (or priests) carrying a lance (or sword) that drips blood. This is caught in a silver chalice by one of the maidens. Perceval is supposed to ask about the Grail and the procession and say, "This cup that bleeds, what is it for?" But he politely keeps silent. However, in some versions he does ask why the cup or lance bleeds—in Christian eyes this is the spear that pierced Christ's side while he was on the cross—and this question does part of the trick.

The "trick" or task is/was to restore to health (or sometimes to raise from the dead) the wounded king of that country, and also to remove barrenness from the land, the Wasteland. Straightaway, then, there are questions of fertility involved. Since, also, we are told that the king has been wounded by "having a spear thrust through both thighs" (a strange kind of wound), we need not hesitate to consider that he has been castrated. Apart from this matter and the question of the land's barrenness, fertility/sex elements are further suggested in the view of most scholars that the Grail is actually the magical cauldron of the ancient Celts "from which none goes unsatisfied." The phrase admits of a fairly obvious double interpretation.

It does not require an overactive imagination to see also in the symbolism of the story (and once again most commentators agree on this) the elements of the male and female principles. The lance or sword is the penis, and the bowl is the vagina/pelvis. (While the "king who dies" is also, I think, the sun who dies each year, leaving the land barren until he is raised again.)

What Shuttle and Redgrove in particular appear to have missed, however, though the idea fits so well with many of their arguments, is that the "lance that drips blood" is the penis of a male who has had intercourse with a menstruating woman. The authors point out that the sexual desires of women do reach a peak around the time of menstruation (though, I must add, not quite the level reached at estrus). Given also that the monthly festivals of ancient times were quite definitely celebrating the menstruation of the Moon Goddess (see p. 122), it is possible that a climax to the affair involved the high priestess having intercourse with a chosen male (promised great rewards in heaven), who was then perhaps sacrificed or castrated.

(It is difficult not to keep going off into, nevertheless, relevant tangents at every point here. But later Shuttle and Redgrove suggest that the origin of the Medusa—the hideous woman, whose hair was writhing snakes and whose look turned men to stone—is in the menstruating vagina. Probably men were never allowed to see this most sacred of mysteries, and the only time they did see it was just prior to being sacrificed. The "wounded" king of the Grail story had, after all, been castrated.)

My own main argument in the belief that intercourse with a menstruating woman (the menstruating priestess) was the most important part of the most important ceremony is precisely because of the iron law with which Judaism *forbids* intercourse with a menstruating woman! As we saw in chapter 6, this crime was punishable by an early death, and any child that happened to be born from such an act was a bastard, despite the fact that a husband and wife were involved.

The total denial of the role of blood in all facets of Jewish life (as in significant aspects, too, of Gypsy and native life) really tells us that Judaism was originally a *blood-worshipping* religion. Tales of vampires and werewolves are faint memories of such practice. In the subsequent Cro-Magnon turnaround on these matters, all such central features of the Old Religion were repressed. For this reason menstruation is today known as "the curse" and a very great number of other derogatory names. It was, therefore, probably once "the blessing."

Far-fetched? Well no, I'm afraid not. "Bless" and "blood" are the same word. (And to bless was originally to sprinkle and consecrate with blood.) Moreover, bless/blood is the same word as bloom and blossom, meaning to sprout, grow, or flower. So there we are once again squarely back with fertility rites.

Shuttle and Redgrove pursue their theme with a consideration of the Song of Solomon. The real significance of this Biblical poem is not far below the surface, as the authors show. And the Song of Solomon is, of course, part of received Judaeo/Christian tradition. This at least is no Celtic yarn!

Before we come to the Song, it is well worth pointing out that the "Christianization" of the Celtic Grail legend may itself not be quite the cover-up job it looks. The sick king of the Grail story is called the Fisher King, and the castle is by the sea. This slight hint is actually of great importance, and well worth a detour.

The fish was the old symbol of Christianity and, as such, its use was very widespread. (Christ himself made some of his disciples into "fishers of men.") The Greek word *Ichthus,* meaning fish, was used as an acrostic to refer to the Christian faith—the initial letters of the word formed, in Greek, the first letters of the sentence "Jesus Christ, Son of

God, Savior." But the fish symbol is actually far, far older and is found in the most ancient folklore we have in the Near and Middle East. In Syria, for example, the fish was worshipped and could not be eaten, except by priests in order to sanctify themselves. But in ancient Egypt it was precisely priests who could not eat it; and various cults in Egypt considered the fish sacred. Perhaps most interestingly from our point of view, the Mystery cults of Eluesis laid strict prohibition on the eating of fish. The Carthaginians sacrificed fish to various gods, and these were prescribed votive offerings also among the Romans and Etruscans on certain occasions. Again most interestingly for us, fish was regarded as the most suitable food for the Jewish Friday night ritual meal, which ushered in the sabbath itself. (In Jewish folklore the fish is said to be particularly protective against the evil eye.) The Catholic eating of fish on Friday is certainly a further echo of these matters.

The sign of the zodiac, Pisces, is two fish tied together by the tails. It derives from a Greek account, in turn derived from a much older Egyptian one, of Aphrodite and Eros springing into a river to escape from Typhon, whereupon they were turned into fish.

Then, finally, one or two theorists have tried to suggest that the Christian use of the fish derives from the "savior fish" of India. But we need not be concerned to ask whether one of these *derives* from the other. A better explanation is that both originate from a common source. In the Indian legend Manu, a kind of Indian Noah, spares the life of a young fish and rears it in captivity. It foretells to him the deluge and instructs him to build a boat. Later Manu releases the now large adult fish into the sea. When the great flood does come the fish returns again to help Manu.

Comment is superfluous in this case. But does it not begin to look as if all this at first sight so diverse and unconnected material is actually all of a piece? The temples of early historical religions seem all to be in part built of materials plundered from one single prehistoric temple—the Temple of the true Old Religion. Our suspicions here will grow, not diminish, as we go along.

Taking especially the line in the Song of Solomon, "thy navel is like a round goblet, which wanteth not liquor," Shuttle and Redgrove show this to be a prudish mistranslation. "Lap," not navel, is the correct translation—that is, vagina or cunt. The liquor of this goblet is then the fluid that lubricates the vagina during sexual arousal and intercourse. This fluid is, of course, absolutely essential to pleasurable lovemaking.

A rather promiscuous Jewish friend of mine once remarked that he preferred making love to Jewish girls "because they produce more fluid."

This leads us on to the question of the pleasure of lovemaking. The more sensuous and arousing the intercourse, the more chance that the intercourse will result in impregnation of the female and the birth of a child. The more vigorous the male's ejaculation, for example, the more chance that a sperm will successfully complete its long and difficult journey. A good ejaculation knocks hours if not days off that mighty journey!

Cunt and tit and fuck are curse words in modern western society. But they were once blessings. For, as every prostitute and non-Mary White-house lovers know, the use of such language dramatically stimulates desire. How strange of the western God to forbid such joy of sex, but to have organized it so that those who defy Him on the issue produce more children.

Joy in sex is indeed one reason why "Neanderthal" breeds faster than "Cro-Magnon," and produces more pregnancies, more full-term pregnancies, and more vigorous babies. The milk of a mother of a child conceived in sensuous love is said to be sweeter hence the wine *Liebfraumilch.*

These matters are important at any time for the survival of a species. But how vital they become when we realize that among true Neanderthals (as opposed to "Neanderthals") one third of the population was dead by the age of twenty, and virtually all the remainder by the age of forty. Cro-Magnon's actuarial statistics were also of a similar order.

The main argument of Shuttle and Redgrove's book, *The Wise Wound,* is that menstruation in women is a physical concomitant, an outward sign, of considerable inner mental powers. Menstruation, they argue, was worshipped and held sacred in part because of the mental and psychic powers it betokens—as well, of course, because it is a sign of fertility. They show, for example, that women dream more toward and during the nights of menstruation. This, they suggest, is a sign of greater creative potential at this time.

Certainly there is no difficulty whatsoever in showing a clear connection between dreaming and creativity, in both men and women, at the present day. It is almost commonplace for writers, artists, and designers to report dreams as being a direct and literal source of their inspiration, for example, individuals like R. L. Stevenson, Coleridge, Goethe, Jung, and Blake. Two of those named (Goethe and Jung) also functioned as noted scientists, and many full-time scientists (including several Nobel prize winners) likewise attribute major scientific discoveries to dream—Niels Bohr, von Stradonitz, Otto Loewi. Even more to the point here is that Penelope Shuttle and Peter Redgrove continuously and deliberately use dreaming and related forms of trance in the production of their own outstanding fiction writing and poetry. More of that in chapter 11.

But these authors claim that because woman's menstruation, and everything that goes with it, is vigorously repressed and despised by modern society (the pejorative terms we have for menstruation would almost fill a book by themselves), the time of the period for modern women tends to be one of pain and distress and anger. This general position does not simply apply to menstruation, of course. Any attribute that society decides is unwelcome frequently becomes a source of mental, and then physical, i.e., psychosomatic, pain—the color of your skin, the size or smallness of parts of the body (Adler's organ inferiority), your religious beliefs, and so on.

Some idea of the extent of the suffering produced by the denial and repression of the menstrual experience is contained in the copious statistics listed by Shuttle and Redgrove. I produce here only a sample of their list:

84% of crimes of violence committed by women were during the premenstruum; most rapes are committed while the victim is menstruating; suicides increase during the premenstruum and menstruation; nineteen out of twenty-two Hindu women who committed suicide by pouring kerosene over themselves and lighting it were menstruating; five billion dollars are lost annually in the US due to menstrual absenteeism; 45% of 276 acute psychiatric patients were admitted to hospital during the paramenstruum; of 185 admitted for depression, 47% were in the paramenstruum; 50% of 156 newly-convicted prisoners' crimes were in the paramenstruum; 54% of alcoholics and 56% of thefts were in the paramenstruum; of 94 disorderly prisoners studied, 35% were menstruating.[1]

Backing up these statistics, the law of several countries treats menstruation during the commission of a crime as an extenuating circumstance. And the burial of a female suicide in consecrated ground was permitted if the woman had been menstruating at the time of death.

All in all a rather remarkable set of circumstances by any standards. Such statistics and other related evidence leads us to suspect strongly that persecution of witches throughout history has been in large part the persecution of the menstruating, sexual woman; and, of course, of the genuinely magical/creative powers that are linked to sexuality.

A word of caution here, though. We may not take the statistics given totally at face value, even though the authors have, of course, reported them accurately. As the authors themselves agree, we do have to examine the methods and methodology used by the various investigators in collecting the data, and even the very attitudes of the investigators, because such matters do exercise a significant influence on the outcome of any investigation. Briefly, researchers tend to find whatever it is they set out to look for. All of us, always, are liable to the danger of "creating" facts. So it is virtually certain that an independent or skeptical investigator would be able to reduce the percentages involved after examining or repeating these studies.

Nevertheless (and I speak here as a psychologist), we can take it that the figures given do express a genuine trend and substantially reflect a real situation.

I also fully agree with Shuttle and Redgrove that both menstruation and dreaming are (significant) elements within a still greater framework. This is the framework of the total autonomic nervous system and its chief evolutionary product—the "unconscious" intuitive mind. (I use the word unconscious, incidentally, simply because it is the term that our society—grudgingly!—recognizes. I myself prefer the term "alternative consciousness.") The intuitive mind is vitally involved in matters like psychic healing, clairvoyance, telepathy, and the production of paranormal phenomena generally.

Modern, western society does direct, massive violence to women and the unconscious intuitive mind. It further does violence to the whole spectrum of creativity. For the autonomic nervous system and its superstratum, alternative consciousness, contribute one half of our creative powers.

But here a further word of warning. The reverse of this statement is also true. "Neanderthal" society does direct, massive violence to the male psyche and the conscious rational mind. It further does violence to the whole spectrum of creativity. For the central nervous system and its superstratum, normal consciousness, contribute one half of our creative powers.

To put it simply, too much objectivity damages our intuitive, subjectivity-based powers. But too much subjectivity damages our objective rationality. We need *both* sets of attributes if we are to be and to remain sane. A "balance" is the equilibrium of two matched weights. But we are today unbalanced. The major problem of our present society is that we have almost completely lost touch with the "Neanderthal" part of ourselves. Modern religion, even Catholicism, does not meet this desperate need of our psyche—hence the flight into extreme, uncontrolled forms of witchcraft and spiritism and—yes—communism as frantic attempts to save ourselves and our society. These desperate attempts, themselves offering not a solution, but a different form of sickness, are the direct product of our overscientific, overrational, material-istic, fascist, authoritarian, patriarchal society.

The evidence for these claims is extensive. Shuttle and Redgrove provide us with one form of it. Their sources show that menstrual tension is greatest in those women who strive hardest to keep to the conventional roles that modern masculine society dictates to them. (I hope we can see now that the loss of "ancient wisdom" and the ills of modern society are in part connected situations.)

Reverting to the ancient wisdom itself, Shuttle and Redgrove suggest that the famed red powder of the alchemist, which could allegedly turn base metals into gold, is none other than a dim, distorted memory of the menstrual religion. (To smear red ochre on sacred objects and sacrificial victims is commonplace in ancient religion—see pp. 73–74, for example.) The red powder originally symbolized the blood of the menstruating goddess. By medieval times that connection had been forgotten. Only a magical red powder was remembered.

Andrew Tomas gives us several typical "case histories" of the alleged phenomenon:

> After a long search they found an old copper chest under a column. It contained a parchment with strange signs and letters, and four jars of reddish powder. Seiler expected to find gold coins in the box and was so disappointed that he thought of throwing out the contents. But the old monk became interested in the document and insisted that the powder be preserved. The aged friar finally came to the conclusion that the red powder could be the precious transmuting compound of the alchemists. Then Wenzel Seiler stole an old tin plate from the abbey's kitchen and after covering it with the red powder the plate was heated in the fire. As if by magic, the tin plate shortly became solid gold![2]

The idea of converting base metal to gold seems to be only a distorted and still more symbolic version of the Grail story of the power of the red contents (allegedly Christ's blood—but originally menstrual blood) of the Grail or cauldron to revive barren land and to cure infertility. Remember one of the reported healing properties of the stones of the megaliths— causing a barren woman to conceive. Originally it was the whole complex worship of the moon/mother goddess, including the menstruation elements, that maintained the fertility of crops and mankind and transformed each year the barren land. Or so its devotees believed.

Shuttle and Redgrove draw attention to Bruno Bettelheim's interpretation of the story of Sleeping Beauty, and I would like to add my own comments. Bettelheim suggests that this is really the story of a father who tried to keep his daughter from reaching puberty and becoming sexual. The twelve blessings are the twelve years of the girl-child before puberty. The curse (of the thirteenth uninvited fairy) is the menstruation that comes in the thirteenth year. Or perhaps rather, as I would suggest, the blood which flows when a girl is deflowered. In the story Beauty "pricks" herself on a spindle: but "prick" is also a slang word for penis.

It seems to me that the Sleeping Beauty story is the story of all fathers, who must one day lose their beloved daughters (who remind them so much in looks and youth of the wife they once married, but who has now grown old) to other men. There is no doubt at all that the act of first intercourse releases a residual instinctive mechanism in a girl that bonds her to the man who deflowers her. (Hence the overlord of a manor used to insist on having the first intercourse with all newly-married women—*the droit de seigneur*—thereby both symbolically and literally bonding her to him.) At the time of first intercourse the "Oedipal" bonds between father and daughter are broken and replaced by the girl's independent sexual activity.

Today in the Jewish religion thirteen happens to be the age at which boys undergo the ceremony of manhood. Was this once, in the dim past, the time when girls (also) were ritualistically deflowered—that is, made women—another possible meaning, of course, of the lance which drips blood—in the sight of the goddess?

To use a coarse phrase from our own society, when they're big enough they're old enough. Neanderthal peoples certainly reached puberty earlier than modern Europeans do (as it happens Jewish—and also African—boys and girls reach puberty on average a year earlier than Europeans) and Bettelheim's "thirteen years" is really rather late for that. Let us not forget that a third of Neanderthals were dead by the age of twenty. They had no time for hanging about as far as childbearing was concerned.

A good point is made by Shuttle and Redgrove about the word "superstition." It means literally "that which stands over"—i.e., survives—from previous religions and cultures. It does not automatically mean, as the superrationalist sneeringly insists, "that which is bunkum."

Etymology links us also to some other fascinating possibilities and actualities. These authors draw our attention to Erich Neumann's claim that the words "man" (that is, mankind) and "moon" were originally the same word. Neumann challenges the orthodox view that "man" (which *also* means "mind" and "spirit"—there is no argument about that) is from the root "men-," while "moon" is from "me-," which means basically "to measure," and so comes to be "moon" (by which we measure time), "menstruate," and so on.

It is an interesting suggestion but remains very much a minority view. I would like to accept it, because this interpretation would enable us to say that mankind once thought of itself as "the people of the moon." However, I am afraid I still side with orthodox opinion in this case.

But the issue led me to a realization no less remarkable, which this time has the support of orthodox etymologists. I was wondering if "mother" had any connection with these matters. The first syllable of "mother" is based on the child's lipword (particularly when feeding at the breast) of m-m-m. It occurs in a great many languages (as mummy, mama, mutti, and so on). To my absolute delight I discovered on checking that W. W. Skeat, one of the pillars of the etymological establishment, considers that "mother" and "measure" and "moon" *are* all from the same root! (By way of explanation he suggests that the mother is the one who regulates or measures the household.[3]) This is wonderful news, for now we need have no hesitation in considering the Moon Goddess and the Mother Goddess as one and the same figure. ("Mother" is then "she who regulates society" or the world itself.)

Straightaway all the suggestive cross-references between these two are now validated. It is real cement for the theoretical edifice this book is building.

To bring us back to the starting point of the chapter, Shuttle and Redgrove consider that they have answered the three great riddles of the Grail legend, and I would agree with them. These riddles are: (1) Whom does this Grail serve? (2) The world is the Grail and the Grail is the world: what is the Grail? (3) Where is the Grail castle, that is surrounded with water, that is everywhere at once, and that is invisible?

The answer to the first question is "humanity" or "mankind." The answer to the second is "the moon"—for the world is governed and fertilized by the moon, but the moon is held in the earth's orbit. The answer to the third question where is the Grail *center?*—is the vagina/womb of woman. It is surrounded by fluid and is hidden, although everywhere, because it is internal. (And even in a naked woman standing and walking normally the vagina is not seen.) It is the moon that governs the functioning of the womb (Grail castle) so the links of the riddle intertwine satisfactorily.

Woman, the moon, the Moon-Mother Goddess, and the menstrual cycle are seen again and again to form the oldest heart of the Old Religion. We had better have another look at women.

Note: Having given these matters careful further thought, I am now convinced that the Gypsy taboos of not allowing a woman to touch herself below the waist after she has touched herself above the waist (and vice versa) without washing, and of not allowing her to wear one continuous dress (see chapter 6) are in origin the same as the Jewish religious practice of strictly and permanently separating meat from milk in kitchen and diet. The meat here represents the menstruating vagina, and the milk the feeding breast.

There are no "mere" Freudian puns. When a woman is menstruating her breasts do not produce milk. Once she is pregnant, the breasts produce milk, but the menstrual bleeding stops. (Breast-feeding a child also prevents the renewed onset of menstruation.) If the Goddess herself (the Moon) took such care to separate and isolate these two processes, then mankind could do no less.

The true origin of these taboos in the Gypsy and Jewish religions has, of course, long been forgotten.

10

The Land of Women

I am black, but comely, O ye daughters of Jerusalem. . . .
As an apple tree among the trees of the wood, so is my
beloved among sons.

— SONG OF SOLOMON

The ancient, poetic name for Ireland is Erin. I think everything I want to say in this chapter could be summed up by this name: it is a feminine word, meaning peace.

Throughout Celtic mythology we find many stories of a marvelous land across and sometimes below the water. It has many beautiful names. It is called the Land of Promise, the Divine Land, the Land Beneath the Waves, the Land of Eternal Youth, the Pleasant Plain, the Land of the Living Heart, and the Isle of Apples; but it is also called the Land of Women, the Maidens' Land, the Land of Ever-Living Women, and the Isle of Women.

The significance of these tales is twofold. They express, on the one hand, the deep longing of the human psyche for that which is both eternal and beautiful. More than any other the mythology of the Celts actualizes and evokes the magical world to the point where we feel we can simply reach out and touch it, Look, there it is . . . almost.

However, aside from expressing and fulfilling (almost) a deep and genuine desire of the human psyche, I believe these tales are also a last, dim memory of an *actual* land—a land, or a time, known long ago. As we look at the material content of the stories we shall come upon many items with which we have already become familiar in this book. We shall later also find other stories like those of the Celts—though certainly not displaying their range and power—as far away as Japan. The parallels we find in these other mythologies will once again help us to think in terms of a common source.

The Celtic stories often tell of some well-known hero or warrior. Typically he will meet with a woman—perhaps in the countryside, perhaps in a castle—who offers to take and often does take him to the wondrous lands of which we are speaking.

Such is the story of Bran in *The Voyage of Bran*. One day Bran hears music behind him, which he finds is being played by a woman from "unknown lands." She tells him that where she comes from there is eternal sweet music and everlasting joy. Grief, sorrow, old age, sickness, and death are unknown. People make love "without crime." They are sinless and immortal. The crops grow without being tended. The rivers pour forth honey. . . .

Bran goes with her over the sea to the "fifty islands" that make up this paradise. (This "fifty" may not be unconnected with the fifty that Robert Temple has researched so well in his *The Sirius Mystery.*[1]) *En route* they pass Manannan. Manannan is the god of the sea—and so the implication is that the islands are part of his kingdom. Indeed, Bran himself is not sure if he is on sea or on land.

In all these stories the traveler meets the marvelous women of the land, who sometimes form the majority of the inhabitants, and who in any case usually live apart from the men (or gods) in their own part of the kingdom. The women—or goddesses—are the ultimate authority. The females are, in fact, always goddesses rather than mortal women. And these offer eternal life to the male travelers if they will only stay and love them. (It is, of course, the female principle begging the ungoverned male principle to resume the old liaison.)

Usually, however, the travelers/heroes tear themselves away and return home. But there either, like Bran, they find that they have been away for centuries and that they themselves are remembered only in legend, or when they set foot on their native land they turn straightaway into ashes, or wizened old men.

(Here, of course, we have general links with stories like those of Rip Van Winkle, whose stay of a "few days" in the magic mountains proves to be one of many, many years. And then also with stories like those of Odysseus, for example, when he and his men stayed in the land of Circe.)

In fact the stories, although telling of the wonders and joys of the Land Beneath the Waves, are really counseling the warrior, the male, not to stay. In some stories he does not even go in the first place. So in the case of Dunlaug O'Hartigan a fairy woman offered him two hundred years of life and joy, an existence without death, cold, thirst, hunger, or decay—if he would but put off the combat he was facing for one day. But he preferred death to "dishonor." And so he joined battle and "foremost fighting, fell."

The Land of the Living Heart, then, is at best a trap. At worst it asks for the betrayal of courage and manhood.

Elements that recur over and over again in these stories of the marvelous country are: the ethereal, supernatural music; the supernatural fruit trees (usually apple trees); timelessness or the slowing of the passage of time; food and drink that never fail to satisfy; making love without sin; and everlasting beauty and youth.

Apart from the so-to-speak common or garden magical food in that land, there is also a special kind of magical food, which is sometimes spoken of as a mead or beer; and sometimes as "crimson nuts" or "fragrant berries": "certain fragrant berries of which it is said no disease attacks those who eat them, but they feel the exhilaration of wine and old mead; and were it at the age of a century, they would return again to be thirty years old." (So the food makes you feel "high" rather like alcohol does.)

This "magical food" or "fairy food" is what fairy tales all over Europe warn one against eating—so that here again is a common element reaching beyond Celtic boundaries into general European folklore.

Frequently after a trip to the Land of Promise, and especially after eating the magic fruits, the hero wakes to find himself alone, in a deserted spot or in an empty castle. Not only have the companions of the previous night vanished, but sometimes the very buildings.

My use of the word "trip" in the last paragraph and the meaning of that word in modern hippie jargon do suggest a very good explanation for some aspects of these mysterious voyages and the wonders experienced. Do they not sound like the visions induced by hallucinogenic drugs—and not so much by "magic mushrooms" as perhaps by opium?

I am not suggesting that magic mushrooms were generally available to the Celtic public (though Peter Redgrove tells me they grow in Cornwall). But it seems possible that magic mushrooms (though not opium) were available to the Druids, for their own use, and for use with a very occasional outsider (like a king) whom they wished to impress. In support of that view, let us not forget that the contents of the mystical Celtic cauldron *were* also said to grant inspiration. The smaller details likewise fit well. Those who have tried hallucinogenic drugs know how they distort one's perception of time—and how even quite banal music can sound absolutely beautiful.

At any rate, as far as the Celts were concerned, there existed or had once existed "fairy food," along with magical women (priestesses, goddesses) who could transport you to another land, where things ran along very different lines to the ones you were used to.

Let's in fact, try translating these stories into a more modern vernacular.

"Look, there used to be these incredible women. Or rather, there still are, but they're not here. They're over the sea somewhere, or they live under the sea, in the most beautiful place. And they can do things to you you wouldn't believe. They can cure *anything*—any illness. And if you're old they can make you young. Well, they can certainly make you feel young, which is the same thing. In fact, as long as you keep on taking the tablets you stay young and beautiful and sexy—well, forever, really.

Of course, once you're there, once you've started all this stuff you have to keep it up. Otherwise all the so-to-speak debts you've been collecting catch up with you rather suddenly. But as long as you keep running you're all right. Anyway, these women . . . "

The withdrawal symptoms of the drug addict today, from whom supplies of the drug are withheld, are well-known to us. They become very "old" very quickly; they turn into ashes. *Is* this one of the things we are talking about in the old fairy tales? I think so.

Remember in *Goblin Market* the girl who hearkened to the fairy music after dusk and went with the elves and ate their apples? How she became sick thereafter and could not eat or sleep for longing for the goblin fruit? Her sister went to the goblins (who would not sell her any fruit) and let them rub the fruit all over her lips, though she was careful not to eat any, and then went back to her sister, who licked the other's lips, and was cured. Is that not a story of the gradual weaning from a hard drug, like opium?

I do very much want to say here that the beautiful goddesses *are real.* These figures are, I think, the distorted memory of the high priestesses of the Moon-Mother Goddess and the *old* Old Religion. (And the goblins and the elves of Europe are also real. They are the actual Neanderthal people, and the fairy food is the various natural drugs—the earth magic—they knew so well. That is all part of it.)

There is plenty more evidence yet.

Some of the Celtic stories tell how wisdom is obtained in the Land of the Gods/Goddesses by eating salmon. (So here we are back with the fish of the last chapter.) This is called the Salmon of Knowledge. What a very odd expression! Of course, had the story said the Apple of Knowledge or the Tree of Knowledge that wouldn't have struck us as odd at all.

Now the cat is really getting out of the bag. Manannan, the god of the sea and the lord of the Land of Eternal Youth, has a palace on the Isle of Arran, which he called Emhain of the Apple Trees. Why? Because the apple tree was sacred to him. (In Welsh—Brythonic—mythology this same god is called Manawyddan. After a battle with the *sun* god he was

one of the *seven* to escape. . . . And then he became guardian of the marvelous cauldron "that never failed to satisfy." The contents could also
produce inspiration. . . .)

Before we go into the further implications of what has been said, crucial aspects of the material so far must be emphasized.

The first is that the Land over the Water is *never* associated with
death or life after death. It has *nothing* to do with an afterlife or any
notion of heaven. Also ruled out in it are any questions of guilt or
penance. Love-making, in particular, is without any sin. A further,
extremely interesting point, not so far mentioned, is that in the Land
over the Sea there is no such thing as personal possession. As one legend puts it, there are no such words as "mine" and "thine." Another
states that "all things are held in common." Finally, the leaders of this
society are females.

The above account—stripped of its supernatural content that, I have
suggested, can be understood mainly in terms of hallucinogenic drugs—
is, in my emphatic opinion, a description of *an actual way of life.* A real
way of life, that once actually existed.

What I think we have here is an—admittedly highly idealized—description of the way of life of the Neanderthal tribes. It was a way of life radically, and indeed diametrically, opposed to the life led by Cro-Magnon
man. Cro-Magnon's life was rooted in the concepts of (1) ownership,
(2) male dominance, and (3) pair-bonding, that is, the union of one man
with one woman. Neanderthal life had no concept of personal ownership (least of all of owning territory or land), was female dominated
(both religiously and economically—let us not forget that "mother"
means "regulator" or "manager"), and did not practice pair-bonding.
The men and women of the tribe made love "freely" and children were
reared by the tribe as a whole. We also find this last practice in Pacific
island communities to this day, incidentally.

I need hardly point out the relevance and incidence of these matters
in present-day views of the (ideal) socialist communist state: free love,
absence of personal possessions, collective social responsibility, equal

rights for women. All of these, of course, were actually put into practice in the early kibbutzim of Israel.

Plant life and plant eating (vegetarianism) also played a greater part in Neanderthal society: as did conversely animal life and animal eating in Cro-Magnon society. Of course, this is *not* to suggest that Neanderthal never ate meat, or that Cro-Magnon never ate fruit and nuts. But we see these two emphases repeated in the vegetarian tendencies of left-wing, progressive groups to this day (and a rejection, for instance, of hunting); and conversely in the steak-eating practices of sportsmen, athletes, business men, and other right-wing, male-dominated subgroups.

I have hinted several times that the Neanderthal way of life described in the Celtic legends is highly idealized. I am quite sure that the reality of it was often unpleasant and desperate. The fact that one third of real Neanderthals were dead by the age of twenty (of malnutrition, disease, accident, and probably, sporadic—though not highly organized—fighting) is quite sufficient evidence for this statement.

But it is the case that (1) anything that lies back in time develops a rosy hue, and (2) that of which one is deprived becomes highly desirable. Both of these statements can be verified by reference to our own personal experience. But both have been tested experimentally at a prosaic level. Students were asked to write a factual account of their holidays. Six months later they were asked to write the same essay again. Comparison of the two essays showed a significant decrease of unpleasant items in the second attempt. In a study of deprivation, children from poor areas and children from wealthy areas were asked to estimate the size of coins from memory. The poor children significantly overestimated the sizes as compared with wealthy children.

Especially in tribes and peoples with a greater admixture of Neanderthal nature and culture, we find vigorous and emotionally-charged memories of Neanderthal life, which, however, are by no means inaccurate in terms of their general content.

We can now go on to look at some further stories of the Land of Promise—or, to give it now its *Greek* name, Elysium.

First, a close relative of the more general Celtic Land of the Living Heart is the Welsh or Brythonic Avalon. Avalon is, again, an island and is also called the "Isle of Apples" (*avall* means apple tree). This island "lacks no good thing," crops grow readily, and so on. It is ruled by a Virgin Queen and is mainly a land of women.

Associated here is Nimue, the Lady of the Lake (who gave the sword Excalibur to Arthur). She is said to live in a wonderful palace in a rock beneath a lake.

Both Avalon and this lake are associated with Glastonbury. It was to Avalon that Arthur was taken to recover from his wounds after fighting Mordred. And we have a very interesting account of that particular story. This account is itself evidence that an older Arthur existed before the one that we have now.

A groom arrives at a castle in Italy. Here he finds Arthur lying sick from his wounds. He is told that these wounds "break out every year afresh."

Here, of course, we are once again back with the wounded fisher of the Grail story. The "wounds that break out every year afresh" are a clear indication of an annual death/rebirth fertility epic. What I myself assume this epic as being is as follows. Every year, at midwinter, the sun and the lands die. The moon, of course, never dies in that sense. She is the same all through the year. She is the persistent and enduring one. Through her influence the dead sun (the dying king) is renewed and brought back to life. And then he, revived, also brings life back to the land.

Now let us turn to the Elysium (Elysion) of early Greece. This land is also called "the Islands of the Blest." Its detailed description parallels very closely the descriptions of the Celtic tradition. *The Mythology of All Races* has the following to say:

> The parallel between the Celtic and early Greek conception of Elysium is wonderfully close. Both are open to favoured human beings, who are thus made immortal and without death. Both are

exquisitely beautiful, but sensuous and un-moral. In both are found islands ruled by goddesses who sometimes love mortals . . . and both are over-sea.[2]

There is no doubt that the Celtic and Greek legends here share a common source.

There are further parallels to both in the legends of Scandinavia and Germany. But the references are much scrappier. (In my own view this is explainable in terms of the greater Cro-Magnon influence among these peoples.) Again, however, in the magical land of the gods time elapses as in a dream. The food of the fairies and gods must not be eaten. It is this that destroys the sense of time and that causes warriors to turn their backs on duty. A far stronger parallel to the Celtic and Greek legends is found in Japan and it is hard not to think that here again we have precisely the same legend.

The legend concerns the Buddhist goddess Benten (who is the same as the Hindu Sarasvati), one of the daughters of the sea god. (Celtic Manannan was also the god of the sea.) There are many extremely beautiful shrines to this goddess along the coast. One of her shrines is the "Isle of the Temple"—an island where, reputedly, neither death nor birth occurred. It is an actual island, situated in the Inland Sea. When the tide rises, the extensive temple buildings are enclosed by it, so that they appear to be floating on the sea:

> Another spot famous for the worship of Benten is Chikubushima in Lake Biwa. The island rises steeply from the water and its cliffs are overgrown with evergreens. The poets are never tired of singing of its beauty, and popular fancy attributes all sorts of fairy wonders to the place. There stands a shrine dedicated to Benten, whose music is heard in the waves and ripples that beat against rocky cliffs, and whose image is seen hovering in the sky when the moon transforms the island and its surroundings into a realm of silvery light. It is said that, on a certain day in spring, when the full moon is in the sky,

all the deities and fairies of the country meet at Chikubushima and make up a great orchestra.[3]

In this account we see that Benten is clearly associated with the moon; in fact, *is* the moon. She rules over the spirits of the earth and the woods (the rivers, the groves, and so on). In her realm beings are immortal (neither birth nor death occurs). We have the association with "over the water" and a strong emphasis on music, which even seems to come from below the water. (While writing these paragraphs the phrase "the pipes of Pan" came to my mind.)

We can now begin to firm up on certain associations and connections, which we have been constantly touching upon. We are certainly involved here with music, poetry, and the arts. The magic cauldron also gives "inspiration," presumably to the artist. In the Greece of the seventh century BC, we have another island, mainly peopled by women, and devoted to the arts and to the worship of the moon. It is the island of Lesbos in the Aegean. Aside from giving the words "lesbianism" and "sapphism" to our language, the poetess/priestess Sappho and her followers endowed Greece with a fine tradition of lyric poetry and music. Here we are talking about real people and real achievements. But can we doubt that they consciously formed part of the traditions we have been discussing?

The Amazons also enter into our calculations at this point. As most people know these were a semimythical (but undoubtedly partly real) nation of women, ruled by a queen, who chose to run their affairs apart from those of men. (They would occasionally visit men in order to become pregnant. But afterward they only kept and reared the girl babies.) They founded several towns—including one at Lesbos.

A common story told of the Amazons is that they cut off their right breasts to facilitate use of the bow and arrow. But, *Larousse* tells us, there seems to be no foundation in this story. None of the many pictorial representations of the Amazons show any trace of such mutilation. *Larousse* proposes that the name does not mean *a-mazos* ("no breast"), but that the prefix "a-" means "augmented" or "enhancing."[4] This means that the Amazons were *large-breasted,* either literally or metaphorically. Shades of Neanderthal woman.

Now a rather dramatic jump to the Aborigines of Australia. Australian Aborigines believe in something they call "the dreaming" or "the eternal dreamtime." This dreamtime is claimed to be a formative or creative period that existed at the beginning of things. "Mythic beings" shaped the land and brought forth the various species. The mythic beings no longer exist, but they did not die. They were transformed and became part of ourselves. And, actually, they were not basically different from men in the first place. Moreover, they have left tangible evidence of their physical presence on earth.

Without undue forcing, I believe we can see in the Aboriginal account of the dreamtime a reference to an earlier, magical species of man— Neanderthal. The choice of the word "dream," especially to describe something real, is a very interesting one.

What do Aborigines say about women? What is their attitude toward them? Well, women are totally barred from taking any part whatsoever in religious affairs. This is a stronger prohibition even than that practiced by the Jews, who at least allow women to attend religious services, but nevertheless then segregate them entirely from the men. And a menstruating Aboriginal woman, who touches items belonging to a man or walks on a path used by men, may be put to death. That attitude is a good deal stronger than the Jewish ritual bath!

What on earth could such savage reprisals be, except a backlash to a once all-powerful superior?

Vestiges of the old, old practices still remain even among Aborigines. There are shrines (totemic increase centers) where women may be mystically impregnated. And, as noted, the totem group consists of blood relatives on your mother's side.

I believe that all stories worldwide of once paradisal or magical conditions (also of legendary lands and retreats said to exist at the present time, like Shangri-La) are dim, distorted, and sometimes deliberately disguised accounts of life as once lived by Neanderthal. Atlantis also comes into this category.

My statement applies equally to a concept like Zion, the idea of the promised land that has burned so strong in Jewish hearts these last two thousand years. The "real" Zion is not even a town or a village. It is a place in the hills near Jerusalem. Yet Jerusalem itself is called a "daughter of Zion" (and in view of the patriarchal overlay of modern Judaism, the use of feminine is itself remarkable). Jerusalem is even called "the virgin daughter of Zion"! Is she not then (like the Sabbath bride) the High Priestess of the Zion/Neanderthal people?

And, then, what of the "Promised Land" of Moses, the land of milk and honey? Is that not the selfsame entity that the Celts called the Land of Promise? There, too, the rivers ran honey and the crops grew without tending.

Further help comes from the legend of the Garden of Eden, one of the myths at the very heart of the Judeo-Christian tradition. This is a heavily disguised and masculinized account, which, in any case, has more than one layer of symbolic meaning. Its inhabitants (Adam and Eve) are, however, immortal in the first instance. They are "without death or birth" as we normally understand those terms. And their subsequent "crime" was sexual, sensual lovemaking.

Where did they get the knowledge of sensual love? Why, from the Apple of the Tree (which is the Tree of Knowledge). The magical Avalon was the Island of Apples. (And all over ancient Europe men were warned not to eat of the "goblin fruit"—the magical apples, perhaps.)

As we saw in the opening chapters, there is good ground for assuming that the "apple" referred to in all these accounts is the Moon-Fruit, which grows in the Universal Tree. The round apple is the symbolic moon.

Virtually all fruits are round, as are all nuts and berries. Women are round (with apple breasts) and become even rounder when they are pregnant. All these are round in honor of the moon, whose fruits they are. The sun is likewise round, and his direct action is responsible for the growing and swelling of the fruit. But he, in turn, is governed by the moon, who raises him again each year from his death. In the same way, although it is man who makes woman pregnant, he can only do so *because she is fertile,* and she is fertile only because of the action of the moon. The moon is the ultimate mover and controller of everything.

This was the sin of Adam and Eve: that they discovered this Old Knowledge of the Old Religion. *That* was the *forbidden* knowledge.

Incidentally, the apple in the stories is not an apple. Apples are temperate zone fruits. For this reason, the "apple" of the Old Testament has been suggested to be a pomegranate. But it isn't this either. "Apple" is really a purely symbolic term. It is "*the* fruit," "the *roundness,*" in fact. "Roundness is all," Browning might have written. In fact, he wrote "ripeness is all," but that will do, too.

There is one more very intriguing point. Again and again, from Ireland through to Japan, we find the suggestion that the magical world is an island. It is over sea, or over water. In some cases it is even said to lie below the sea. (And here, as already suggested, we can also tie Atlantis into the general web we have been weaving.) The god of the sea (or his daughter) in some sense has charge of this domain, though authority is vested in the ruling queen or goddess. And sacred fish, the inhabitants of the sea, are a further persistent element in the stories.

I do not think we can dismiss these elements. They are too persistent and too central.

There are two possible types or levels of explanation, and, in fact, I think both are involved.

One is that the sea has always been a symbol of the unconscious mind. (The reason for this, in my view, is because the cerebellum, the physical seat of the unconscious mind, has in the course of evolutionary time been covered over by the newly-developed cerebrum, the seat of the conscious mind. So the cerebellum is a kind of neurological Atlantis.) The fish represent the mental contents of the unconscious.

But I think we also need to be literal about the Islands of the Blest. And I think we can find literal explanations.

I consider that European Neanderthal culture (and so here we are talking about Neanderthal 1a—see pp. 59–60) and the rule of the moon goddess came to its flowering during the years 70,000–30,000 BP. At this time the Würm glaciation held Europe in its iron hand. Incredibly, *classic* Neanderthal managed to survive on the actual ice sheets of Europe, and under these pressures became, as we saw in chapter 6, in our eyes the least human of our relatives. But the other European Neanderthals retreated down below the ice sheets into southern Europe and the Near and Middle East. Here they were never far from the waters of the Mediterranean. Fish was a significant, staple item of their diet—not just those from the sea itself, but those of the many, mighty rivers and lakes.

(In such climates, too, grew the opium poppy.)

Certain islands were made the holy of holiest places, where priestesses lived in isolation. Perhaps, on certain feast days, the general population visited those islands. Inland tribes would send delegations, composed mainly or entirely of priestesses.

The idea of a vast communications network suggested here is not far-fetched. We have clear evidence of such a network operating in pre-Celtic Britain.

It is probable that Sappho and her fellow female and male poets on the island of Lesbos in the seventh century BC were consciously continuing, or reviving, an antique tradition that they had real knowledge of—in much the same way as the witches of medieval Europe continued and knew of the traditions of the Celtic Druids.

Ecstasy, inspiration, drug-induced visions, music, poetry, sensual love, lesbianism, and homosexuality mingled on these islands.

The artist in historical times has also never moved far from these matters.

11
Artists, Poets, and Priests

*The procedures are a continuum, and the trance is of
various levels and depths. It can start as mere attention
and deepen so that one seems to have gained a new mind,
new sense-organs. It is difficult to remember what one
has done when one is back in the ordinary state, and this
is why the poetry is such useful messages from the other
place. The messages can (a) give one actual information
(b) comfort one in adversity or depression that there is
a larger world, more vivid, better in every way than the
ordinary senses pretend (c) poetry correctly read produces
a trance in the reader in which he is able to tap these
abilities; this makes him write more poetry if he is a poet,
but if he is, say, a doctor, it will help him in the intuitive
side of his work, and it may for all I know give gardeners
green fingers.*

—Peter Redgrove

Certainly up to ten thousand years BP, the only "home" or refuge that the
creative (particularly the creative-artistic) individual could find in human
society was in the priesthood. Human society, at that time, had no "leisured class" and nobody could be spared from the pressing affairs of the
twenty-four-hour working day. These affairs involved (1) fighting (defend-
ing/conquering), (2) finding food (gathering/hunting), (3) the rudiments

of domestic or home life (making clothes and cooking vessels, rearing children, and the like—either in one fixed spot, or on the move). Nobody could be, or was, spared from these tasks—except the priesthood.

There is good and still accumulating evidence that the priesthood was the first, and for a long time the only, profession that human society was willing to "carry," and to exempt from the common duties. In modern terms, the priesthood was funded out of taxes. The stone megaliths of pre-Celtic Britain, with their enormous investment of time, labor, and finance are ample evidence of the power that priests had to divert capital and revenue to their own ends.

Not that the priesthood was considered by the people as any kind of luxury or inessential aspect of society. On the contrary, it was an absolute necessity. It was the priests/priestesses who ensured the supply of game and wild crops, guaranteed the fertility of the tribe's women and the health of its babies, turned the tide of battle in their people's favor, or shielded them from the worst effects of attack. They functioned also as doctors, treating the sick and the mad. And they were also the repositories of the tribe's history, traditions, and laws, which they learned by heart as part of their profession. At night, while the people snatched a few hours rest around the campfire, it was the priests who lifted the people's hearts with tales of their past deeds and their glorious future, who fed and exercised their imaginations with song and poem and story. And it was the priests/priestesses who organized the great religious feasts that were the highlights of the year, the injection of magic that carried the people through the grim days between.

With the later development of proper agriculture and the rise of great civilizations like Sumeria and Babylon (though Jericho is a flourishing city already 11,000 years ago), other "leisured" or supernumerary classes come into being—economists, military advisers, agricultural advisers, diplomats, and so on. But still the priesthood had the lion's share of the cultural and spiritual action, and it was still in the priesthood that the cultivated, talented, and artistic individual found his or her home. And the poorer the society, the more this remained true.

The poet today is the descendant, both culturally and psychologically, of those ancient priests. Perhaps I should have stressed "psychologically," because important though the cultural links are, it is the psychology of the poet/artist/visionary that is, as it has always been, the single most indispensable asset of human society. In case any scientist reading this feels left out—don't. The visionary scientist and the visionary poet are one and the same.

Robert Graves has always been quite clear that he (like all visionary poets) is the direct cultural descendant of the ancient priests and priestesses. He writes: "Since the age of fifteen poetry has been my ruling passion and I have never intentionally undertaken any task or formed any relationship that seemed inconsistent with poetic principles." As a result, he is "nobody's servant" and lives away from the pressures of modern urban life "on the outskirts of a Majorcan mountain village . . . where life is still ruled by the old agricultural cycle."

In his book *The White Goddess,* Graves shows that the Welsh poets of early medieval times were conscious bearers and direct descendants of the Druidic tradition. His argument is based partly on "two extraordinary Welsh minstrel poems of the thirteenth century, in which the clues to this ancient secret are ingeniously concealed." In fact, all "European poetic lore is ultimately based on magical principles, the rudiments of which formed a close religious secret for centuries."[1] An ultimate descendant of this brotherhood and practice is seen in the Welsh Eisteddfod (though Graves considers this but a sanitized and castrated remnant of the original) and in the work and thought and feeling of a few present-day poets.

Looking back to the origins of the great poetic tradition Graves tells us that: "The ancient Celts carefully distinguished the poet, who was originally a priest and judge as well and whose person was sacrosanct, from a mere gleeman. He—the poet—was in Irish called *fili,* a seer; in Welsh *derwydd,* an oak-seer, which is the probable derivation of Druid."[2]

This is extremely interesting information. The poet, originally, was synonymous with the priest and the psychic. (The gleeman, incidentally, is an Anglo-Saxon figure who approximates in function and scope to the music-hall artist of the Victorian era—a song, a recitation, some juggling, an anecdote, and so on.)

Sappho, the seventh-century BC poetess, and her poet/musician friends on the Greek island of Lesbos were certainly part of the same tradition as the Celtic poets, with similar functions. They (among much else) lend support to Graves's view that the priest-poet existed throughout greater Europe.

Graves maintains that all "true" poets today (as opposed to versifiers and doggerelists) are still in the great magical tradition. I agree with him—except that I believe this to be not a cultural but a psychological heritage. To say that all outstanding poets of the last two centuries or more all consciously realized at a very early age that there *was* a tradition, and made a decision to join it, will not stand up. It is not true of Peter Redgrove, for instance, whom I am sure Graves recognizes as a "true poet." In any case, Graves himself provides us with the evidence we need.

No, the case is rather that becoming a visionary poet is something that happens to you by reason of a psychological endowment, which would find poetic expression even if all poetry books in the world were burned before your birth. Fortunately Graves tells us that his own present position is the outcome of a psychological predisposition and nature, not the result of any cultural indoctrination. Speaking of poetic truth he remarks that "the Goddess . . . demands either whole time service or none at all."[3]

This is a psychological statement. It is the statement of an inner need and compulsion. It is "the love that will not let me be" (as the Christian hymn has it). Earlier, too, Graves spoke of poetry as his "ruling passion." A ruling passion is not a cultural artifact.

My own basic proposal in these matters is a contribution not only to helping us understand aspects of the ancient mysteries but toward helping us understand that greater mystery that lies behind all local variations— the mystery of the evolution of mankind and of life itself.

When Neanderthal and Cro-Magnon met and mingled to produce ourselves, modern man, I believe each side made a unique contribution. This was at one level a cultural cross-fertilization; but at a deeper level it was a genetic one. Neanderthal contributed our religious/intuitive genes and Cro-Magnon our scientific/logical endowment.

Now, as argued in earlier chapters, this mingling worked very well up to a point, creating a well-endowed and vigorous hybrid. But this was also an unstable hybrid, with the union of the opposing natures by no means entirely complete or carried through in all respects. Where an individual is highly endowed in respect of both ancestries, however, *and* where he or she cannot cope with the tendency of the two to tear themselves apart, we have what we term a genius or the true visionary.

Many of us, all too many, fail to unite the two sides of our dual nature. And especially in individuals where the two endowments are unequally matched in the first place, we end with the man or woman who is "just a priest" or "just a scientist." This individual spends much of his or her time overindulging and glorifying the one aspect, while denying the other.

Among the true visionaries (what Graves calls the true poet and what we can with equal justice call the true scientist), we have Goethe, Jung, Blake, Schiller, Einstein, Schopenhauer, Nietzsche, da Vinci—as well as poets like Dylan Thomas, W. B. Yeats, Wordsworth, and so on. Among these I would also place Graves himself, and Peter Redgrove.

Before going on to discuss Peter Redgrove, both for himself and for his so valuable insights, let me tie in here the opening remarks of this chapter. I said there that in the ancient past and to a considerable extent even in recent historical times, the gifted individual took refuge in the priesthood. We have plenty of evidence that many of the "priests" were full, two-sided human beings. For it was they, after all, who masterminded the building and aligning of the megaliths, the pyramids, and temple/observatories of Europe and the Middle East. These were mathematically accurate and astronomically sound. They were (as well as being the homes of poetic inspiration, earth magic, and medicine) scientific laboratories. We have already indicated the scientific contributions made by these laboratories (in chapter 8 and elsewhere).

As late as the nineteenth century, a monk, Mendel, discovered the laws of genetics by observing the plants in the abbey garden, some thirty-five years before they were discovered by the scientific establishment.

Peter Redgrove read Natural Sciences at Cambridge (where he obtained his place by Open Scholarship). Prior to this he had had extensive treatment for schizophrenia. Breakdown and severe mental stress are, sadly, only too often part of the legacy of genius—as in the cases of Jung, van Gogh, Nietzsche, Einstein, Goethe, Beethoven, and so on. When he survives the disintegrative experience, the gifted individual is often able to build the insights obtained into his adult creativity.*

As scientist Redgrove's credentials are more than adequate. As poet and novelist he is quite outstanding. A majority of critics and other poets consider him one of our most important living artists. (This is a judgment the reader can easily verify for him or herself—and I suggest they begin by reading Redgrove's novel *In the Country of the Skin*.[4])

But we are here concerned with Redgrove as priest-poet, as a living present-day representative of the priest-visionaries of ancient times.

Given that we can show individuals living and creating at this moment as once allegedly did the mystical priests of former times, then we have yet another powerful argument in favor of the *real* existence of those perhaps otherwise only hypothetical individuals.

Peter Redgrove is resident poet at the Falmouth School of Art in the west of England. Here he "teaches" poetry to his fortunate students by leading them into their own inner kingdom. I am quite sure that any Druid or pre-Druid priest would immediately recognize and approve of what Redgrove is doing. The following are a few of Redgrove's comments— and, of course, the quotation at the head of this chapter is another:

---

*My comment here is not to be interpreted as a recommendation for undergoing mental illness—a thoroughly irresponsible suggestion made if not by R. D. Laing himself at any rate by many of his disciples.

> Poetry is produced in trance, is training for trance, and produces trance (the English language needs a better word, since trance suggests the suspension of thought; of course it is nothing of the kind).

> We [Penelope Shuttle and Peter Redgrove] use procedures very much like automatic writing in our own work. I also teach simple automatic writing techniques to my students in conjunction with autohypnosis relaxation exercises, and they seem to do very well with these. As for ourselves, all poetry is done in trance . . . trance is produced by various means, the strongest being reverie after sex.[5]

(Peter Redgrove lives with Penelope Shuttle, who is herself a gifted poet and novelist. Their working together as coauthors, both in respect of fiction and nonfiction, clearly resembles the functioning of Sappho's "amatory" poet colony on Lesbos. And, once again, I am sure both these situations resemble the magical-poetic activities of the priesthood of the Old Religion.)

I am happy to say that Peter Redgrove never resorts to drugs in the production of trance. In this, at least, he differs from the ancient priests. I have myself always insisted, incidentally, that drugs should never be used. They are quite unnecessary. All forms and depths of trance can be achieved by other means.

Trance, as Redgrove and I use the term, is *not* mindless immobility. It is an active (sometimes a very active) reverie—a state in which many scientists report that they have made major scientific discoveries. Probably the deepest and most complete form of trance is dreaming, and in dreams also, as we know, major artistic and scientific inspiration emerges.

I have proposed that the intuitive mind and the logical mind function in the following respective ways. The function of the intuitive mind is to convert information into experience. The function of the logical mind is to convert experience into information. In the *whole* person these processes will take place simultaneously—or more precisely, with constant oscillation between the two, as a kind of alternating current.

Peter Redgrove expresses the same idea in a different way. He states that the data of science are experienced as poetry by creative scientists; while the data of poetry are experienced by the creative poet as science. Science, of course, means knowledge. Redgrove considers it symptomatic of the schizoid thinking of our modern society that it separates the disciplines of poetry and science by dwelling on the differences between them instead of the likenesses. Redgrove insists that the insights of science (as opposed to the grim plodding through the experimental verification of the insight subsequently) are arrived at by the same mental machinery or set that brings the images of poetry.

(Interestingly the words "artist" and "poet" are in some languages the same word as "person"—in Java, Polynesia, and elsewhere. In English "whole," "holy," and "healthy" are all the same word. This situation again tells us that the true poetic vision—and the true scientific vision—can only be achieved by the *whole* person using his total mental equipment and not just isolated aspects of it.)

Redgrove argues that all "magic" is "sex-magic," and I agree with him. Neither he nor I, of course, are using either of these terms simplistically. But here are a few of the connections in these matters.

At the beginning of this century Freud went on record as believing that, despite appearances, the content of dreams is always sexual. Much later in the century scientists discovered how to monitor at which times a person is dreaming during sleep. As a result of the application of this technique, it was established that males had an erection of the penis during 80 percent of the time they were dreaming. And it is now established that females likewise experience clitoral arousal during the same proportion of dreaming time. The close connections of dreaming (the strongest form of trance) and other forms of trance with creativity have already been established. Therefore, there is a close connection also between creativity and sex.

In his function as scientist Peter Redgrove has drawn my attention to the importance of skin as a vehicle of complex experience. He points out, among other matters, that skin evolves from the same embryonic layer as the brain itself, the ectoderm. Many of Redgrove's books and articles are concerned with the skin. (Apart from his novel *In the Country of the Skin,* one of his collections of poems is titled *Sons of My Skin.*) I have to admit that I have very much overlooked the skin in my own work. But what strikes me about it at once is that here, *par excellence,* is where the conscious and the unconscious mind meet "face to face."

Touch is not only essential to us as part of our normal psychological development (see chapter 7), it is also our ultimate means of verification as far as the physical world is concerned (as Werner Erhard is always reminding us). "Can I *touch* it?" is always one of our basic criteria. "Is it *real?*" These are vitally important aspects of the skin. But the skin is equally geared to our unconscious needs and reactions. The completely unconscious psychogalvanic skin response is what is used in the lie detector, and the similar monitoring instruments employed in word-association and other tests by psychiatrists.

Redgrove's comments on negative and positive ions are still more interesting. "Negative ions" have more than once been trotted out as some kind of cure-all for mankind's total ills—just as have posture, breathing, eye-exercises, vitamin enrichment, and a host of other notions. Each of these, in turn, has very much suffered from being promoted as a cure-all. None is or can be—though each "method" can and does make a real contribution to our well-being, a fact that is lost sight of during the pernicious oversell.

So it is with "negative ions." There remains solid evidence that the presence of negative ions is beneficial to us, and the presence of positive ions harmful.

Redgrove reminds us that the hot, dry winds that wreak such havoc with the human nervous system—the khamsin and the scirocco of the Middle East, the Föhn of Austria, the mistral of France—are supercharged with positive ions. Conversely, waves breaking on the shore, a waterfall of fountain, a downpour of rain (and a shower in the bathroom!) are releasers of negative ions. This can explain why a day at the seaside can set us up physically and psychologically, why we are drawn to walk at the waves' edge, why many holy shrines are situated at waterfalls and springs. Candles are also generators of negative ions, which is possibly why we burn them in church and at shrines (and during the Friday night Sabbath supper). (Candles do also generate an equal number of positive ions, but it may be that we are able to make better use of the negative flow, so giving us a net "negative" profit.) But most important of all, the rising moon increases the balance of negative ions in the atmosphere! What a marvelous discovery!

Can it be that Neanderthal was more conscious than we ourselves both of the presence and benefits of negative ions? Again, I think so.

It has been shown experimentally that negative ion radiation augments the production of alpha waves in the human brain. These arise, in any case, during meditation and contemplation. Redgrove is convinced that the use of negative ion generators (they can be purchased from companies like Medion Ltd) also improves the quality of both sleep and dreaming, and of one's sex life. He is now trying to have these suggestions tested experimentally. Meanwhile C. A. Laws (a director of Medion) reports that an Italian biologist has shown improved activity in the gonads (sex glands) of animals after neg-ion radiation—and that one Harley Street consultant recommends the use of a neg-ion generator in the treatment of impotency.

The aim in this chapter has been to show that Peter Redgrove is a living example of the poet who is also a priest (he says, "if we had a proper, that is, psychologically useful religion, it would of course be highly poetic"), and who is also a scientist. As a bonus we have further added to our moon-lore, have found one possible reason for the choice of certain places as shrines, and see again that the ancient wisdom may have been truly wise.

Here, too, is a good point to look at some comments made by an internationally recognized scientist, Carl Sagan, who is nevertheless implacably opposed to the idea of paranormal phenomena (telepathy, clairvoyance, psychic healing, and the like)—but who is currently turning up evidence that may (and should) result in his own conversion "to the true faith." With luck, Carl Sagan will soon be considered a visionary scientist and a poet.

At this point we are concerned both with the mystery of evolution and the ancient/modern mystery of telepathy.

CARL SAGAN

In his book *The Dragons of Eden,* Sagan first dismisses dreaming (along with many kinds of what we can call "alternative" phenomena) remarking: "Perhaps those people who can do with only a few hours sleep at night are the harbingers of a new human adaptation that will take full advantage of the twenty-four hours of the day. I for one freely confess envy for such an adaptation."[6]

However later he comments, uneasily (because he is too intelligent not to see the important implications): "The fact that mammals and birds both dream while their common ancestor, the reptiles, do not, is surely noteworthy. Major evolution beyond the reptiles has been accompanied by and perhaps requires dreams."[7]

Well, yes, Dr. Sagan.

But there is a statement of still greater consequence:

> There is, for example, an African fresh-water fish, the Mormyrid, which often lives in murky water where visual detection of predators, prey or mates is difficult. The Mormyrid has developed a special organ which establishes an electric field and monitors that field for any creatures traversing it. This fish possesses a cerebellum that covers the entire back of its brain in a thick layer reminiscent of the neocortex of mammals.[8]

Is it so unthinkable that this device of the primitive Mormyrid, based on its cerebellum, could be the foundation and forerunner of a telepathic faculty in a highly-evolved organism? And also of dowsing and scrying? Precognition and clairvoyance, of course, cannot be explained simply by such a "field" notion, for they also break the laws of serial time.

So, we look forward to welcoming you, Dr. Sagan. Perhaps, too, in the light of these comments you will not, after all, find the material of the next chapter so totally unthinkable. For the moment, we leave the last word to Peter Redgrove, who began this chapter:

> *And in their slithering passage to the sea*
> *The shrugged-up riches of deep darkness sang.*

12
Scrying

The digging so far consists of a twenty-eight foot deep
exploratory shaft. Not only was the psychic amazingly
accurate in locating a new deep site which had no surface
indication to recommend it—a site most archaeology
professors said couldn't possibly exist—but the
psychic was also amazingly accurate in the geological,
chronological and archaeological details he predicted we
would encounter in our digging. Crude stone tools have
been recovered throughout the shaft as predicted: changes
in geology have occurred at the exact depths predicted
and radiocarbon dating proves the very early dates
predicted. Of the fifty-eight specific predictions tested so
far, fifty-one have proved correct. That is eighty-seven
percent accuracy.

—PSYCHIC ARCHAEOLOGY

This is in no way the first time that psychics have helped archaeologists to find hitherto unknown sites, as Geoffrey Goodman's book relates. But Goodman's own experience is recent (*Psychic Archaeology* was published in 1977) and extensively corroborated. We need no stronger evidence.

This psychic ability that some sensitives possess seems on the one hand related to psychometry. Psychometrists, by holding or touching an object belonging to a person (living or dead), can describe in detail scenes and localities associated with the owner of the object, whom, of course, they do not even know. Other psychics can receive telepathic impressions of a place they have never been in and know nothing of through the agency of another human being, who is actually in the place acting as sender. Russell Targ and Hal Puthoff have described some highly successful research into this phenomenon. But specific senders can be totally dispensed with in the case of yet other psychics. Ingo Swann, for example, is able to describe the nature of specified localities thousands of miles away, simply by being given a longitudinal/latitudinal reference on a map grid. (See again Targ and Puthoff, *Mind-Reach*.[1])

The "psychic archaeologist," however, looks below ground and discerns objects that no living human eye has ever seen. The ability to look below ground reminds us most obviously of the talent of dowsing, whereby the presence of the hitherto unknown underground water, oil, minerals, and so on is detected by the psychic standing at surface level.* But most interestingly, some sensitives and dowsers claim to be able to perform the act of dowsing simply by looking at a map of the area. And so once again we are back with Ingo Swann.

Certain aspects of these perhaps linked human abilities are tentatively understandable in terms of some kind of radiation or wave emissions. The dowser, standing above running water or a particular kind of mineral deposit, may unconsciously sense wave or particle emissions that the substrate is giving out. Not altogether dissimilarly, a sending person in a given location may somehow "broadcast" thoughts that the receiving individual picks up. Neither of these suggestions is then at variance, in principle, with the ideas of orthodox science. Professor John Taylor is currently engaged in an attempt to prove that some kind of conventional electromagnetic radiation must be involved in such cases.

---

*So strong is the evidence now for "conventional" dowsing that even *New Scientist* ran a cautiously favorable article on the subject "Dowsing Achieves New Credence," 8 February 1979.

And yet that explanation cannot really hold for the ability of the psychometrist to get in touch with the past of a deceased person—or the future of a living one! Even in the first case it is not easy to see how the ring or diary or scarf, which the psychometrist holds, can have absorbed and retained the "thought impressions" of its now dead owner. And how can the object possibly do so in respect of events that have not yet happened? Here we have not just "embarrassed" the physical universe of the orthodox scientist—we have stepped outside the normal space-time universe altogether.

The use of a map or a map reference *only* in the production either of a description of a locality or, still more remarkably, an in-depth dowsing survey, also poses very real difficulties for any straightforward radiation hypothesis.

It is virtually certain that in the range of cases just described we are talking about more than one ability, more than one set of variables. Nevertheless, there is an old term that was used to cover all of them—"scrying." If we define scrying as "the ability to obtain information other than by means of the known senses," we can continue to use it ourselves, as long as we do remember that more than one ability is involved. Scrying is crystal-ball gazing—with or without a crystal ball!

The siting of ancient shrines and megaliths was certainly sometimes due to the recommendation of "scryers" in the matter. (Perhaps all priests were genuine scryers, perhaps only some were.) But conscious or even purely fortuitous factors could also enter into the choice of site, and it is not always easy to sort one of these reasons from another.

For example, if we plot the point of the Mayday sunrise on the east coast of Britain on a map and then join that point to, say, Avebury— "the mightiest in size and grandeur of all the megaliths"—by drawing a straight line and then continue the line beyond Avebury, a remarkable thing occurs. We find we have on this line half a dozen or more major prehistoric shrines and monuments.

As most people interested in these matters already know, such straight lines derived from important points in the solar and sometimes lunar calendar (the midsummer/midwinter solstice, the equinoxes, and so on) are called ley-lines. Though some or even many instances are arguable, others, such as the one just mentioned, seem incontestable.

The first point I would want to make about these straight lines is that they are not in themselves mystical. The lines originate in fully-conscious (and very careful) observation of the heavenly bodies. We know this because we ourselves have been able to discover their objective basis. (In any case, as I remarked earlier, straight lines are always the hallmark of consciousness.)

But what caused the shrine builders to site their shrines at particular points on the line? The sites are not equidistant from each other, for example.

Now, sometimes we can find reasons that we can at least understand, even if we do not think much of them ourselves. There may at a particular site be an outcrop of strangely-shaped, though perfectly natural, rock that suggests a human figure, a crouching animal, or whatever. (Actually that seems rarely a reason in Britain, though it is common in some parts of the world.) Or perhaps the spot is the highest for some distance. Or perhaps there is a deposit of salt here, or a good vein of flint (another important commodity), or a well of good water, perhaps having outstanding mineral properties.

We can cobble together a number of reasons like this—but, actually, these "account" for only a very small proportion of the sites. What other lines of reasoning can we involve?

A clue is found straightaway in the mention of a well. Is it a natural well, or man-made? And, if man-made, how did the ancients know this was the right place to sink a shaft?

So we are back to dowsing and scrying. It is claimed that many ancient sites are, in fact, placed directly over running water, sometimes even over a convergence of underground streams. And, in some cases, as mentioned, wells have been sunk, suggesting that this is really rather a strong explanation.

In passing here we must mention the astounding discovery of Xavier

Guichard, a French philologist who published a remarkable book in 1936. Actual copies of this book can today only be found in French museums, but a good report, along with some of Guichard's startling maps can be found in Francis Hitching's *The World Atlas of Mysteries*.[2] Briefly, Guichard found a vast network of *prehistoric* towns, mainly sited in France, but reasonably frequent in Germany, Italy, Greece, and Spain, and occasionally reaching as far as Poland and Egypt. All of these towns had names based on an Indo-European word meaning a meeting place (alès, alis, or alles). These were invariably sited either on rivers (which is not surprising) or by a man-made well to salt or mineral water: that is, to health-giving spa waters.

Guichard's research did not stop there. Finally he was able to show that these very numerous towns lie either on such obvious lines as the summer and winter solstice and the north-south meridian; or on the lines of a "compass" that divide the total horizon into twenty-four equal segments, a standard tool of later Greek geographers. The single center of all these radiating lines is the town of Alaise in France.

(I am moved to make one single, tangential comment here. Eleusis is one of the derivations of this name. And that name is also famous for the celebration of the Eleusian Mysteries.)

Now, clearly the actual sites that are found along Guichard's compass lines were not put there by an act of God, in that sense. None of the other towns are equidistant either from Alaise or from each other. And plenty of other spas and watering places exist away from the lines (although *they* do not have the name of Alaise or its derivatives). So clearly what happened was that the ancients went along these (to them) important compass lines until they found a place, by dowsing presumably, where they could sink a well; or of course, found a convenient river. And *there* they founded a shrine or meeting place, which eventually became a town.

(We ought to note very firmly here that we are talking about *prehistoric* Europe. And the kind of vast communications network operating over many, many thousands of miles that we have here is precisely the kind of network I have argued in respect of the still more ancient (?) Neanderthal and "Neanderthal" peoples and their religious practices.)

We have still by no means exhausted the possible "mystical" reasons for the siting of ancient shrines and megaliths. In the previous chapter we noted that some shrine sites are producers of negative-ions, which exercise a beneficial effect on the human nervous system—fountains, waterfalls, and breaking waves, for example. (Was this why Benten's shrines were sited along the water's edge?) We noted also that the moon favorably influences the negative ion balance of the atmosphere. Is it possible that the moon's influence on certain rocks or geological structures yet further augments the supply of neg-ions? I would like to see researchers in this area examining all ancient sites carefully to see whether they in anyway, perhaps only at certain times, generate neg-ions.

It is known that neg-ions facilitate the production of alpha brainwaves, and that these, in turn, are associated with meditational states. Peter Redgrove believes that the presence of neg-ions also facilitates better sleep and enhances dreaming. In ancient Greece seekers would often spend the night sleeping at a shrine in order to receive a dream from the deity. . . .

We know, too, that neg-ions have an influence in respect of sexuality and fertility. Many of the ancient shrines were reputed to be capable of curing barrenness.

So there are reasons enough for suspecting that ancient shrines may be potent natural generators of neg-ions. (Two questions would then remain: did the ancients have any concept of, or theory concerning, neg-ions? Or did they simply say—and know—"this place is right"?)

Neg-ions are but one possibility. A wide range of both known and unknown radiations and emissions remain as further possibilities to explain the real or reputed properties of shrines, including, of course, the electromagnetic properties of the planet itself.

The straight ley-lines themselves, as I have emphasized, are conscious artifacts. The shrines and sites along them, however, appear to have been chosen by the unconscious, intuitive mind, or as I prefer to call it, by alternative consciousness. In line with this second statement we find that the shrines themselves are usually round, are sometimes sunk into the ground, and are often associated with water. These matters are all symbols of the unconscious mind.

Incidentally, I do not make statements like these lightly. They are not just associations I have plucked out of the air. I have supported and defended such views at great length in my earlier books. And in the companion volume to this one I intend to confront the scientific community with further neurological and electromagnetic evidence that it will be hard put to refute, much less ignore.[3]

So the ancient shrines and megaliths were very much a yin-yang phenomenon. They partake both of conscious and unconscious human impulses. They stem from a time when even we in the west managed for a while to get the balance right. But that situation did not last and it was left to the people of the east to recognize and foster, for a while longer, the wholeness of mankind.

There is one last important item in this chapter. It is the answer to this question: whether by scrying it is possible for at least occasional, highly gifted psychics to perceive the nature and structures of physical matter *at the molecular and atomic level?*

Obviously, if this were to be or to have been possible, we would have an explanation for the apparent knowledge of atomic structure that we find not just in ancient Greece but long before (see chapter 7). It would also help us to understand how it was that in one or two cases medieval alchemists seemed to have some knowledge of atomic number. We know that alchemists were privy to ancient traditions and sources of information, like the Kabbalah, which in some cases were never written down, or had been but recently.

I would regard my suggestion here as nothing more than a very speculative footnote—but for one event and one person—Marcel Vogel. I was present on an occasion when Vogel demonstrated his ability to project a precise mental image telepathically into the minds of an audience. Some fifty people out of five hundred experienced the complex image that Vogel projected—and I was one of them. Since I did not believe that *anyone* possessed the ability to communicate telepathically at will, I was all the more dumbfounded than I might otherwise have been. (My book *The Paranormal* contains a full account of the incident.)

On this same occasion, Vogel told us that he himself could enter a plant telepathically or clairvoyantly, and study its biochemical composition and processes at the molecular level. He also said he could cause others to share this experience. He attempted to demonstrate this ability also during the lecture—but it did not seem, as far as I could judge from the reactions of the audience afterward, that he succeeded in that attempt.

However, the fact remains that this remarkable man considers that he himself is able to scry at the microscopic level. The question remains however, whether he is *really* doing this, or only imagining that he does. Since he is Senior Chemist at IBM, he obviously has the technical information stored in his head that would enable him to generate a very real-seeming experience. I suppose, if he were willing, his ability here could be tested experimentally. A plant could be injected with bacteria, for example, and he asked to describe and identify them by his method.

I am not a lover of the experimental approach in respect of paranormal affairs—for the whole emphasis of repeatability is at variance with the quixotic, personal, unpredictable nature of paranormal events. However, if Vogel *could* demonstrate his ability under experimental conditions, it would be a famous victory.

At any rate, the possibility remains: the ancient psychics may have been able to obtain information concerning atomic/molecular structure by paranormal means. And it is an ability, therefore, that modern psychics might, with practice, develop.

13
Neanderthal Now

Only a stocky barefoot girl of twenty sometimes came
hesitantly down the path to our camp to deliver eggs. . . .
Short, thickset and massive, her body was still not the
body of a typical peasant woman. Her head, thrust a
little forward against the light, was massive boned. Along
the eye-orbits at the edge of the frontal line I could see
outlined an armoured protuberance that, particularly in
women, had vanished before the close of the Würmian
ice. She swung her head almost like a great muzzle
beneath its curls, and I was struck by the low bun-shaped
breadth at the back.

—LOREN EISELEY

One can observe even the Neanderthal type at any
public gathering.

—OSWALD SPENGLER

These are Neanderthalers.

—DMITRI BAYANOV AND IGOR BOURTSEV

Neanderthal man exists among us at the present time—in two senses.
First, you can observe him "at any public gathering"—and I personally
know one or two splendid examples. That is to say, *he is part of our own*

178

genetic inheritance. You and I are part Neanderthal. More of this aspect again later. There is, however, a still more astonishing sense in which this statement is true. *It is absolutely clear that pockets of unmixed Neanderthals have survived in Europe, Russia, Asia, and America up to, and including, the present day.*

I hope with all my heart that the one shot by the soldiers of Major General M. S. Topilsky in 1925 in the Pamir mountains was not the last. There is every reason to hope not. In 1959 Y. Merezhinsky, Professor of Ethnography and Anthropology at Kiev University, saw another several hundred miles further west in Azerbaijan. And there have been several other reported sightings.

It is a difficult choice to know where to start with the mass of fascinating material that has emerged on these matters. (I am, incidentally, deeply grateful to Francis Hitching for drawing my attention to it.) On the one hand, I want to report and discuss the material in its own right. On the other, I want to link many points in it with the views I expressed, on general theoretical grounds, in *The Neanderthal Question.* The new material on Neanderthal is, from my own point of view, remarkably supportive. Not only that, but if Neanderthal is still alive today, this helps us to be sure that he has been a force to be reckoned with throughout our own history and prehistory. What I shall basically do is present the recent material from Russia as the main theme of this chapter but interpolate it with cross-references to my own position and to this present book.

My hope is that by the end of the chapter no one will be able to doubt the reality and authenticity of Neanderthal as a historical force. Time is running out on us desperately in respect of Neanderthal, in many more ways than one.

Let us start with excerpts from the detailed account given by Major General Topilsky, actually written in 1925, and published in *Moscow News* in 1964:

> We recovered the body all right. It had three bullet wounds. . . .

At first glance I thought the body was that of an ape; it was covered with hair all over . . . the chest was covered with brownish hair and the belly with greyish hair. . . . In general the body hair was very thick . . . there was most hair on the hips. . . . The colour of the face was dark and the creature had neither beard nor moustache . . . the eyes were dark and the teeth were large and even and shaped like human teeth. The forehead was slanting and the eyebrows were very powerful. The protruding jawbones made the face resemble the Mongol type of face. The nose was flat with a deeply-sunk bridge. The ears were hairless and looked a little more pointed than a human being's with a longer lobe. The lower jaw was massive. The creature had a very powerful chest and well-developed muscles . . . the hands were slightly wider and the feet much wider and shorter than man's.[1]

What a superb account. We shall see how very significantly it agrees with other wholly independent accounts and drawings down through historical time.

In my own writings I had hypothesized that Neanderthal had brown eyes, and large ears standing well away from the head at the top and perhaps actually pointed. These were *hypotheses* only, because we have (or rather had) only skeletons of Neanderthal to go on. No trace of the ears or eyes or any other soft part survives. My hypotheses were based partly on the assumption that the fairy tales of Europe are, in fact, garbled accounts of the *actual encounter* (of Cro-Magnon man) with Neanderthal twenty-five to thirty-five thousand years ago. In fairy stories dwarfs, trolls, pixies, and even fairies have large pointed ears. On the same basis (i.e., a study of fairy stories), I also assumed that European Neanderthal was hairy—and in this respect quite unlike African and Asiatic Neanderthal. In the case of so-called classic Neanderthal, trapped in glacial Europe, it was reasonable to assume that this body hairiness had been taken to an extreme.

Most delightful of all in Topilsky's account is the remark "the eyebrows were very powerful." I have repeatedly emphasized that, in my opinion, the eyebrows of Neanderthal grew as very thick, pronounced tufts (as we see to an extent in Leonid Brezhnev in Russia, and Dennis Healey and Joe Gormley in Britain). Coming on top of Neanderthal's very pronounced brow ridges, we have a perfect model for the horns of the Christian devil—who, incidentally, is also often drawn with pointed ears. These "horns" of Neanderthal, again, further reinforced Cro-Magnon's opinion that this type of man was subhuman. For only animals have horns.

On to another account. This was written by an anthropologist, Michael Wagner, in 1784:

> Here you have information about the wild boy who was found a few years ago in Rumania and was brought to Kronstadt, where in 1784 he is still alive. . . . This unfortunate youth was of the male sex and was of medium size. . . . His eyes lay deep in his head. . . . His forehead was strongly bent inwards. . . . He had heavy brown eyebrows which projected out far over his eyes and a small flat pressed nose. . . . His mouth stood out somewhat . . . with a dirty yellowish skin . . . the back and the chest were very hairy; the muscles on his legs were stronger and more visible than in ordinary people. . . . He walked erect but a little heavily. It seemed as if he would throw himself from one foot to the other. He carried his head and his chest forward. . . .

The most marvelous aspect of this account is that Michael Wagner and his contemporaries *had never heard of Neanderthal man.* The first fossil skeleton of this species was discovered and named in 1856. Paradoxically, the most valuable aspect of Wagner's account is that, from our point of view, *he was writing in complete ignorance.*

You cannot, however, imagine with what delight I read this account, actually far longer than given here. "heavy brown eyebrows which projected out far over his eyes . . . small, flat-pressed nose . . . forehead strongly bent inwards."

The flat, bridgeless nose is another attribute that I myself hypothesized for Neanderthal. The nose as such is not found in fossil skeletons. Both it and any associated cartilage decay to nothing.

The "throwing himself from one foot to another" is again especially exciting. Anthropologists and biologists, having studied the pelvis and other bones of *Australopithecus,* a cousin of ours who was around some two million years ago, believe that this creature waddled. I myself proposed that a lesser version of this waddle would also have been found residually in Neanderthal man (who had a broader, heavier pelvis, shorter legs, and so on, than Cro-Magnon man). I pointed out that a form of splay-footed, slouching walk can be fairly readily observed in Jews and some African groups, though, of course, not only in such groups. Charles Chaplin's immortal tramp walked in this way—and I believe that the tradition of the circus clown is, like goblins and dwarfs, another stereotyped memory of actual Neanderthal.

These points were all speculation on my part. Little did I know that Wagner had already confirmed my hypothesis almost two hundred years before!

We can now tap in, with every confidence, to a rich vein of accounts and sightings running from the earliest historical times to the present day, and that extend from Europe through Asia to North America.

The chronology of the reports here is based on the excellent summary in Francis Hitching's *The World Atlas of Mysteries.*[2] This, in turn, is partly based on the long article by Dmitri Bayanov and Igor Bourtsev in *Current Anthropology.*[3] Bayanov and Bourtsev's article is the most fascinating piece of writing I have come across in a very long time. It deserves to be extended into book form as a matter of urgency.

Already in the seventh century BC the Epic of Gilgamesh describes the "wild man of the steppes." He is "shaggy with hair in his whole body . . . with the wild beasts he drinks at the watering-place . . . strength he has."

Then an item of great interest—a drawing on a bowl from either Carthage or Phoenicia, and also dated seventh century BC, which shows four hominoid figures entirely covered with hair attacking a settlement. They are armed with stones, which they are in the act of throwing. Perhaps the most exciting feature of the drawing is that the figures have pointed ears (see figure 10, p. 186, for one of them).

In 86 BC a captured satyr was brought before the Roman general Sulla. Passing mention of similar figures is then made from time to time by important writers and chroniclers from all over Europe and the Middle East. The report of an Arab, Makdisi, in the tenth century AD is interesting because it places the home of these creatures in the Pamir mountains—where nine hundred years later Topilsky's soldiers shot and killed just such a being. The Pamirs are a northerly extension of the Himalayas. In the twelfth century AD another Arab reported satyrs (or *nasnas* in Arabic) to be common in Turkestan, only two or three hundred miles north of the Pamirs. It is, of course, in the Himalayas proper that we have the legend of the Yeti or Abominable Snowman.

A sculpture in the fabric of a thirteenth-century French church shows a "wild man and peasant" (see figure 9). This portrait is clearly drawn from life, and the Neanderthal qualities of the "wild man," including the all-over body hair, are marvelously in evidence. Bayanov and Bourtsev point out that the cranial vault, the size of the facial skull, and the "seat" of the head all betoken Neanderthal.[4]

Figure 9. Wild man and peasant from a thirteenth-century French church (Notre Dame, Semuris, Provence).

Of course, as we realize, Neanderthal was not heard of officially until 1856.

As late as the eighteenth century a medical textbook published in Peking shows a drawing of a biped primate, standing erect on a rock with one arm stretched upward. This is a completely serious book that Emanuel Vlcek (of the Archaeological Institute of the Czech Academy of Sciences) describes as "a standard textbook of the natural history of Tibet applied in Buddhist medicine." He notes that the authenticity of the illustration is supported by the fact that among the many illustrations of animals of various classes (reptiles, amphibians, birds, mammals in the book "there is not a single case of a fantastic or mythological animal, such as those known from medieval European books (dragons, water monsters, demons, etc."). The creatures of this Chinese text are actual living animals observed in nature. Significant is certainly the fact that the manlike figure is shown standing on rocks, and is not drawn in association with a tree.[5]

Now we reach present times.

The Abkhazians (who live to the east of the Black Sea in the neighborhood of Azerbaijan) tell of the wild men they call *abnauayu.* (It is itself interesting that so many peoples from the Black Sea through to the east China coast have each a special name for the wild men, which name is common coin and known to everyone.) The Abkhazians report the capture and domestication of one of these creatures, whom they named Zana. She was covered with reddish hair, with a flat nose and powerful jaws. Physically she was very robust. *She left several children by human fathers.* One of these was exhumed by Professor Boris Porshnev, Director of the Modern History Department of Moscow Academy. He confirmed it to have Neanderthaloid features.[6] (This information that the "wild men" and human beings *can* interbreed, of course, offers quite crucial support for my proposal that Cro-Magnon mated with Neanderthal.)

Several thousand miles further east the Kazakhs (Cossacks) also once captured a male, wild man. He, too, had a body covered with thick, reddish hair. He had a sloping forehead, massive jaws, a small nose, and pointed ears—and prominent eyebrows.

A Mongolian scientist named Rinchen collected many eyewitness accounts from the Gobi desert region (we are now a couple of thousand miles further east again) of wild men *(almas),* who had sloping foreheads, prominent eyebrows, large jaws, and were covered with reddish-brown hair. A group of these were seen as late as 1927.

A further case from the Pamir mountains: a geologist, Zdorik, was told by locals of the capture and subsequent escape of a *dev* (an "unclean spirit"). Then he himself saw one in 1934. Among the peoples of the other side of the Pamir mountains, Porshnev collected numerous accounts of eyewitness sightings between 1930 and 1950.[7]

These accounts are sufficient for our purposes, though we have by no means exhausted the supply.

The points to emphasize and to bear in mind are these. The various accounts come to us over a very long time-span and a very wide geographical area. (We are talking about a swathe of land running from Germany in the west through to the Pacific seaboard in the east, and embracing the whole of southern Russia, Tibet, northern China, and the Middle East, including parts of North Africa.) There are consistent points of agreement in all descriptions—the massive muzzlelike jaws, the very extensive body hair, the pointed ears, the sloping forehead, the projecting eyebrows, the bridgeless nose, and the great strength.

There is one item of disagreement running through the accounts—but from my point of view this serves to make these tales more, not less, authentic, as we shall see. The disagreement is that some reports state the hair and body hair of the creatures to be curly, others that it is straight. Figures 10a and b show this difference between the two types clearly.

The silenus (of which figure 10a is an example) is a creature mentioned not merely in Greek mythology but also in Greek history, and he is one member of a clan that includes satyrs, nymphs, fauns, and pans. From the descriptions and alleged habits of these creatures, we can assume they are all but variations on a single theme. (Pausanias, a Greek geographer, remarks that sileni are only elderly satyrs.) In the light of

(a)   (b)

Figure 10. The curly and straight-haired varieties of the "wild men."
Note in both cases the "seat" of the head, and in the second
figure the pointed ears and shambling walk.

what we now know, we also realize that these are not *mythical* creatures,
but *actual* creatures.

The horns of Pan and his colleagues are, as I have been proposing
for the past ten years, based on the projecting brow ridges, further augmented by tufted projecting eyebrows, of Neanderthal man: that is, of
these men. As to the flattened brows of Neanderthal, why, the goat has
just such a flattened brow, and pointed ears, too. (It actually looks, by
the way, as if when Neanderthal men fought each other, they did so by
lowering the head, charging, and butting each other. Eskimos today still
do this.)

The phrase "the pipes of Pan" comes again to mind. This kind of
music and dancing in respect of these "mythical" creatures ties in well
with what we know of the Old Religion. The legendary association of
music with Pan and his fellows is one we will do well to bear in mind
also when considering the question of Neanderthal man and speech.

But to come back to the curly and straight hair. Most (though not
all) reports of curly hair in wild men come from Europe, and most
(though not all) reports of straight hair from the east. I believe we are

talking about two quite distinct varieties of Neanderthal—in my terms, of Neanderthal 1a and 2, respectively. The admixture of 1a in modern European populations is responsible for the curly hair we find in Europe today alongside the Cro-Magnon straight hair; and the admixture of type 2 in the east is responsible for the straight hair of the Chinese and Japanese. (Straight, blonde hair in Europe and straight, black hair in China are, we must emphasize, two totally different phenomena. The cross section of these two types of hair, and all associated features, are absolutely different.)

The differences observed in accounts of "wild men" in Europe and Asia tally, therefore, with differences observable in these same geographical areas today, and that, in any case, my own theories predict.

Returning for a moment to the ancient Romans and Greeks, the naturalist Lucretius Carus (first century BC) has this to say about a race of early men: that they had "larger and more solid bones within, fastened with strong sinews traversing the flesh; not easily to be harmed by heat or cold or strange food or any taint of the body." They were like "bristly bears." At night, when sleeping, they wrapped themselves around with leaves and foliage.

(As it happens, chimpanzees do just this at night. And I have repeatedly proposed that Neanderthal man is most closely related to the chimpanzee, while Cro-Magnon is most closely related to the gibbon.)

Lucretius Carus's account is altogether too accurate and too detailed to be based on anything but fact. He is clearly reporting eye-witness accounts still current in his own day.

Using Greek "myths" as our basis, we today speak of "nymphomania" and "satyriasis." These are two forms of unbridled lust. They imply that one of the major preoccupations of the wild men was promiscuous and frequent sex.

How well this ties in with our knowledge that sex, in both its literal and more evolved forms, was the very heart and center of the Old Religion. Such a religion would be wholly appropriate for a type of man who was by nature sex-mad; or should we say, sex-sane.

At this point an anonymous objector interrupts: "Oh, but one can't go on taking hints from old myths as proof."

Well, as it happens, we have good evidence from no less a figure than the philosopher Albertus Magnus (1193–1280) that the "mythical" sexual lusts of the satyr and the nymph were very much reality (as, of course, were the creatures themselves).

Magnus describes the recent capture in Saxony of a pair (one male and one female) of "forest dwelling hairy monsters." The female died of blood poisoning as a result of dog bites. But the male lived on and even learned the use of a few words (a most important observation). But, says Magnus—a wholly typical Cro-Magnon chauvinist—the creature's lack of reason was evidenced by his ever trying to accost women and exhibit lustfulness. (Wagner's wild boy also, after he had been in captivity a while and his initial fears overcome, behaved thus: "as soon as he saw a woman he broke out into violent cries of joy, and tried to express his awakened desires also through gestures.")

Only modern, western man can or could—and *does*—believe that "intelligence" and "sexuality" cannot coexist. But Neanderthal man—as well as the lives of the great majority of our most outstanding creative artists—says otherwise.

NEANDERTHAL, THE WILD MEN, AND THE POWER OF SPEECH

Many authorities, including Boris Porshnev, who is otherwise extremely positive in this cause, believe that Neanderthal man lacked the power of speech. I think this view is based on a misunderstanding of the available evidence—and that below this "misunderstanding" lies a powerful layer of emotional prejudice against the idea, a prejudice we have already encountered many times in this book.

There are two strands in the argument against Neanderthal possessing speech. One is the linguistic behavior (or, as is claimed, the linguistic nonbehavior) of captured wild men in historic times. The second is the study of fossil skulls of prehistoric Neanderthal, and the inferences drawn from such study concerning the mouth, palate, vocal cords, and voice box of Neanderthal, none of which soft items we actually possess; for these decay, leaving no trace.

Taking the wild men of Europe, we must first understand exactly what it is that we face here. It turns out to be no less than the greatest crime and the greatest indictment in the already appalling record of "civilized" man's behavior. And in documenting this crime we do not in any way need to *imagine* what happened to Neanderthal man. We know from our own recent behavior in respect of the Tasmanian Aborigine, the Gypsy, and the Jew.

For example, during the last century, as well as before, the British settlers in Tasmania amused themselves by hunting and shooting the Aborigines. As a result of this "pastime," the last full-blooded Tasmanian Aborigine died in 1876.

A word in passing in memory of Tasmanian "Neanderthal." He differs—or rather differed—from the Aborigines of the mainland in being an even more extreme representative of the type than they are themselves. He possessed the broadest nasal index ever recorded. While mainland "purebreds" have brown skin and wavy hair, the Tasmanians had black skin and woolly hair and were shorter. The nasal notch was very deep, the mouth very prognathous, and the head shorter and broader than in mainland Aborigines. The projecting brow ridges were very exaggerated. *These Tasmanians had very heavy body hair.*

The skull characteristics of the now extinct Tasmanians are found in fossil skulls on the mainland, and all characteristics occasionally among the present southernmost coastal tribes. Those observations tell us that the Tasmanians were part of the very first waves to reach Australia. Later arrivals were either of slightly mixed blood or had undergone further evolution.

The Tasmanian Aborigines had left India between 50–100,000 years ago. They show us that the population of southern India of those times (especially in respect to features like body hair) was much closer to

Neanderthal norms than it is today. There has since been considerable mingling with Cro-Magnon types.

Although the last Tasmanian Aborigine died in 1876, there still exist several thousand Tasmanians of mixed blood. So we see that the white settlers had no objections to "screwing" the females. Many of these females must have been kept alive in captivity (apart from the few that probably escaped back to their own people), for otherwise we would have no mixed population today. Zana, the red-haired wild woman, was obviously treated in a similar way.

Not only did the white settlers have no objections to "screwing" the aboriginal women, I suggest they actively sought the opportunity. For "Neanderthal" woman arouses very ancient, atavistic desires in "Cro-Magnon" (just as true Neanderthal woman did in true Cro-Magnon 35,000 years ago). There is, as it happens, ample evidence that ancient instinctive responses can survive intact though unused in a species for many millions of years.

The French today recognize the impulses I am talking about in the phrases "*aimer la boue*" and "*senter la boue*" ("loving the mud" and "smelling the mud"). These impulses are one reason why some men today, despite adequate respectable sexual connections, still like to visit prostitutes. A French woman acquainted with my books recently wrote to ask me whether I thought men found women wearing black silk stockings and black underwear arousing because of the stimulation of ancient instinctive responses. And my answer is, yes, I do think so. (In this connection the comments on the heroine and antiheroine of the romantic novel in chapter 6 are relevant also.)

The Gypsies bring us to another aspect of the Neanderthal question. These people (for whatever reason) set out from India two or three thousand years ago and reached Europe via Egypt and the Middle East. Here they found they were unable to assimilate (which, certainly, in many cases they did not even want to do). They had too much of the "Neanderthal" about them. They were darker skinned than the average European, they were moon worshippers, they were deeply into the mystical and the magical, they had a distinctive language of their own (which, though Indo-European in origin, is only distantly related to European tongues and is not recognizable as related to the layman), and their own distinctive music and culture, including partial rule by a tribe-mother.

What happened to the Gypsies? They were always moved on by the local European populations. They were blamed for any crimes committed in their vicinity and for the spread of disease. They were the subject of pogroms, during which the women were violated.

Apart from the mixed babies produced by this last, no doubt also some Gypsy women practiced prostitution for a living (even though Gypsy law strongly forbids this). There is no doubt that Gypsies also stole and unwittingly helped in the spread of infectious diseases (which is not to suggest that Gypsies are "dirty" either by nature or culture). As so often in human affairs, the very suspicion of law-breaking and other undesirable behavior itself produces such behavior. If you are going to be blamed for sheep-stealing, then you may as well do it. And if people hate you, then why not hate them? And if you can swindle the haters, why not do so?

So the cycle goes on and on. Gypsies, forced on to the periphery of life, became increasingly *parasitic* on life. Increasingly they "lived off" the peoples and lands they passed through.

Only the advent of modern European society, its relative affluence, and its occasional attempts to do the right thing prevented the Gypsies from becoming full-fledged "wild men." (Though this "rescue" did not stop them figuring on Hitler's extermination list.) The text I am preaching here is, I hope, clear. What nearly happened to the Gypsies *did* happen to the surviving groups of European Neanderthals following the Cro-Magnon takeover.

Then we come to the Jews. Their fate at the hands of fascism in Europe has been well documented and, thank heavens, continues to be. But how many people even today realize that the Nazi holocaust was but a continuation of two thousand or more years of altogether similar, if slightly less systematic, persecution?

I have argued in my writing that the Jews, from the point of their very inception, possessed a slightly greater admixture of Neanderthal genes than any other people in Europe and the Middle East. The Jews are an extremely ancient group by any standards—their day-to-day calendar alone takes us back six thousand years. They also have a core of mystic traditions unequalled, I think, in intensity and complexity by any other. These traditions clearly reach right back into the heart of the moon religion of ancient Europe.

The point here is this: two thousand years (conservatively) of unremitting persecution (Jews in the Yemen, for example, were forced to live below ground level) have noticeably strengthened the ratio of Neanderthal genes in the Jewish population (and to a lesser extent the same has happened also to the African-American). "Neanderthal" is tougher and hardier than "Cro-Magnon" in all kinds of ways. And, incidentally, I defended that view long before I read Lucretius Carus's comment: "not easily to be harmed by heat or cold or strange food or any taint of the body." The selective pressures operating on the mixed Neanderthal/Cro-Magnon population are moreover subtle as well as obvious.

True Neanderthal was by nature nomadic. And even when he inhabited one general area for lengthy periods, we have evidence that he never considered he *owned* the place in question. (We see this same attitude today in Eskimos, Bedouin, and North American Indians.) Cro-Magnon was exploratory by nature (which is *not* the same psychological commodity as being nomadic). And when Cro-Magnon came to a new place that he liked, he said "right, this is mine." He now *owned* the new place and defended it as his territory. (It is clear, too, that psychologically the male personality regards bonded females as an extension of territory.)

Now, when it came to a choice (in mixed populations) between standing and fighting (defending "your" territory) or picking up your belongings and moving on, the "Cro-Magnon" element urged the former, and the "Neanderthal" element the latter. So more Cro-Magnon gene-bearers died fighting than Neanderthal gene-bearers. This is just one example of several similar arguments.

Have we now learned something else about the fate and character of the "wild men?" I believe so. But there are more important points still.

For the first of these we go back to Tasmania. The Tasmanian Aborigines originally arrived at this island by boat from the Australian mainland (though there was a land bridge until 7000 BP). Here they remained genetically isolated for many thousands of years. They were always a small population, for without farming or agriculture this limited territory would support just so many. Although there were several distinct tribes, there was still not enough genetic diversity in the total island to enable the mechanisms of forward evolution to function adequately. Perhaps somehow recognizing what was wrong, the tribes now fought each other continuously—and the prize they fought for was the other tribes' women.

Nevertheless, this was no cure. Archaeologists, digging down through the layers of Tasmanian civilization, find that the culture gets more advanced and more complex as they go *backward*. In other words, what was taking place in Tasmania was not evolution, but devolution. At some point in the past, the Tasmanians even lost the knowledge of how to build the boats that had brought them from the mainland, as well as their knowledge of fire.

Can we understand that the fate of too small a gene pool finally overtook also the relic Neanderthals of Europe and Asia? Surviving, true Neanderthal man, at some point in fairly recent prehistory, began to devolve.

This situation explains the circumstance that so much puzzled Boris Porshnev and still puzzles others: namely why, given the fact that Neanderthal had good knowledge and use of tools; showed many advanced cultural practices, such as ritual burial of the dead and the construction of altars; knew how to cure skins for bedding and clothing (tying the clothes together with thongs through buttonholes); understood herbs; and lived (wherever else) comfortably in dry, well provided caves—why is it that the present wild men appear to possess and exhibit none of these cultural practices and artifacts? They, the wild men, seem to have no tools (although they throw stones); do not wear clothes; often sleep in the open; apparently have no knowledge of fire or cooking—are in short without civilization. They *may* also have no language—but that is a question we will look at below.

What has happened, then, is that this once highly-evolved and civilized people have been reduced to a level actually *below* that of some animals—by the direct action of other so-called "civilized" people.

There is still another point. It has long been recognized by psychologists that, in condition of stimulus deprivation (including, of course, in prisons and barracks), sexual activity increases. Overcrowding itself leads to increased sex, for self-evident reasons; but there is the question also of lack of alternative activity and diversion. Sex, after all, is free, and it is there for the taking. So, despite everything, birth rates in slums and ghettos are not only always high but even as a regular rule outstrip the punitive mortality rate. The unusually high sex drive of all members of *homo sapiens,* augmented still further by stimulus and cultural deprivation, has more than once saved human communities under threat of extinction. It has also saved Neanderthal (and I use the implication of the present tense quite deliberately). He had a far higher sex drive than us in the first place—and the "unnatural selection" pressures applied to him by his fellow human beings have left him just that one trump card. He has played it consistently: by his nymphomania and his satyriasis, "by his ever-trying to accost women and exhibit lustfulness."

And now back to language.

THE POWER OF SPEECH

Speaking now both as a professional linguist and a professional psychologist, I am quite unable to understand how anyone can even imagine that a hominid like *homo erectus* (who lived some 500,000 years ago, and was almost certainly a direct ancestor of Neanderthal) did not possess language. These hominids lived together in permanent cave sites, cooked their food over fires, and practiced cooperative hunting. I find myself obliged to say "of course they had language." But a majority of anthropologists think otherwise.

When we get as far as Neanderthal—who makes clothes with button-holes and builds altars and holds huge funeral feasts—I personally find doubts about his linguistic abilities slightly idiotic. But feelings are one thing, and perhaps proof is another. So I must try to tackle this question in a way that will cut ice with doubters.

Let us first take the captured wild men of historical times. Or rather, just before that, let me make one or two remarks about the nature of language.

Standing on the train yesterday, I was watching an Arab reading an Arabic newspaper. Now, despite the fact that I have studied modern lan-guages and can even read a little Hebrew, there is still no way that I can accept emotionally that this printed mass of squiggles in the newspaper means anything. Of course I accept intellectually that it does. But emo-tionally I cannot accept that the black marks on that page leap into the Arab's consciousness in exactly the same way that a printed page of Eng-lish does into mine. (Yet, of course, they do.) Or take, say, spoken Chinese. Is there any way that that cacophany of sighs and grunts and bongs can mean anything? Of course not. Oh, well all right, perhaps those noises in some way convey primitive emotions like "eat," "screw," "sleep." But they could not possibly be used to discuss philosophy, nuclear physics, and mathematics, or to write tender, sad, wistfully-mocking, love poems. Could they? So let us, in short, be very, very careful when we approach the question of language in Neanderthal. I should, perhaps, also have mentioned that Arabic makes some of its sounds in the throat, while in Africa clicks also sometimes form parts of words.

It is certain that both the volume and complexity of Neanderthal lan-guage in the wild men of historical times had decayed dramatically along with all their other cultural abilities. Language and culture are but two parts of one whole. We do not, therefore, in principle expect to find very much in the way of language in the wild men—and this amount could be further reduced by another circumstance described below.

At any rate, the wild man described by Albertus Magnus did manage in captivity to master the use of a few words of German. Now, that is not bad at all. For we know that there is a plastic period for language learning in the young human being (roughly up to the age of five). It is necessary for language to be "imprinted" on the personality in those early years. If the plastic period is not taken advantage of, the person will not subsequently learn to speak *any* language. This position is fully confirmed in modern children who for any reason miss the plastic period, like the so-called feral children who grow up with animals. (These are *not* Neanderthal children, they are modern children.) The two then teenage girls, who were found running wild in India early in the present century, never subsequently managed more than a couple of spoken words, despite several years of living back among people and all attempts by teachers. If it is the case, then, that the parents of the wild Neanderthals do not have language, their offspring will miss the crucial learning period (as perhaps those parents did themselves).

So the performance of the wild man from Saxony may not have been bad after all.

But let us look at some of the other reports again. Sulla, the Roman general, reported on the satyr that was brought into his presence in 86 BC. He said that the accents of this creature were "harsh and inarticulate," something between the neighing of a horse and the bleating of a goat. Well, perhaps these were just noises. Or perhaps they were like Chinese bongs and African clicks, only more so.

What of Michael Wagner's young wild man? "The desire for food, of which he now liked all kinds, particularly *légumes* (vegetables), he would show by intelligent sounds." But he was completely lacking in speech, adds Wagner, meaning, of course, speech that anyone could understand. Wagner goes on: "The sounds which he uttered were an understandable murmuring, which he would give when his guard drove him ahead of him. This murmuring was increased to a howling when he saw woods or even a tree. He seemed to express the wish for his accustomed abode."

Well, were the "intelligent sounds" and the "murmuring" the wild man talking to himself? Perhaps we shall never know.

Again there is the point of possible crucial linguistic deprivation during the plastic period. For the question is, who reared the wild Neanderthals that were captured? Was it their parents—and if so, did those parents have language? Or were these Neanderthals isolates from birth—perhaps the very last of their kind in a particular area—and so perhaps reared by wild animals that happened to come across the newborn infant?

If reared by a social animal, like wolves, one would expect to find the Neanderthal running with the pack, and going on all fours, like some of the *modern* feral children already mentioned. (Actually, Wagner's wild boy, though he walked erect, had nobby hardenings on his elbows and knees. Had he perhaps, therefore, gone on all fours at one time?) But if reared by a bear, the young Neanderthal would be instinctively driven away by the mother bear after a few years, to fend for itself. (Bears go on all fours but also often stand erect.) Interestingly, a Neanderthal woman captured in Hungary in 1767 would only eat raw meat. This does suggest that she had been reared by a carnivore, like a bear. At any rate, the hunters who found her were pursuing bear, and she was in a bear cave.

The discussion so far is just one aspect of the case concerning Neanderthal's use of language. There is also the question of the structure of the mouth, throat, and so on. We need to look briefly at this position also—for, clearly, speech is vital to my own concept of the moon civilization of Neanderthal man.

An apparent majority of anthropologists consider that Neanderthal man could not speak. The view is based on a study of fossil skulls and jaws of Neanderthal. These skulls in general exist only as fragments. From the fragments the rest of the skull is inferred or deduced. And from the inferred "complete" picture, further inferences are then made about the missing soft parts (tongue, vocal cords, and so on). Finally, on the basis of these inferences, and after comparison with the soft and hard parts of our own mouths and throats, a judgment is made as to whether Neanderthal could speak or not.

Biologists and engineers lecturing to young students often draw their attention, by way of a warning, to the fact that the bumblebee cannot fly; or at least to the fact that it ought not to be able to. The design of the bumblebee should never have been able to get off the drawing board. Had there existed only fossils of these creatures, biologists would have proposed that this was an animal that had once possessed flight (or was in the process of developing flight) but had now lost it. This bee might have been capable of bumping along off the ground on occasion, but that would have been the limit. In fact, of course, the bumblebee not only flies well but makes its living by flying.

This story, as I said, is often used as a warning to biologists. I wish it were used more often as a warning to anthropologists; although, fortunately, the case for Neanderthal being able to speak does not rest upon such hypothetical arguments.

It does not even need to rest on arguments like those put forward by David Burr, an anthropologist at Colorado University. He undertook an examination of the statistical and sampling methods used in the studies that supposedly produce the "proof" that Neanderthal could not speak.

There are highly technical matters involved here, which we will not go into. (Those interested can naturally consult Burr's paper for themselves.[8]) But he reduced the number of "reliable" Neanderthal skulls to a mere thirty-eight. (These are, in principle, those with the lower-jaw present.) He then performs a statistical analysis of these skulls. His conclusion is that "when all measurements are taken in combination and size factors deleted, no morphological differences between Skuhl V, Broken Hill and the more modern groups exist with respect to vocal tract anatomy."

What Burr is saying is that there are no significant differences between Neanderthal and modern skulls in respect of their suitability for producing speech as we know it. Some of the ancient skulls considered were between 150,000 and 600,000 years old.

These comments and conclusions are certainly very interesting for us. But again my own case does not rest there. My case is that I (just like Loren Eiseley, Oswald Spengler, and others) see around me, in particular, male individuals that I can in no way distinguish morphologically (that is, in terms of their anatomical structure) from fossil Neanderthal, and many more others still who possess some of Neanderthal's attributes.

These males have the short, thickset body-type with its barrel body and head set low into the shoulders on a short, heavy neck. Sometimes (though not always) this head is also set forward in typical Neanderthal style. I observe that this person has pronounced, projecting brow bridges, a massive jaw, a prognathous (muzzlelike) mouth with broad, even teeth, but recessive chin. He is short in stature, has large hands and ears, broad feet—and so on and so on.

I also observe—though we cannot confirm these features from a study of fossil Neanderthal—that the eyebrows are often heavy and projecting, that the individual is usually dark-haired and dark-eyed, that he walks with the feet slightly splayed. When seen on a beach, I observe that these males are as a rule covered with body hair, also on the back, upper arms, and hips. Do not take my word for any of this. Make your own observations from now on.

In a review of *Total Man*, the sociologist Professor Ronald Fletcher said that all I was asking psychologists, anthropologists, and biologists to do was "just for once to lift their self-conditioned eye-balls from their microscope tubes, to look out of the windows, and consider what is there."

I am still asking.

Now finally, and this is the central point here, these living individuals, whom I can in no way distinguish morphologically from fossil Neanderthal, speak every jot as well as you or I. No—much more than this. Clear examples of this type are found among *our finest thinkers, scientists, writers, actors*—whatever you will. More of this shortly.

AMERICAN NEANDERTHAL

There is also a relic population of Neanderthal in North America. Numerous sightings during this century strongly suggest that we may also not be too late to save some of these people, too.

This American representative of Neanderthal is called "sasquatch" or "bigfoot," as a consequence of large tracks left in the snow.

As it happens, we can tie in this additional evidence of Neanderthal survival with Geoffrey Goodman's "psychic archaeology."

Asia and America are joined by a land-bridge of islands in the far north. During warm interglacials this island chain is readily negotiable by primitive man.

Already by 500,000 BP *homo erectus* possesses fire and cooks his food. He is widespread in Africa and China, and the Chinese group is, if anything, more advanced. It does not stretch the imagination to consider these people reaching North America already at that time. *Erectus* is almost certainly ancestral to Neanderthal. It stretches the imagination still less to consider Neanderthal proper crossing the Bering Strait around 100,000 years ago.

Officially, that is, according to the orthodox view, man first entered North America by the Bering route only some 25,000 years ago. However, Goodman's excavations have produced materials (crude stone tools, and the like) that have been reliably dated, in terms of the layers in which they are found, as being of the order of 100,000 years old.[9]

Orthodoxy does not on the whole challenge that the tools and artifacts are genuine, nor that the soil layers in which they are found are as old as claimed. But it insists that the tools must have been introduced into these layers by accident at a much later date. Orthodox scientists are not willing to accept the evidence presented at face value; though under other circumstances there is no doubt whatsoever that they would accept it.

Of more interest still from my own point of view is the fact that Goodman's dig is in Hopi Indian territory, and that Hopi legend supports the kind of dates Goodman has produced. We have met the Hopi Indians several times before in this book. They make use of the number thirteen in their religious ritual (pp. 83–84), and they draw mazes that unmistakably echo maze drawings found in India, Greece, and Britain (p. 126).

The Hopi say (no doubt correctly) that their first ancestors came to this continent from islands ("stepping-stones") across the sea. They say that their first world was destroyed by fire, the second by ice, and the third by water. Here they could be referring to volcanic activity, glaciation, and the flooding that follows deglaciation, respectively. Goodman, who is also a geologist, establishes volcanic activity 250,000 years ago and glaciation 100,000 years ago in the mountains near San Francisco where the Hopi live.

This is certainly one tenable view, though I do not myself feel we necessarily have to assume that the Hopi have lived in one particular area for the last quarter of a million years. At any rate, the geological references contained in these legends are certainly most interesting. Many other writers have found the Hopi Indians to be the most intriguing of the North American tribes. They may, perhaps, have the closest cultural and genetic links with ancient Neanderthal. Possibly, at the cultural level, they have actually adopted aspects of Neanderthal legend.

Speaking again of Neanderthal, this may be the right moment to draw attention to the markedly backward-sloping foreheads of the Maya Indians in South America. This feature is clearly seen in the many drawings of themselves that the Mayas have left us, and it has been widely remarked.

Reverting then to sasquatch and bigfoot, it is very possible that when mixed modern types entered North America from the Asian continent 25,000 years ago they found there a native population of purebred Neanderthals. These, perhaps, in part retreated before the newcomers, in part died fighting them, and in part intermingled with them. (The mixed type—ourselves—is, in fact, superior to Neanderthal in any straight takeover situation; it is really only in conditions of deprivation that Neanderthal has the upper edge.)

Interest centers on those who "retreated before the newcomers." They, in all probability, are the wild men of the American and Canadian mountains.

IN PRAISE OF JEWISH "NEANDERTHAL"

Neanderthal characteristics are found today in each and every human population on this planet. But the distribution of these characteristics is not entirely even. Asiatics are probably the group that show most on average, with negroid types next (and especially the now extinct Tasmanians). In Europe, collectively speaking the area where Neanderthal traits are least in evidence, the characteristics are more in evidence in the south and the east, and less in evidence in the north and the west. The Celts, living in the far west of Europe, are an exception. But, as we have seen, they are really a migrated people from the southeast.

In these various global areas also, as I have indicated in chapter 6, we are talking about admixtures of different *varieties* of Neanderthal. In Europe and the Middle East the variety of Neanderthal in question is type 1a.

The greatest admixture of type 1a is found among the Jews.

Before I go any further with my comments here, I had better point out that I am myself half-Jewish. My father was a Polish Jew and, before he changed it, the family name was Zuch. So let us have no misunderstandings at this point.

All human populations on this planet are, in my opinion, without exception the result of the genetic crossing of the Neanderthal and Cro-Magnon varieties of man. We are a hybrid species. Our vigor and inventiveness and the meteoric rise (as geological time goes) of our civilization is due to what biologists call "hybrid vigor." (And there was *no* intervention from outer space.) Unfortunately, we are also what is called an unstable hybrid.

Through whatever quirk of fate, the best—that is, the most successful and the most stable—mixing of the two parent genetic endowments took place in the peoples of the Middle East. Or maybe this is not so surprising, for it was here, somewhere round about present-day Israel, that pure Neanderthal and pure Cro-Magnon first met. ("And there appeared to me two men, exceeding big, so that I never saw such on earth . . . as grasshoppers we seemed to ourselves and so we seemed to them.") That the two types did indeed mix we know from the fossil skeletons with strangely mixed features that were found on Mount Carmel.

These brand new, instantly gifted genetic hybrids were initially widespread in the Middle East and much remarked upon. ("When the Sons of God came into the daughters of men and they bore children to them . . . these . . . were the mighty men of old, the men of renown.") Interestingly, and I think accurately, this statement from the Book of Genesis speaks really of Cro-Magnon males "screwing" Neanderthal females. This was no love match, but a lust match, such as the Tasmanian aboriginal women and the wild woman Zana were also later to suffer.) The very successful mixed types now prospered and spread, absorbing and genetically displacing first the remaining pure Neanderthals (with the exception of the relic Neanderthal tribes that withdrew themselves, and held on to the present day—and whom I am basically discussing in this chapter) and then many thousands of years later also pure Cro-Magnon in Europe. And so the whole sense of *being* a successful hybrid was lost—even though we all of us are such, although in varying degrees.

Lost, that is, by all groups except one—the Jews. They kept the memory of our fantastic biological adventure alive down through the tens of thousands of years that followed. Over such a great span of time, naturally, the verbal body of tradition (just like a geological stratum of rock) kept cracking and rearranging itself, and getting mixed with other later layers. But still with care we can recognize and tease out the fragments of the original story—as I have just done in the quotations from the Old Testament.

Knowing that a miracle had happened (which to us is biological, but to them was simply magical) and knowing *that they themselves were the outcome* of that miracle, they determined to preserve themselves, for all time, as the living proof that divine forces were directly and deliberately at work in human destiny. They now, therefore, set up quite deliberate cultural and religious barriers, so that either to cease being a Jew if you were one, or to become one if you were not, was almost impossible. Of course, they had to be pretty firm and ruthless about this whole process. They had, for example, savagely to repress certain purely Neanderthal elements. Only with a great conscious, cultural effort—and at a very high price—did they succeed in "getting it together." But they *did* get it together. And having built their ship, their ark, they all climbed aboard and set sail down through the millennia. And the builders had built well "for the ship endured on the face of the waters."

So far these comments are perhaps not better than purely cultural speculations. But there are two levels of solid proof.

The first is the quite incredible level and range of ability manifested by the Jews. There is not one single other people or nation in the world, real or fabled, that comes anywhere near them. For example, though representing less than one percent of the world's population, the Jews produce no less than twenty-five percent of the world's Nobel prizewinners—and *that* is despite a two-thousand-year background of the most appalling persecution, degradation, and social deprivation that human beings have ever undergone, with the exception of pure Neanderthal himself. And what list of the world's ten greatest men could fail to include the following: Christ, Einstein, Freud, Marx? Nor are the achievements of the Jews "just cultural." The only man ever to win seven gold medals at one Olympic Games, at the same time setting seven new *world* records, was the Jew, Mark Spitz.

My second level of proof is yet more incontestable, if that is possible. It is the physiology and anatomy of the Jews.

If you want to see Neanderthal 1a alive and well and walking about, go and study your Jewish friends. If you do not happen to have any, study prominent Jews in public life. Elliot Gould the film star, for example, though uncharacteristically tall and so forth, has splendidly armored

Figure 11. Immanuel Velikovsky, an
outstanding thinker and visionary.

frontal brows. You will need to catch him at the right angle to see them, for the camera (and perhaps makeup) tend to flatten them. But once you catch sight of them, you will be astonished that you have not noticed them before. As regards sloping foreheads, Henry Kissinger is a reasonably good example. For strong, tufted eyebrows I would recommend both Ian Mikardo and Lord Goodman in Britain.*

But by the way of instant example, figure 11 shows the profile of one of our most outstanding modern thinkers and visionaries, Immanuel Velikovsky. We see clearly the projecting brow bridges, and we note the slope of the forehead. Although one cannot be sure on the basis of this picture, the extended back of the head almost certainly houses a large cerebellum—which is both a Neanderthal feature and, in my opinion, an indispensable part of the equipment of the great visionary-artist-scientist. Appropriately enough, Velikovsky also possesses many Cro-Magnon features—the high-bridged nose, a high skull-vault, and strong projecting chin.

(The high-bridged, Jewish nose, which most people think of as

---

*Film stars are most easily studied. Two *non*-Jewish actors with strong brow bridges are Marcello Mastroianni and Tommy Lee Jones. As can be seen in the illustration in appendix 1, Cro-Magnon had no such ridges.

typically Jewish, is neither that nor typically Neanderthal. Neanderthal had a flat or snub, bridgeless nose. But this type of nose is far more common among Jews than outsiders usually realize. Arthur Koestler puts the incidence of such noses at 20 percent.)

An important point: redheadedness is fairly common among Jews. So much so that there is a saying in central Europe that all redheaded Poles are Jews. (My own beard, as a young man, had a touch of red in it, though nowadays what is not black is grey.) This rufousness turns up quite surprisingly in otherwise dark-haired families.

Can it be just coincidence that the reports of the wild men and women down through the ages say: "covered with reddish hair," "thick reddish hair on its body," "covered with reddish-brown hair?"

Whether on some intuitive basis, or because he was familiar with the reports on satyrs and wild men, William Golding gave his Neanderthal men red, curly hair in his novel *The Inheritors*.

There is one very last point. It is rather technical and I do not, therefore, want to go into too much detail here. In body-type theory one of the main subdivisions is the so-called pyknic body type.[10] This type in many ways corresponds closely to the Neanderthal type—deep-chested, large-stomached, short-limbed, bull-necked, and so on. However, this type, in males, is said often to go prematurely bald in early life. Do I agree or not? The answer is yes and no.

I am, on the one hand, quite emphatic that baldness is a Cro-Magnon characteristic, and that Neanderthal men did not go bald at all. At the same time, I agree that many male individuals of the pyknic type do go bald. The answer to the apparent paradox here is that there are *two* pyknic types, which we can call pyknic A and pyknic B. The two types are readily distinguishable. In pyknic A the skin is tight and shiny, the eyes are small, and the ears regular or again small. In pyknic B the facial skin is always loose and "leathery," with much folding that increases with age. (Somerset Maugham's heavily-folded face in later life is a good instance, or that of W. H. Auden.) I suspect that the skin is also much *thicker* in the B type. The eyes and ears are large, and the head as a whole is massive in relation to the body. This type not only has a full, vigorous head of hair in later life but often shows no recession of the hairline whatsoever, even at the temples. The hairline remains as we see it in young male children and in women at all ages.

Several well-known Jewish writers are excellent examples of this type—but you will have to find them on the beach to observe their extensive, all-over body hair!

This last point is a puzzle for orthodoxy. Orthodoxy maintains that high levels of male hormone are responsible for hairy chests *and* for male baldness. How is it that pyknic B has very extensive body hair but no trace of balding at all? The answer is that pyknic B is a different variety of man (that is, Neanderthal) where the rules are different. (Chinese and Asiatic males show no balding, and negroids show less than Caucasians—though in these cases body hair is notably absent. But these again are a different *sub*variety of Neanderthal—see chapter 6.)

I long ago predicted that because Neanderthal characteristics would tend to be found on the fringes and at the bottom of our modern social heap, therefore less male baldness would be observed there.

In September 1977 *Psychology Today* reported the results of a study that showed that winos and other inhabitants of Skid Row showed less male baldness than business men and other establishment males. I was, of course, delighted with this verification of my prediction, which runs absolutely counter to normal expectation. We would expect poor diet and poor hygiene and poor health to *increase* the incidence of baldness. Vigorous head-hair showing no trace of male pattern baldness can also be readily observed in all tramps and "gentlemen of the road" in western countries.

THE YEAR OF THE HUMAN BEING

At this very moment the remnants of a human community that has been relentlessly persecuted by ourselves for twenty-five thousand years is suffering and dying in the central mountain ranges of Russia, China, and

America. Their level of subsistence is somewhat below that of a self-respecting animal.

These people are both our cousins and our ancestors. And it is not yet too late to save a handful of them.

We have just had the International Year of the Child. My urgent plea is now for an International Year of the Human Being. Let all the nations of the world now mount a joint expedition to find and rehabilitate these rejected aspects of our own being.

Let these *people* then be a living symbol to us that the Nazi holocaust or the Tasmanian massacre will never again be duplicated. Such a symbol, far more so than any space station or Jupiter probe, might be able to bind us all together in our common humanity.

There is no need to venture into outer space in search of complementary intelligent life. We have it right here on our own planet.

My hope is that while, unfortunately, we cannot expect too much from the magazines supporting and purveying scientific orthodoxy, the journals and magazines devoted to fringe science and futurology can be persuaded to take up this cause. Why not a fundraising campaign? Why not an appeal to the growing number of progressive scientists and biologists, who are turning seriously to the study of unorthodox phenomena?

For apart from the direct psychological and spiritual value to ourselves and the world we inhabit in what I am proposing, there is still a further bonus. It is very likely that these relic Neanderthals are highly gifted in respect of psychic and paranormal abilities. Such abilities, perhaps, have contributed to their, after all, startling survival.

But if we should act too late, how would we ever forgive ourselves?

Perhaps this Year of the Human Being I envisage might even lead us into the Age of the Human Being.

14

The Christ

I had finished writing this book and already delivered it to the copy editor. I was sitting dozing late on Saturday evening, having watched some television, when the full significance of the Christ story suddenly became clear to me.

I have left the rest of the book untouched so that the reader can see for himself and herself how I had all the pieces of the puzzle in my hand, yet without seeing the final step and the final picture.

The Christ story is none other than the yearly slaying and resurrection of the sun god at the hands of the moon goddess.

Let us consider the evidence step by step. Christ's "birthday" is Christmas Day, 25 December, and four days after the shortest day of the year, or winter solstice, 21 December. It is widely agreed by scholars that this date was chosen by the Christian leaders to capitalize on the greatest pagan festival of the year, the Saturnalia (17–24 December—see chapter 3). But the real reason, I suggest, is more subtle. It is in fact to *perpetuate* the Old Religion.

Christ is resurrected at Easter. This of course is the time of the pagan Spring Festival. And again scholars agree that the placing of Easter is specifically designed to take over the ancient pagan festivals of this time (the Green man and so forth). The *actual* date of Easter is, we must emphasize, fixed by the moon.

In literal fact the "dead" sun is "resurrected" already on 22 December, on the day after his death. But it is in the spring that the promise of his annual resurrection is first fulfilled, in the greening of the fields, which is the renewed gift of life on earth (to all men and all creatures). Christ is killed by the "weak" thirteenth member of the group, Judas. It is of course in the short thirteenth half-month of the thirteenth moon that the sun dies. Judas therefore is the "weak" or "evil" thirteenth month.

Equally the resurrection of the slain god also takes place in the thirteenth month. Clearly therefore the thirteenth Tarot card—see p. 18— and the sun/Christ legend are very closely associated indeed. That thirteenth card, Death, as I have indicated, is very much the card of Death *and Resurrection.* It was the most *holy* card or symbol of the Old Religion, although today thought of as the most cursed.

Most interestingly, in the Christian legend Christ dies late on Friday, on the eve of the Jewish sabbath (which is *Saturday*). First thing on *Sunday* morning the stone is already gone from the sepulchre and the tomb is empty. Christ has been resurrected at this point, *so perhaps already the day before;* that is, on the day after his death. (Nobody went to look at the tomb on Saturday, because that was the sabbath.)

The other fact of special interest is, of course, that we have good reason to believe the Jewish sabbath to be none other than the great ceremony of the washing of the goddess's "menstrual linen"—an occasion that was originally celebrated yearly (perhaps at the winter solstice), then monthly, and finally every seven days (see chapter 8).

I wrote the words "weak" and "evil" in quotations just now because these are the pejorative terms of the sun religion. In the original purely moon religion these "curses" would have been "blessings" (see p. 133).

Now I think we can understand why Christ called his disciples fishers of men, and why the fish is the ancient symbol of Christianity. For he is the "Fisher King" of ancient Celtic legend, who is killed/castrated by the priestesses of the Grail (symbolically, by the priestesses of the moon, but actually by the moon herself) and whose "wounds break out every year afresh." The sun, the Fisher King, dies of his wounds each year at the hands of the moon and is then resurrected by the grace of the moon.

The Fisher King of the Celtic legend is wounded by having a spear thrust through both his thighs. Christ receives the spear wound in his side (and the blood from the wound is caught in the Holy Grail). But, as we have seen, the "spear through both thighs" really means "the knife through both testicles." No doubt the blood of that castration was also received into a cup. In terms of chapter 9, this operation of removing the male genitals, so that the blood flows, is symbolically that of turning a man into a menstruating woman.

We are in the habit today of associating the sea with woman. And yet we can now see that this idea that the sea is a man and a king is perfectly logical in terms of the ancient moon religion (and also, paradoxically, why we today associate the sea with the feminine). The ancient Japanese, the ancient Romans, the ancient Hindus, and the Celts all firmly speak of the *god* of the sea (Neptune, Manannan, and so on).

The sea is ruled by the movement of the moon. It rises and falls at her will, just as does the sun. Therefore the sea *is* the sun, in the sense that it is another personification of the male principle that obeys the eternal feminine.

This was why, for instance, the temple of Benten (the moon goddess) in Japan was built so that the rising tide actually rose up into the lower parts of the building—and then receded. This was, in a general sense, the sea paying homage to the moon. In a particular sense, I suggest, it represents the erection, entry, and orgasm of the penis into the womb, followed by its detumescence and withdrawal. In the old religion all things were seen and understood to be one. The rise and fall of the sea is the male principle making love to the female principle. (For the earth is the female principle.)

(How often, incidentally, in the prepermissive days of films, was the crashing of waves on the shore used to suggest the hero making love to the heroine.)

Christ walked on the water and had the fish as his symbol—and fed

the five thousand with fish at the miracle of the loaves and the fishes—
because he is the god of the sea (and, simultaneously, the god of the
sun).

Once one begins to look at the Bible story in the light I am suggesting, every detail becomes significant. The feeding of the five thousand
employed loaves and fishes symbolizes the union of land and sea. The
bread is the fruit of the land, and the fish are the fruit of the sea. In this
"miracle" the two principles are joined, as indeed they should be. And
by their union mankind is fed—which, I propose, is the original meaning
of the miracle story. The point not to forget, only, is that the land is the
female and sea is the male.

Christ's attributes as sun god are so obvious as not to need mention.
The halo or nimbus that surrounds his head is the sun itself. He is also
the Prince of Light, the light of the world, the glorious radiance, and so
on. Churches, with their magnificent stained glass windows to admit
and transform the light, the most magnificent of which face the rising
sun, are clearly sun temples.

I have written on these aspects in great detail in my earlier book *Total
Man.*

But here is the solution of another mystery. Lucifer, the Devil, in etymological terms, is also the Prince of Light, specifically the "Bringer of
Light" (Latin *lux, lucis* = light). We can see that his "fall," as the Christian religion describes it, is only his yearly obeisance to the moon. It was
Lucifer's bowing to the old religion, to the moon, which was his "crime"
in the eyes of the sun worshipper.

I have repeatedly tried to show in this book how ancient religion
consists of two layers—of an old moon religion overlaid by, and to an
extent combined with, a sun religion. But it is clear that the old moon
worshippers continued to consider that their religion was the true one
and the only one. For this reason (in the west) they continued, secretly,
to practice it independently at the heart of public sun worship. *They
never accepted the sun religion at all.*

That is why (as we saw in chapter 3) we find stone penises carved inside the altars of Christian churches, why a complete Celtic altar is built into the fabric of a church in Paris, and labyrinths are inlaid in the floors of medieval cathedrals.

Some of the practices of rank and file moon worshippers were undoubtedly performed without any real understanding of why they were done or what exactly they represented (just as the Catholic Marranos of Portugal lit candles in the cellar on Friday nights without realizing this to be a Jewish ceremony). But quite clearly many of the leaders of the Christian Church knew exactly what they were doing and why.

This view gives much credence to Margaret Murray's arguments concerning such matters as the significance of the Order of the Garter, and her belief that highly-placed officials were secretly following the old religion.

I would now make this firm statement. All "secret societies" with ancient traditions (like the Rosicrucians and the Freemasons) were, and are, so far as they are guarding anything, guarding fragments of the knowledge of the old moon worship. Here we include also the Knights Templar proper, not so far mentioned in this book. They were publicly said to be the guardians of the Holy Grail, which alone is hint enough. They were quite clearly following in secret aspects of the old ways.

All old secret societies, then, and all formalized ancient and occult wisdoms—such as the Jewish Kabbalah, of course—as well as Druidism, witchcraft, voodoo, and the like, *all* these are lineal descendants of the old moon religion. But the really astonishing thing is that *so is Christianity itself.*

Christianity springs from the Jewish religion. Judaism, as we have seen, has the clearest and most detailed links with the old moon religion to be found anywhere in Europe or the Middle East. (Jewish circumcision, incidentally, is certainly the symbolic act of castration that turns a man into a menstruating woman.) The Jews are also physically, let alone culturally, the most "Neanderthal" people found in the world today. And even as Christianity was being formed out of Judaism *somebody* (and more than one person) saw to it that the essence of the old moon religion was incorporated and enshrined within it. Thus, for instance, Christ and the twelve disciples form a coven of thirteen.

It was an incredibly skillful piece of window dressing.

The Virgin Mary is the Moon-Mother Goddess. In the Catholic religion her importance has grown continuously over the centuries—though here we are talking about a psychological rather than a political development, as already discussed. Her son is subordinate to her, just as Zeus was originally subordinate to Rhea, and Osiris to Isis (see chapter 8 and elsewhere). The blood that figures so prominently in Catholicism and Christianity generally is ultimately the blood of menstruation—but also, clearly, the blood of the castrated male sacrifice at the midwinter solstice. This blood was probably drunk by the priestesses. Today in the Catholic Mass the blood of Christ is drunk. Nothing of the Old Religion has, really, been lost.

In worshipping Christ we are in reality worshipping and reenacting the old fertility rites of the old moon worship. "Though your sins be as scarlet, I will wash them as snow" *must,* for instance, be a reference to the washing of the moon goddess's "laundry" after her menstruation (see again chapter 8).

Christ's coming into the world to bring us eternal life, and his conquering of death, is to be understood not literally, but as the age-old fertility rite. The death of the old year allows the birth of the new year. The present generation (of man, of animals, of plants) dies to make way for the new generation. Without death there can be no regeneration. Death therefore is the key to (eternal) life.

I believe this last is a biological statement, in line with the material examined in chapter 7. I believe that the old moon worshippers (Neanderthal) well understood the principles of evolution and saw that life moves on and evolves only because of the eternal reshuffling of the genetic deck of cards. They understood, I believe, that each generation is only the vehicle for the time traveling genes themselves (the "selfish gene" described by Richard Dawkins). We individually die: but our genes are immortal.

In all this I do not mean to imply, however, that a person called

Christ did not really exist. I am quite sure he did, and that he possessed remarkable paranormal powers. The point is that the leaders of the old moon religion saw to it that the story of his life and death perpetuated and enshrined the eternal "truths" of the Old Religion. These secret moon leaders must have been people of great public importance, and it is fascinating to speculate who they actually were. Probably Joseph of Arimathea was one, "this wealthy and influential secret disciple of Jesus," who, according to legend, also brought the Holy Grail containing Christ's blood to Britain.

On the assumption that the Shroud of Turin is genuine, as I think it is, then Christ actually did receive a spear wound in the side. This, I suggest, was inflicted by a secret follower of the Old Religion, and he and his accomplices saw to it that some of the blood was taken. It was, as it happens, Joseph of Arimathea who requested Christ's body from Pilate—at which request Christ's body was tested with the lance thrust (an odd method?)—and who also bought the actual shroud, took down the body, wrapped it in the shroud and placed it, packed in spices, in the sepulchre that again he, Joseph, had already provided. Joseph and his allies, I further suggest, visited the tomb the next day (or during that same night) and removed the body, so that it should be believed that Christ had been resurrected.

The trail of the Turin shroud again leads, suspiciously enough, to the Knights Templar. Ian Wilson, in his book *The Turin Shroud*, suggests that the famous Mandylion portrait of Christ—which Wilson considers to be nothing other than the shroud, folded, so as to reveal only the face—passed into the keeping of the Knights Templar in the twelfth or thirteenth century.[1]

I am very inclined to accept Wilson's evidence on this point. I will mention some of it in a moment, but for me it is entirely logical that the Knights Templar, being as I suggest one branch of the lineal descendants of the followers of the Old Religion (the moon religion) and active at the time of the crucifixion, should have been in a position to acquire the Mandylion/shroud. And would very much have wanted to do so.

Just to point up the connections between the activities of the Templars and the events of Christ's death a thousand years earlier, the Templar Knights were so called because they were initially given land close to the site of the ruined Temple in Jerusalem. (This spot is the Holy of Holies of the Jewish, Muslim, and Christian religions alike; and it is very nearby that the spot called Zion is said to be. Zion, as I showed in chapter 10, appears to be none other than a reference to the land of the moon goddess.)

Moreover, in their secret ceremonies, the Templars were alleged to prostrate themselves before the shroud, shouting the Saracen word "Yallah." This word, of course, embodies the Arabic "Allah," but it is also not all that far from the Hebrew "Yahweh" (Jehovah). This word is later further distorted (?) to "Selah," according to Wilson. ("Selah" itself is a word without either translation or meaning, which reference books rather helplessly suggest may be a liturgical or musical notation.) But to me this word sounds like "Shiloh," originally a very important name and site in early Jewish history, and again very close to Jerusalem. Shiloh was, in fact, a kind of forerunner of Jerusalem itself. Moreover, the word is occasionally used to actually signify "the Messiah." "Selah" or "Shiloh" *might* therefore be a variant or diguise for Zion, in my sense. All in all we seem here to be touching on a tradition that is very old, rather central, and yet mysterious.

Our suspicions are confirmed rather than dispelled when we learn that Psalm 67 figured centrally in the special Templar Mass . . . "then shall the earth yield her increase . . . " and that: "Like the Grail, the Templar 'idol' [see below] was regarded as having fertility properties; one account specifically states it was 'the Savior' who 'makes the trees blossom and ripens the harvest.'" We are squarely back with fertility rites and a fertility worship.

More arresting still, for myself, is the fact that a Templar portrait of a head is found in England near Templecombe, Somerset, and dating from the thirteenth century. It resembles in general form the Mandylion head. But this portrait has "a reddish beard!" Shades of Neanderthal once again!

It is further the case that the much-rumored "Templar head" or "idol," one of the central features of Templar mystery worship, was the object not just of intense veneration, but the inspirer of the most intense fear. "It seemed to me that it was the face of a demon. . . . Every time I saw it I was filled with such terror I could scarcely look at it, trembling in all my members." That quote, from an actual Templar, is but one of many available concerning this innermost mystery of the Order. As Wilson says, "if we are just talking of the Mandylion head, this fear is very hard to account for."

I myself propose that the Templar "head" was an object of worship that had an independent genesis from that of the Mandylion/shroud—but that, certainly, the shroud was held to be a powerful version of it, one that separately confirmed and supported the Templar belief. The Templecombe portrait is, possibly, one pale version of other more formidable paintings. Those other paintings, perhaps, showed a red-haired Medusa face: Medusa being in origin (see chapter 9) nothing other than a stylized depiction of the menstruating vagina, and the castrated male turned into a woman. (Incidentally, though I have not stressed this point before, if European Neanderthal was red-haired, as I strongly believe, we have here another good associational link between Neanderthal and the worship of blood. Neanderthals saw themselves as marked with the blood of the goddess.)

All these precise details being as they may, what is quite clear is that in practice *today* Christianity is a fertility religion, certainly nothing less and perhaps nothing more. (I would remind the reader again that "blood," "bless," and "blossom" are all the same word.) It is of course also a very sick religion, in that it tragically denies the very sexuality on which it is originally founded. The sickness of Christianity is but one instance, though a major one, of the sickness of all mankind: that is, of our "divided self" and our "divided society."

In summary, then, despite all persecution and all attempts to eradicate it, the Old Religion—the moon religion—survives among us. In this respect it is just like Neanderthal himself.

15

New Wisdom for Old

It was common rumour that Elphin Irving came not into the world like the other sinful creatures of the earth, but was one of the Kane-bairns of the fairies, whilk they had to pay to the enemy of man's salvation every seventh year. The poor lady-fairy—a mother's aye a mother, be she Elve's flesh or Eve's flesh—hid her Elf son beside the christened flesh in Marion Irving's cradle, and the auld enemy lost his prey for a time. . . . And touching this lad, ye all ken his mother was a hawk of an uncannie nest, a second cousin of Katie Kimmer, of Barfloshan, as rank a witch as ever rode on ragwort.

—THE WITCH CULT IN WESTERN EUROPE

Was there an ancient wisdom? My own answer is yes. I do not think we shall ever be able to discover its full extent and scope. The size of the nuggets we find washed down into historical times, however, do suggest that the mother lode was considerable.

People nearer to the ancient times than ourselves, like the Jewish kabbalists, knew this, and they tried almost frantically to preserve this heritage for modern times. Unfortunately, I think they went about it in the wrong way. Or rather, that which they preserved was already so distorted and decayed or deliberately disguised that the trees could no longer be seen for the wood.

The alchemists who came later were in even a worse way. The early kabbalists were at least working with a memory of something that had once been. The alchemists had only a memory of the memory.

So they believed that there was a "red powder" that could "transform." It could transform that which was dull and lifeless and corruptible into that which gave out life and brightness, and that was eternal. Well, let's see now, muttered the alchemists. That must be—well, say lead into gold. After all, lead is dull and lifeless and corrupts, while gold shines and is incorruptible. No other element affects it and it lasts forever.

As I think we have seen, the "red powder" was actually the symbolic representative of the moon's menstrual blood. And that which it transformed was the lifeless land of winter into the productive land of summer, or the barren woman to the pregnant mother. The moon's blood promised not eternal life but the eternity *of* life, in the sense of its eternal renewal.

Nearly all the so-called ancient wisdom (the books of spells, the magic signs, the secret rituals) is like this. It is a memory of a memory, in itself without direct value: except, that is, as a signpost, as the bearer of the message—"there *was* once something else that was wonderful." Or rather—there *is* something else that *is* wonderful! This is the message for us today.

There *is* another way of going about things than the conscious, logical, scientific, masculine way. There really is a magical way. The lowest or base form of this is intuition. The highest form is clairvoyance.

We have today sadly lost touch with this whole area of our being. Only struggling minority groups have kept even the memory of it alive. Part of the problem is that one of our ancestors (Cro-Magnon) had very little endowment in these respects, simply by construction. (But *he* was endowed with the logical, objective, out-turning mind, which is our other great gift.) Luckily our second ancestor (Neanderthal) was very well endowed intuitively and magically.

To reach and revive that aspect of our being, that endowment from our shadow ancestor, we must "Neanderthalize" ourselves. This does not mean at all that we must lose or abandon our Cro-Magnon inheritance.

It means we must bring up the shadow side (which is also the "feminine" side) into full partnership.

One of the ways we can do this individually is to go about with the idea that magic is both real and here-and-now. It *is*. The "kingdom of heaven" (the "land beneath the waves") is within you. Accept, therefore, that magic (clairvoyance, scrying, far memory, and so on) is real. Here is a Cartesian motto for you: "I breathe, therefore I am clairvoyant."

The "nonlogic" of that statement is quite deliberate. We are in a different area than logic.

This is the main aspect of it all. But there is another aspect, too, something for the scientist this time. What the scientist must do is very carefully sift all the ancient writings and beliefs, in search of nuggets that he can use for his own purposes. In many cases he will find new starting points for his own inquiries.

Here is a very recent instance of what I am talking about. In this case science made the discovery in its own right—but it could have been made far, far earlier—and was, intuitively.

It has now been established that eating fresh garlic rapidly reduces the level of blood cholesterol. Cholesterol is strongly implicated as being the main causative agent of heart attacks. Blood cholesterol levels drop appreciably within *two weeks* of beginning the garlic diet.

In ancient legend, one of the items the blood-sucking vampire is said to fear is fresh garlic. So you see? This recent discovery of science was known long, long ago.

The puzzle (for scientists, that is) is how ancient people could have known about this property of garlic. If we are talking about actual Neanderthal (the people of Shanidar cave, for example), scarcely any of them could have lived long enough to have experienced heart attacks in any case. But even if they did, by what process was it discovered that garlic *prevented* heart attack? A great mystery for the scientist. I do not myself believe that any experimental process of trial and errror was involved. Some psychic or psychics simply looked at garlic and said, "This is good for that which hurts the heart."

In all details the legend preserves the symbology (the logic of the symbols). For in the legend it is through the heart that we kill and drive out the blood-sucking vampire.

The kind of wisdom we have here, and the form of the legend itself, strongly remind us of the form and content of the Prometheus legend of the liver that self-renews (see pp. 91–92).

In the companion book to this one I shall be reporting on tribes in Indonesia, whose religion appears to describe actual functions of the brain: functions that modern psychology and neurology have only just begun to recognize. I could not include this account here, because it requires as background a detailed look at brain theory. The trail led too far away from the central subject matter of this volume.

As I said, it does look as if the mother lode of ancient wisdom was very considerable indeed. And as I also said, scientists must as a matter of urgency begin to take ancient legend seriously, and see it as a major source area for their own research.

What we "progressives" must beware of on our side are the dangers of too much, or misunderstood, "Neanderthalizing." The process can easily be taken too far, resulting only in a similar undesirable imbalance in the opposite direction.

For example, I remarked in earlier chapters that true Neanderthal was more of a vegetable eater than a meat eater. And actually the large stomach with its long intestine, and the broad flat teeth, are the mark of the typical vegetarian. But when and if we recklessly try to Neanderthalize ourselves psychologically by weird vegetable diets that avoid meat in all its forms, tragedy is not far away.

The *Observer* of 4 February 1979 carried this report.

> Children of parents who adopt faddish diets run a real risk of suffering from malnutrition. If babies are fed on the same eccentric foods as their parents, they can quickly show symptoms of diseases more familiar in the context of a natural disaster in the Third World— kwashiorkor, marasmus and rickets. It is a form of malnutrition

which has been familiar in the United States for some time, and has now been reported for the first time in Britain. Doctors from two London hospitals report in the *British Medical Journal* on four cases of malnutrition in infants resulting from faddish diets. Three of the babies had been fed on a macrobiotic infant food known as kohkoh, which is made up of rice, wheat, oats, beans and sesame flour. The other baby had been given only breast milk and uncooked fruit and vegetables since birth. All four were grossly underweight and suffered other symptoms of malnutrition. . . . Far from being grateful the parents in three cases objected strongly and the hospital had to obtain court orders before the children could be treated.[1]

Neither the pursuit of "alternative consciousness," any more than the pursuit of science, should ever be allowed to result in us abandoning our common sense.

Some may be wondering why I have had so little to say about astrology. Certainly, like all other memories and legacies of former times, the practices and beliefs of astrology should be sifted carefully for nuggets by scientists. The role of the moon in the evolution of our species is already one major nugget, which scientists should now evaluate further. But I have not said much about astrology for two reasons. One, because Michel Gauquelin and Hans Eysenck are currently sifting this material (and have already produced results); and two, because the massive superstructure is fairly clearly a late addition and extension to whatever it was the true ancients knew and believed about this topic. To me, therefore, it is just another memory of a memory, having very little objective value. (Its supporters consider it to be entirely objective, but there I think they are wrong.)

Where astrology does have value—along with Tarot cards, the crystal ball, and the ouija board—is in serving as a vehicle for clairvoyance. This is a *subjective* value. Now, if the metaphor of astrology—and I personally believe it to be a metaphor—helps you personally to establish touch with your own clairvoyant abilities, that is absolutely fine. Any metaphor that helps one to do that is valuable.

As I have already indicated in chapter 7, a metaphor is really an explanation that isn't (at any rate as far as the objective mind is concerned). The "explanations" of the intuitive mind are subjective—that is, they are meaningful only to those who believe in them. They are not public explanations, but private ones, like the ones children invent.

As I just said, any metaphor that works for you is, of course, valuable. However, I believe in one sense we are better off devising metaphors that suit our own age and time than in using those of past ages (despite the fact that "pastness" is itself a valuable ingredient in awakening our shadow mind and arousing the necessary emotional involvement). For the danger is always that we shall end up thinking that these past metaphors are objectively real, and that they are not just extensions of our own personalities but "something else": something ineffable, sacred, untouchable, unchangeable. They are, of course, none of these things. Nothing is sacred, untouchable, or unchangeable (neither in science nor in religion). There are only extensions of ourselves, which are tools or means for our greater understanding and the development of our abilities.

We see the danger I just mentioned in respect of the so-called chakras of the so-called etheric body. I personally think that there is very little chance that these exist in any objective sense. There is even less chance of there being seven of them (see chapter 2). But believers in them are quite convinced that they exist in an objective sense and that they indeed number seven. They have lost all sense of this being just a useful metaphor (they are a kind of internalization of the seven stars of the Plough). *If* it is useful. I am not sure that the number seven has any real right to go on being part of our modern paranormal metaphors at all. I think thirteen *has* and should probably be reinstated. For at least natural woman still ovulates/menstruates thirteen times a year.

This is the point really. Although our metaphors are necessarily, and quite rightly, *invented,* that is, *made up*—are in a sense only "working fantasies"—there *is* nevertheless something called subjective reality of which they partake.

Our subjective reality does have the habit of changing itself even from minute to minute (like the shadows of clouds scudding across the countryside); but some of its elements are relatively constant. The moon is one, and thirteen is another. We should and can always turn back to them.

But seven? I think not. I think the fact that the modern purgers allowed it to stay on is enough evidence of its actual valuelessness as a magical symbol.

So really the idea is for us to retain only what is useful for us from the ancient wisdom, and then to build this into a present (and future) wisdom of our own. This new wisdom then takes its place alongside the new know-how—that is, science—at its left hand; so that we as a people are once again jointly ruled by the two eternal divinities, the moon goddess and the sun god—by Isis *and* Osiris.

Skeletons in Our Cupboard

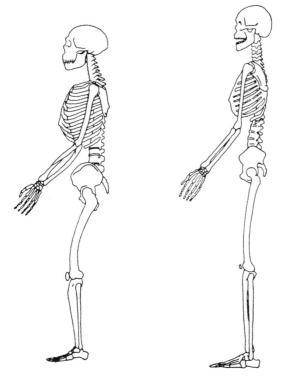

(a) Neanderthal Man   (b) Cro-Magnon Man

Figure 12. Full skeletons and heads (see 12c and 12d on next page) of Neanderthal and Cro-Magnon are shown. The chances of either of these forms of man being descended from the other are virtually nil. ("This hypothesis has been abandoned"—Professor Ralph Solecki, *Shanidar: The Humanity of Neanderthal Man.*)

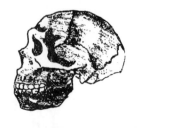

(c) Neanderthal Skull   **(d)** Cro-Magnon Skull

Both physical types are found in our population today, more obviously in males. Look around you for the prominent brow ridges of Neanderthal. You will be surprised how obvious these are once you start looking. They tend to be associated with a short, thickset physique and dark, curly hair.

APPENDIX 2

Inner Space and Outer Space

Geoffrey Ashe is one of the serious writers who tentatively subscribes to the idea of an intervention from outer space somehow beginning our civilization. Robert Temple is another. It is not an idea that I myself find appealing or feel the need of. But I am not going to be so dogmatic as to say that no case at all can be made out for it.

Of all those who have written on the subject only Robert Temple has, in my opinion, produced worthwhile objective evidence to support it. In his book, *The Sirius Mystery,* he presents his thoughtful scholarly case, based primarily on his study of the Dogon tribe in Africa.[1]

It is a remarkable case that he offers and a remarkable book. So much so, that it has carried traditionally hostile scientific critics with it. Perhaps its greatest triumphs over skepticism were a cautiously favorable review in the magazine *Nature;* and the BBC *Horizon* program devoted to debunking the theories of von Däniken introduced Temple as the only responsible researcher in this field.

Like many others, I have continuously examined and thought over the evidence of *The Sirius Mystery* in the two years since I first made its acquaintance. For a long time (like Temple himself), I could see no alternative explanation to the visit by extraterrestrials he proposes. Now there is one, I think.

First, a look at the material presented in the book.

There is living today in Mali, West Africa, a tribe known as the Dogon. Though they are in outward physical appearance much like any other African tribe, it is clear that some of their remote ancestors were not African. These came probably from the Near or Middle East, moving then perhaps through Greece to Libya, whence they traveled south through the Libyan oases of the Sahara, and finally southwest toward Timbuctu. Here they mingled with the local African population, losing their language and their Middle-Eastern appearance, but preserving and bequeathing to the Dogon their strange and complex religious beliefs.

For us now these events were an incredibly fortunate accident. For what we find among the Dogon today are religious practices and attitudes that are in all probability several thousand years old, preserved for us in time like a fly in amber. These are beliefs that, in their country of origin, had long since been dismantled and forgotten—except, as Temple shows, for scattered fragments and remnants still surviving in the legends and folktales of many lands.

The Dogon worship the star Sirius. In so doing they enact complex rituals and follow complex religious dogma. What the dogma states in essence is this: it says that the star Sirius (Sirius A) is orbited by another star—an invisible, dark star (Sirius B). The Dogon insist, however, that this other star, Sirius B, is more important than Sirius A. Yet they say that Sirius B is very tiny. They call it *po tolo* or "seed star." The *po* seed is the smallest grain of cereal known to the Dogon.

They go on to say that this tiny star nevertheless is of an enormous weight. They say it is made of a metal so heavy "that all earthly beings combined cannot lift it." It weighs the equivalent of "all the iron on the earth."

This is still not all. The Dogon say that Sirius B does not go round Sirius A in a circle (which would probably be the natural assumption for a primitive people to make), but in an ellipse—a flattened or egg-shaped circle. Nor is Sirius A at the center of that ellipse (again the most logical assumption)—it is at one end of it. So in the course of its orbit around Sirius A, Sirius B is sometimes very close to it and sometimes very far away (see figures 13a and b). (The average separation between the two stars is twenty times the distance from our own planet to our own sun.) One of the ways in which the Dogon express this situation is to say that the dark star has to pursue its twin till the end of time, but is never capable of reaching it. Finally, they say that Sirius B completes its orbit round Sirius A once every fifty years.

In summary, what the Dogon are telling us here—in nonscientific language, of course—is that they understand the mechanics of binary systems and elliptical orbits, and the nature of collapsed dwarf stars.

So much for what the Dogon say. What are the scientific facts as established by modern astronomy? The facts are that Sirius *is* a binary star system composed of Sirius A and Sirius B. Sirius A is a normal star at a midpoint in its life cycle; but Sirius B is a star that has collapsed under its own gravity, what we today call a "white dwarf." The vast mass of the originally normal star has been compressed into a relatively tiny volume. Because of this compression, the material of the dwarf star has enormous weight. A cubic foot of matter from Sirius B would weigh two thousand tons. With powerful modern telescopes *we* can actually see the tiny speck of Sirius B emitting its faint light—first seen in modern times by Alvan Clark in 1862, and first photographed only in 1970.

Astronomy also states (since Kepler, 1571–1630) that the major body of any binary system—the movement of a planet around a sun, or of one star around another—remains in the vicinity of one of the two foci that all ellipses possess, while the minor body follows, or describes, the path of the ellipse (see figure 13a).

Finally, modern science agrees that the periodicity of Sirius B around Sirius A is fifty years.

It is absolutely obvious that the Dogon people, a primitive African tribe, did know all these facts long before modern astronomy. There is no argument about that aspect of the affair and all critics and reviewers agree with this. The mystery and the question is *how* did the Dogon gain their detailed and accurate knowledge.

Temple's answer is that the ancestors of the Dogon were given this

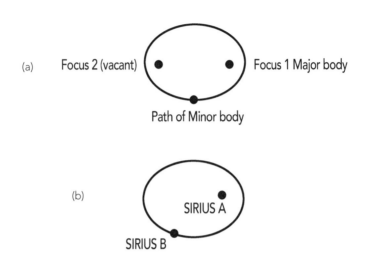

Figure 13. (a) Elliptical path of a minor stellar or
planetary body around a major body. (b) Orbit of Sirius B
around Sirius A (as also drawn by the Dogon tribe).

information by spacemen traveling from Sirius to Earth. He does not
come to the conclusion lightly or willingly. He finds himself forced to
it as the only possible answer to the riddle. There seems now to be at
least a partial alternative solution to the mystery, however, that does not
require the intervention of space people. Before we come to this, I have
to refer briefly to other matters in Temple's book.

In it, with great brilliance and scholarship, Temple shows how many
fragments of the knowledge of the Dogon are found all over the Near
and Middle East, reaching occasionally even as far as India, as well as
classical Greece. They are further proof, if we needed it, of how widespread a legend can be, and how long it can survive. Here I can do no
justice to the complex interweaving of threads of legend that Temple
produces connecting culture to culture and age to age. But a brief sample
follows.

For example, the companions of the Greek hero Jason the Argonaut
number fifty. His boat, the *Argo*, is described as having fifty oars, and
these as being laid out "in line around the ship." This is certainly a very

odd way to place oars—for a ship with oars so placed would simply spin round in circles. For this and other reasons Temple takes this legend to be a distorted account of the fifty-year orbit of Sirius B. Moreover, the Jason story itself seems to be a late copy of a much earlier story about Gilgamesh, a Sumerian hero who also had fifty companions. Furthermore An, the heaven-god of Sumeria, had fifty companion gods called Anunnaki. An is represented as a jackal. Again, the dog Cerberus, the guardian of the Greek Hades, originally had fifty heads—while Sirius itself is, of course, the dog-star, in the constellation of the Great Dog *(Canis Major)*. So the fifties, dogs, gods, and heroes weave to and fro and interlink.

Many other items accompany these—the heat of the days that in latter-day Egypt follow the annual rising of Sirius (known as the dog-days), when the hot wind drove men to crime and madness, "which then as now caused a wave of criminal violence in Egypt" (Graves). As it happens the name of that hot wind in Arabic is *khamsin,* which means fifty.

In the wealth of material offered by Temple there is one connection between Egypt and the Dogon that he has missed, but that is well worth mentioning. During an occasional ceremony called the Sigui by the Dogon—and which symbolizes the rejuvenation of the world—the following happens: a rock in the middle of the village is said to light up with a red glow. After this happens the priests then ceremonially dig a small hole and place seeds in it.

What this surely must be is a debased and no longer understood version of what probably happened in the temples of Isis at the first dawn rising of the red star Sirius, heralding as it did the overflowing of the Nile. When the glow of the star shone upon the altar (see p. 234) the priests, perhaps symbolically, placed a variety of seeds upon it in a hollow. This ceremony symbolized and sanctioned the sowing of the new crops in the now once again enriched plains of the Nile delta—"the rejuvenation of the world." (We in the modern west, incidentally, perform a similar though opposite rite—placing *harvested* grains and fruits upon the altar at Harvest Festival.) In all this we have another reason why the Dogon call Sirius B the seed star. It is typical of Temple's concern for the truth that he is not content to *assume* that the red light from Sirius shone on the altars of the temples. He has currently asked Professor John Taylor to test this idea experimentally by building a scale model of a temple and Sirius. (Ultimately, of course, this redness must also link back to menstrual blood.)

At any rate, the Egyptians did disassemble and realign the temple aisles every century or so, in order that these should continue to point directly at Sirius on its first heliacal—or dawn—rising. For Sirius, like most other celestial events, gradually creeps along the horizon due to the tiny, but cumulative difference in length between the solar year and the sidereal year.

Only in quite late Egyptian times did the heliacal rising of Sirius come sufficiently close to the flooding of the Nile to be thought of as "causing" the flood. Nowadays Sirius actually rises *after* the flooding!

The general pattern and the logic of the vast mass of material Robert Temple offers is inescapable. We are seeing the fragments of a once great tradition, now broken up, distorted, and misunderstood. "Misunderstood" is actually an understatement. We ourselves would not understand these surviving fragments *at all,* but for the freak chance that allowed one version of the original tradition to survive, more or less intact, in central Africa. Precisely because the people there (the Dogon and one or two related tribes) underwent no further social evolution, the legend retained much of its original form.

So I am saying, therefore, in summary, that I agree with everything Temple claims and accept all his proofs—except in one vital particular: the explanation.

Here is how I believe matters really went.

There existed at one time an ancient civilization known as Sumeria. The Sumerians, who inhabited territory to the east of Israel around the Tigris and Euphrates deltas, were the forerunners, both in time and culture, of the ancient Babylonians, Egyptians, and Assyrians. There is no doubt that they bequeathed much knowledge and general religious belief and practice to those later civilizations.

The Sumerians were great astrologers—or rather, I think we must begin to say astronomers. For they did not simply regard the stars and the planets mystically. They had begun to study, record, and measure them. The oldest known drawings of the constellations are from Sumeria. We do not, of course, need to imagine that the Sumerians themselves began from scratch. The fact that there are substantial parallels in the names of constellations throughout the whole world, dating back at least 20,000 years (see p. 83) totally argues against this. Wallis Budge, the Egyptologist, firmly though exceptionally believes that Sumeria and Egypt both derived their own cultures from a common source older than either.[2]

No matter if they did or not. The basic fact remains that Sirius would come readily to the attention of anyone observing the sky with any kind of intelligence. For it is the brightest star in the heavens. Moreover, in the Middle East in late times the first heliacal rising of Sirius signals the beginning of the hottest part of the year. To a still relatively primitive mind (inclined in any case to see the heavenly bodies as gods), the star would be the *cause* of those hot days. Incidentally, on rising the star looks red close to the horizon. It is the only body bright enough to produce this optical effect. And the redness of Sirius was, in fact, thought to be a causative factor in the heat that followed its rising.

Aside from these factors, Sirius is a very reliable star. Both the Sumerians and the Egyptians employed it to calculate the "sidereal year" (of 365.256 days), as compared to the solar or tropical year (of 365.242 days).

Already then we can see reason enough why Sirius would readily come to the attention of, and be of direct importance to, any nation whose major pursuit was, in any case, the study of the stars. There is no reason to doubt that its "career" both as a major deity and reference point was already well advanced in Sumerian times.

But in later Egypt, matters of still greater importance attached to it. For then in the days following the first dawn, rising of Sirius, the flooding of the Nile began. This annual flooding, and the deposit of alluvial mud it brought with it, was not only the lifeblood of Egyptian civilization but the source of all its wealth. Rheinhold Merkelbach notes: "the festival of the Nile flood was the greatest festival of Isis."

These are reasons enough why the Egyptians should have been intensely interested in Sirius and had grounds for seeing it as their greatest benefactor. Did not he (or she) bring the life-giving floods, the renewing, refreshing water that came just when the earth was burned to a cinder?

By exactly the same token the Mayas in South America worshipped the Plough, for its rising on their horizon heralded the beginning of the annual rains.

But there is more. Given the logical importance of Sirius to the peoples of the ancient Middle East, and especially to the Egyptians, two things follow. One, it would be worshipped. Two, it would be studied and theorized about. Both these events occurred, and the two are interlinked. For there was as yet no separation, formal or otherwise, between "church" and "state," between things spiritual and things temporal.

Robert Temple writes as follows (but see also the point on p. 231):

> The heliacal rising of Sirius was so important to the ancient Egyptians that gigantic temples were constructed with their main aisles oriented precisely towards the spot on the horizon where Sirius would appear on the expected morning. The light of Sirius would be channelled along the corridor (due to the precise orientation) to flood the altar in the inner sanctum as if a pin-pointed spotlight had been switched on. This blast of light focused from a single star was possible because of the orientation being so incredibly precise and because the temple would be otherwise in total darkness within. In a huge, utterly dark temple, the light of one star focused solely on the altar must have made quite an impact on those present. In this way was the presence of the star made manifest within its temple.[3]

Another reason for the alignment of the aisle might have been to study Sirius. It is well-known that, if one looks up from the bottom of a deep, narrow hole (or outward from a deep cave), the stars become visible even in broad daylight. The tunnel removes the effects of the sun's rays, enabling us to see the stars normally hidden by the sun's light and that, of course, are always there. Looking at Sirius from within one of these temples gave, even at dawn, a heightened view of the star. It is true the priests could only look properly once a year by this means—but that is the point. They were, in modern terms, controlling all the variables involved *except* the state of the star itself. What precise features of it the priests were charting we will come to shortly: for the moment we note only that Sirius does pass through a fifty-year cycle.

I had hoped to make a great deal of this next point, imagining myself to be its discoverer. But Francis Hitching indicates that several others have already thought of this possibility. We can really take it now as established fact.[4]

The fact is that crude but adequate lenses, made from polished natural crystal, were available to the ancient astronomers of Sumeria and elsewhere around 4,000 years ago. As John Irwin remarks in his *Britannica* article: "The effects achieved by looking [at the sky] through a magnifying lens, and especially by looking through two lenses in alignment, are so startling that it is likely that the telescope was 'invented' independently and accidentally many times."

The invention of the telescope is officially credited to Galileo in 1609. Yet we have grounds for believing that primitive telescopes were available to astronomers two or three thousand years before Christ. After all, what were those ancient lenses otherwise for?

A "telescope" is formed once you take a lens in each hand, hold them up to your eye, and align them by trial and error movement. Once this discovery is made, it becomes a simple matter to construct a wooden device that holds the lenses in that position. This is what I suggest the ancient Sumerians and the ancient Egyptians did. The total number of lenses that could be aligned in this way depends and depended, I imagine, on the amount of image-distortion produced by the "crude" lenses. This is a matter for scientists with access to these lenses to check.

We already know that exceptional individuals can see the four main moons of Jupiter and the phases of Venus with the naked eye. This feat must have been still easier in the relatively less polluted atmosphere of four thousand years ago. (The amount of pollutant material in the atmosphere has increased steadily with man's population explosion, and his food gathering and industrial processes. Main contributing factors are: the burning of forest cover to flush game and clear land for farming; the smelting of metal, which began to consume enormous quantities of wood from the Bronze Age onward; and straightforward domestic heating.) Visibility could be, and I suggest was, increased by the building of tunnels such as those found in temples, and also by ascending to mountain tops.

This last point is my own little contribution—my guess is that the reason why most priests (like Moses) traditionally went up on mountains to speak to the gods was because viewing conditions were best up there. And that venue also kept the general public from seeing what the priests' secret practices really were. All priestly affairs were closely guarded secrets. (The Dogon priests, incidentally, only finally described their religious rituals to a deeply respected anthropologist who had lived among them most of his life.) With this proposal, that the ancient priests had access to primitive telescopes, I believe we are now in a position to understand much of the "mysterious knowledge" of the planets and stars (trotted out by writers like Däniken), which the ancients probably did indeed possess. From the telescope and this wholly conscious source comes the otherwise sometimes baffling knowledge of the ancients.

Now, what did the priests see when they looked at Sirius? They saw (and I would emphasize again that many of these features are visible even to the naked eye) exactly what Bessel saw in 1844—a star that wobbled. Sirius A moves its position and "weaves" slightly due to the influence of Sirius B. At times also the star is brighter than at others— and then at yet others twinkles noticeably. This situation is described by the Dogon. They say that when Sirius B is close to Sirius A, the latter becomes brighter. When it is at its most distant point from Sirius A, there is a twinkling effect, suggesting several stars to the observer. "If you look at Digitaria then it's as if the world were spinning" is how the Dogon put it. (Digitaria is the botanical name for the *po* seed, and the name Temple uses for Sirius B.)

Studying the star over many centuries—and we have no problems of continuity here—the Sumerians/Egyptians would have observed that the time gap from one "most bright" to the next "most bright" (or from one "most twinkling" to another) was fifty years. They could calculate this interval precisely by studying the yearly appearance of Sirius in the temple tunnels. And so the periodicity of the cycle was established.

So much for observation. What about theory?

The old Arab name for Sirius is Al Wazn, giving the modern name Wezen, which means "the star that seems to rise with difficulty from the horizon." Temple takes this to be a garbled reference to Sirius B that, as we know today, is a collapsed white dwarf of superdense, superheavy material. I think it is too—but not necessarily in the sense Temple understands it. I do not think the reference is garbled. I think we can take the Arabic name literally.

Back in ancient Egyptian times we have a very bright (the brightest) and very powerful star—powerful because it causes the Nile to flood, scorches the earth so that nothing grows elsewhere, and induces mad, ungoverned human behavior. Yet this bright and powerful star scarcely succeeds in getting over the horizon—though, in view of its power, we would expect it to rise like the sun. Instead, after it first shows (nowadays at the beginning of August), it rises slowly (as it were with difficulty) to its high point over the next five months. This is never a very high "high point"—in England, for example, the star is never seen more than 29° above the horizon. The reason is that Sirius is essentially a star of the southern hemisphere. It is visible in northern latitudes only during the winter months, and then always low on the horizon.

Moreover, this "reluctant" star also wobbles and passes through a fifty-year cycle of changing appearance. What might cause a star to wobble? Perhaps the presence of another star. What would cause a repeating fifty-year cycle? Why, the orbiting of another body, circling the star just as the moon circles the earth (drawing the tides with it and affecting the menstruation and pregnancy of women as it does so).

But why was it not possible to see that orbiting body (Sirius B)? Perhaps because it was invisible or black or dark. (The Dogon do refer to it as the dark star). Or perhaps it was very small? Or even both. But if small, it would need to be very heavy. Why? Because (a) it caused the mighty Sirius to wobble, and (b) it prevented the mighty Sirius from rising above the horizon.

I believe that from these possibilities alone the ancients could have decided finally that Sirius B—"the companion," as we shall see they called it—was small, dark, and heavy. In this thinking they were aided also by the operation (both consciously and unconsciously) of the major principle of the conceptual universe—that of duality, or yin yang. Dualistic theory would necessarily urge that the brightest star in the universe (and, therefore, also the largest as far as the ancients were concerned) would logically be orbited by the darkest and smallest star in the universe—yet one equally powerful in its own way.

I have shown in earlier books how fundamental and permanent the concepts of dualism and duality are to all times and cultures. Sometimes a society gives undue weight to one side of the total equation (as, respectively, did moon cultures on the one hand, and sun cultures on the other) but the totality is always implicit even when (or perhaps especially when) the opposite is denied. Only in a few cultures, like those of ancient China or aboriginal Australia, was equal or more or less equal importance given to both sides. But it seems we may have to add Sumeria and Egypt to that list. For the later crystallization of the dual principle in Egypt was the overriding cult of Isis and Osiris. And, most interestingly and in support of my view, we find the identification of Sirius A and Sirius B, respectively, with these two.

It is impossible to reproduce all the points of that particular argument;

for these the interested must go to *The Sirius Mystery* itself. But we note first that there exists no full account of the Isis-Osiris story! "Many Egyptologists have remarked on the irony that we have nowhere in Egyptian sources a full, coherent account of Isis and Osiris—not even in all the sources put together." As in so many of these cases, it seems that this pair were part of the central "mystery." But we do know that Isis is often identified with Sirius. The companion of Isis is Osiris. He, in turn, is often equated with the constellation Orion—and Orion's companion is the Dog, of which Sirius is the chief star. There are other references and legends also that appear to link Osiris both with darkness and the process of orbiting.

The arguments are difficult here for two reasons. One, because, as just stated, they are part of closely-guarded mysteries of which only fragments come down to us. Two, because what we find in middle Egyptian times seems to be already a partly garbled and misunderstood version of an original statement. The real origin of these stories and of what we call the Sirius mystery may well, therefore, lie with Sumeria—or perhaps with the still earlier civilization postulated by Wallis Budge.

CONCLUSIONS

The argument I have presented is, I think, not inferior in logic to that of Robert Temple—but, most importantly, does not involve the giant step of assuming visitors from outer space. My suggestion is that the Sumerians (or whoever it was) arrived at an understanding of the nature of Sirius B for at least partly the wrong reasons (a frequent sign of the working of intuition, which I am not altogether ruling out in this case). The wobble of Sirius A they correctly ascribed to the influence of a large, but invisible—or a small, dark, and very heavy—star. The fact that Sirius could not get very far above the horizon was, to them, additional fuel for these arguments. But that was just coincidence (?), as was the fact that the supposed influence of Sirius was "heavy," as the modern hippie understands that term—that is, produced pessimistic and negative impulses in the human psyche.

I cannot claim to have dealt fully with all of Temple's evidence. But the idea that the ancients possessed rudimentary telescopes does knock a fairly large hole in some of his reasoning—as it does, of course, in the case of much other evidence for extraterrestrial interference.

ANY OTHER BUSINESS

The main purpose of this present book has been to examine interrelationships in man's "inner space." In so doing the book necessarily skirts the question of extraterrestrial visitors and UFOs. Yet precisely these apparently most "outer" elements do seem to be products of our own "inner space," as C. G. Jung well understood and showed.[5]

I am in no position to say with absolute finality—who could be?—that visitors from outer space have never been on this planet. What can be done is to show that most of the evidence usually put forward in defense of such claims is not valid. We should, in my own opinion, do our utmost to show that *all* of it is not valid—and only fall back on the hypothesis of space visitors when we are absolutely forced to. Paradoxically, the attempt to destroy the case (providing the attempt is fair and honest) will in the long run do more for the cause of extraterrestrials than any amount of wide-eyed and naive enthusiasm.

What, we have *no* need of, above all, are phony mysteries. We have plenty of real mysteries without these. The phony variety can only hinder us in our understanding of genuine wonders.

The best case for the intervention of outer space visitors is undoubtedly in Robert Temple's book. And, in all honesty, I must say, that the Dogon descriptions of the precise composition of Sirius B, as well as some of those from the ancient Middle East, do still strongly suggest to me that the individuals concerned really understood the nature of collapsed matter.

But among the lines of attack on Temple's position, as I remarked in an earlier chapter, we can also ponder the major coincidence that the alleged visitors *just happened* to come from the brightest star in the sky (instead of from one of the billions of others), which also just happens to be the star that in late times announced the Nile flood and which also happens to be the star that noticeably wobbles. Similarly, Geoffrey Ashe (see chapter 2) wants us to accept that his outer space visitors just happened to come from the most easily identified constellation in the whole sky, the Plough, the only one that never dips below our horizon and that revolves around the still center of the sky. I think here we are asking too much of coincidence or even of synchronicity.

At the other end of the scale from Temple and Ashe we can simply shovel most of the material offered into the incinerator. Let us glance at everybody's favorite target (or champion, depending on your viewpoint) Erich von Däniken. Jacquetta Hawkes has written a short and definitive piece about Däniken (published in the *Sunday Times* of 15 September 1974) and the following points—only a few of many—are taken from it.[6]

First, Däniken, and writers like him, make errors that almost any schoolboy interested in these subjects would know enough to avoid. Such mistakes—and they are terribly frequent—can really give us no confidence in anything else the writer has to say.

An incredible howler by Däniken is to state that "our galaxy is only a tiny part of the Milky Way, which contains some twenty galaxies." Of course the Milky Way *is* our galaxy (a cross-section of it, that is) and does not "contain" any galaxies at all, apart from itself. Däniken's statement is literally as foolish as saying that a tin of fruit contains tins of fruit.

By way of further example, Däniken believes and claims that Ezekiel (of the Old Testament) witnessed the landing of a space ship in 592 BC. In support he cites the fact that the Bolivian ruins of Tiahuanaco, which he believes to have been the base camp of the extraterrestrials, are assigned to 600 BC by archaeologists. In fact, the date given by archaeology is AD 600.

A final point is the most telling of all. Däniken's illustrations in his various books include "more than forty" well-known forgeries! Note the wording here: *well-known* forgeries.

Now, why is it that Mr. Däniken does not know that many of his reproductions are forgeries? Or does he know that they are forgeries, but not care? And do his publishers not know they are forgeries? Or do they simply not care? Or what?

Running Däniken a close second in terms of popularity are books about what is called the "Bermuda Triangle," or "Devil's Triangle," off the coast of Florida, where allegedly vast numbers of ships and aircraft have disappeared without trace or reason, and where extraterrestrial intervention is one of the "explanations" most strongly urged.

For those interested in finding out how worthless and unjustified this sort of literature is, I recommend L. D. Kusche's *The Bermuda Triangle Mystery Solved.* At the end of this excellently researched and totally damning book the author comments: "It is no more logical to try to find a common cause for the disappearances in the triangle than, for example, to try to find one cause for the automobile accidents in Arizona. By abandoning the search for an overall theory and investigating each incident independently, the mystery unravels."[7]

Before leaving these unprofitable areas altogether, let me comment on one or two other items central to many theories of outer space intervention.

First, the statues of Easter Island. A tiny speck of land, Easter Island is situated in splendid isolation in the Pacific, thousands of miles from continental land, and almost as far from the nearest other island. The statues, as most people know, are giant figures carved from stone, which are set in the earth around the coast looking out to sea. Some of these statues weigh fifty tons. How could a small native population, without proper tools, carve and transport these giant monoliths around the island? A real mystery. Surely visitors from outer space must have had a hand in their genesis. Perhaps the statues (each with a great piece of red rock balanced weirdly on the head) were replicas of those giants from the beyond?

Thor Heyerdahl, the explorer, went to live for a time on Easter Island. He gradually won the natives' confidence and in the end was told their folklore. Following the instructions contained in it, Heyerdahl and the local natives cut one of the great statues from the living rock of the central mountain—using *only* the primitive stone tools of the early natives—and transported the statue to the coast on a wooden sledge as the legends described, and finally erected it. The erection of the colossal piece of masonry was achieved by natives fractionally raising the head with long poles. Each time it was lifted a fraction, other natives were on hand with small pieces of stone that they slipped into the tiny opening, so that the statue could not fall back again.

So that is it. There is no more mystery about the construction of the Easter Island statues. (And the people the statues actually commemorate were, it seems, tall blonde or red-haired Europeans, who first came to South America and from there crossed the Pacific to Polynesia, many hundred of years ago.) Yet, despite the publication of Heyerdahl's book *Aku Aku* back in 1958, many writers are still trotting out the "mysteries" of Easter Island in support of space visitors.

In a fascinating documentary program entitled *The Case of the Ancient Astronauts,* shown at the end of November 1977 on BBC2, the producer and writer Graham Massey gave some marvelous insights into yet other "mysteries." Concerning the Egyptian pyramids, the first point made was that there were several failed and experimental attempts at building them before the builders started "getting it right." The finished pyramids we see today are, therefore, the end product of a lengthy process of trial and error. During the program, moreover, we saw blocks being prepared and raised into place, using the ancient methods, in the construction of a modern copy of a pyramid. There were no major problems. It can be done.

As far as the shaping of the blocks is concerned, which usually excites such wonder, it is, in fact, well-known that "if originally laid down as a sediment, stone will part parallel to bedding planes or stratification." Limestone, used in the pyramids, is a sedimentary rock. This rock, depo ited at the bottom of seas and lakes, is built up in perfectly flat la But sensibly enough, the ancient Egyptians also checked the fla each layer of blocks with a water-level (a kind of early spirit-level as used by modern builders).

The pyramids are, of course, a magnificent engineering achievement for their day. But the method of their construction is not in the least mysterious.

As for the pyramids of Central and South America, the close-jointedness of whose blocks has also caused wonder, we note that: "Almost all rocks have been slightly compressed or have been shrunken by drying or cooling, and therefore show real or incipient parting distinct from the [sedimentary] planes already described. This may follow a regular pattern, giving jointing, which yields rectangular or rhomboidal shapes—forms obviously desirable for use in foundations, walls or pavements." It is also the case in South American pyramids that the close fit of the stones is only in respect of the *outside* layer, not the inner layers. Furthermore, the size of blocks decreases as the wall rises higher. It is relatively easy to find progressively smaller blocks that fit larger ones.

Once again there is no mystery here—though, again, a fine achievement by early man.

What of the gigantic ground designs found on the flatlands of Nasca in Peru? These designs, achieved by removing surface stones to expose lighter stones below, can only be properly seen from a height of three hundred yards or more from the earth's surface. Some of them are outlines of birds and animals. Others are sets of straight lines running for miles. Many writers, Däniken among them, have argued that these are the landing sites of spacecraft. Or at any rate, since they can only be appreciated from the air, the designs argue at least an ability to fly, some-

thing that we would normally believe the Incas and their predecessors

not do.

of the designs suggests that they are probably a gigantic

Gerald Hawkins insists they are not.) When some of

d to the horizon, they mark the summer and winter

orthernmost and southernmost risings of the sun).

ls do, indeed, probably represent the gods of these

ancient peoples, who in one sense certainly "inhabited" the sky. The designs are, therefore, probably meant to placate the gods (perhaps there had been a series of disastrous summers or winters) and to show them that man knew and cared about them. Possibly, even, these early men thought the gods would descend to earth on account of the designs (in the way a hunter will set plastic ducks, on a lake in the hope of attracting the real thing). Alas, the gods never came.

The primitive telescope theory takes care of statements like "the Milky Way consists of very small stars huddled together" (Democritus, fifth century BC) and "the earth revolves in an oblique circle while it rotates at the same time about its own axis" (Plutarch/Aristarchus, first millennium BC). The "oblique circle" is an ellipse, so no doubt both the Dogon and Plutarch received their information from the same source.

In respect of other statements, like those about the nature of atomic structure, the telescope theory does not help too much. (There, perhaps, we must fall back on scrying.) The telescope could also not have played any part in the view expressed by the ancient Brahmins that the universe is 4,320 million years old. Our current estimate is around 4,600 million years. These matters remain mysteries.

I would, however, take even reasonably responsible writers like Andrew Tomas to task for two things. One, for their wide-eyed, noncriticism of the early civilization we have been discussing. Reading even these authors one gets the impression that the ancients were all-knowing and all-wise. Not a chance. The ancient Egyptians, for example, when preparing a body for mummification carefully removed the internal organs of the stomach and treated and stored them separately. But the brain they drew out of the head through the nose and threw away! That was how much *they* knew. The Mayas in South America, for their part, a remarkable people in many ways, never discovered the wheel and never discovered iron!

How was it, I wonder, that Däniken's space men forgot to tell the Egyptians about the brain and the Mayas about the wheel? No, what we seem to see in these civilizations is the idiosyncratic development of man, turning up only what it is that the clever individual happens to spot, and missing the rest. Certainly the ancient Babylonians and ancient Indians had primitive electric batteries and practiced electroplating and electrolysis. Certainly the ancient Greeks had a form of primitive computer, with moving parts made of ceramic. But the nonbrain in Egypt and the nonwheel in South America show us the rest of the picture—the part that is always ignored by sensationalist writers.

My second criticism of, as I say, even fairly responsible authors is in their failure to grade and evaluate items. It is no good throwing, say, the cave paintings of Cro-Magnon (around 20,000 BP), a city sewage disposal system in a city in India (2500 BC), and the *alleged* ability of alchemists in Europe to turn base metals into gold (AD 1200) into one stewpot as if they were all the same events and all bequeathed by the same space visitors—when, in fact, they are separated not just by thousands of miles but many thousands of years.

Däniken, of course, argues for at least six separate space visits. The full total claimed by all different writers probably amounts to dozens. One begins to get the impression that this planet is a kind of Waterloo Station of the universe. And yet not one single, solitary artifact, or tool, or piece of metal, or other material of extraterrestrial origin has ever been found.

The theory of space visitors seems also unreasonable purely in itself. If beings from a highly-advanced civilization were to take the trouble to cross the inconceivable deeps of space to see us, one would imagine they would do so with some carefully-thought-out procedure. Basically they would either decide (1) to interfere in no way at all, or (2) make contact in some systematic, coherent fashion. The first alternative would involve not being seen by anyone, since to be seen is, willy-nilly, to interfere. The second would surely involve leaving behind some permanent, unmistakable "visiting card" and would certainly *not* involve stopping off to chat with isolated individuals of by no means always the highest intelligence, as allegedly happens in the case of UFOs today. But nowhere in the various alleged landings and behaviors of alleged extraterrestrials do we see anything that looks to me personally like reason or planning or coherence. *If* the space men came, then on the evidence they only came to mess around. Why should they bother to do that?

Believers in extraterrestrial visits do often argue that "they" started civilization. Either the visitors operated on our brains, giving us powers we did not have before, or they functioned as teachers, giving us a large and apparently necessary shove toward civilization.

But if such intervention was necessary for us to achieve advancement, why was it not necessary in the case of the space men themselves? Either they made it on their own, or they themselves were helped. In which case, who helped their helpers? You see, you have to start somewhere. Somebody initially had to make it by themselves.

There are other lines of argument. Why is it, for example, that sightings of UFOs in the United States increased fourfold after the release of the film *Close Encounters of the Third Kind* (*Sunday Times*, 12 March 1978)? Had the space visitors heard about the film?

No, not really. This particular finding illustrates what I think to be the real point involved. At least the large majority of UFOs are hallucinations, induced by suggestion. Dozens of psychological experiments have been performed to show that even fully conscious people will see, in general terms, whatever it is they are told they will see, providing the suggesting comes with enough authority or plausibility. Apart from that, hypnotized or semihypnotized (including self-hypnotized) subjects are totally responsive to suggestion. Alcoholics and mental patients likewise see complex, coherent hallucinations. Psychics and mystics also regularly see sights and objects that are not really there. And let us make no mistake about this—hallucinations are not lies or pretense. The subject sees them as clearly and vividly as any real object. The difference is that the hallucinated object or scene (except in very rare cases) cannot be seen by anyone else present at the time. And more importantly still, *they do not obey the laws of the physical universe.* This feature, coincidentally enough, is the hallmark of most UFO sightings (accelerating and decelerating at impossible speeds, soundlessness despite movement through the atmosphere, and so on) usually trotted out as proof of the validity of the vision! Our best conclusion is that in the continued absence of one single scrap of any extraterrestrial, physical, manufactured matter whatsoever, all UFO sightings are hallucinations. Or, just possibly, a form of paranormal event.

I had my own first sighting of a UFO recently. I was walking with Robert Temple (who, incidentally, is also a psychic) over the hills of Warwickshire at dusk, well away from all roads. The sky itself was still quite light, although at ground level the darkness was almost complete. We were talking about matters connected with *The Sirius Mystery*, and our individual plans for future books. Glancing up above my head (I don't know why I glanced up), I saw briefly a shining, stationary irregular object, as shown in figure 14 below. (If I had seen this across country, I would have said that a car windshield had momentarily caught the sun or some other source of light.)

Figure 14.

I hesitated, and while I did so, the object simply vanished. I remarked on it to Robert, but there was nothing more to be seen. Such incidents, in my experience, are especially common when two or more psychics are present at a particular point.

Like C. G. Jung, I myself believe the enormous increase in "sightings" of UFOs in recent years is an outward expression of a deep inner hunger, which our civilization can no longer satisfy. This hunger and its nature is the subject matter of my next book.[8]

Notes

CHAPTER 1: THIRTEEN

1. Stan Gooch, *The Double Helix of the Mind* (London: Wildwood House, 1980).
2. Robert Graves, *The White Goddess* (London: Faber, 1961).
3. Margaret Murray, *The Witch Cult in Western Europe* (London: Oxford University Press, 1962).
4. Richard Cavendish, *The Black Arts* (London: Pan Books, 1969).
5. J. Hastings, *Encyclopedia of Religion and Ethics* (Edinburgh: T. & T. Clark, 1917).

CHAPTER 4: MOON RIVER

1. Alison Jolly, *The Evolution of Primate Behaviour* (London: Macmillan, 1972).
2. Don Smith, *Why Are There Gays At All?* (London: Quantum Jump Publications, 1978).
3. Ibid.
4. June Singer, *Androgyny* (London: Routledge, 1978).
5. Charlotte Wolfe, *Bisexuality* (London: Quartet Books, 1978).
6. Colin Wilson, *Mysteries* (London: Hodder & Stoughton, 1978).

CHAPTER 5: TWO OF A KIND

1. Stan Gooch, *The Double Helix of the Mind* (London: Wildwood House, 1980).
2. Carl Sagan, *The Dragons of Eden* (London: Hutchinson, 1978).

3. W. N. Stephens, *The Family in Cross-Cultural Perspective* (New York: Holt, 1963).

CHAPTER 6: THE NOT SO LITTLE PEOPLE

1. Stan Gooch, *The Neanderthal Question* (London: Wildwood House, 1977).
2. Felix Guirand, *New Larousse Encyclopedia of Mythology* (London: Hamlyn, 1969).
3. N. K. Sandars, *Prehistoric Art in Europe* (Harmondsworth: Penguin Books, 1968).
4. Richard Elen, *Radical Occultism* (London: Wildwood House, 1980).

CHAPTER 7: WISDOM AND KNOW-HOW

1. E. Swedenborg, *Heaven and Hell* (London: Swedenborg Society, 1896).
2. Stan Gooch, *The Paranormal* (London: Wildwood House, 1978).
3. H. F. Harlow, "Love in Infant Monkeys," *Scientific American,* June 1959.
4. Stan Gooch, *The Paranormal* (London: Wildwood House, 1978) and Stan Gooch, *The Neanderthal Question* (London: Wildwood House, 1977).
5. Stan Gooch, *The Double Helix of the Mind* (London: Wildwood House, 1980).
6. Stan Gooch, *The Paranormal.*
7. Andrew Tomas, *We Are Not The First* (London: Sphere Books, 1972).
8. Stan Gooch, *The Paranormal.*
9. Arthur M. Young, *The Reflexive Universe* (London: Wildwood House, 1977).
10. Ibid.

CHAPTER 8: STANDING STONES

1. Aubrey Burl, *The Stone Circles of the British Isles* (London: Yale University Press, 1976).
2. Ibid.
3. Ibid.
4. Robert Graves, *The White Goddess* (London: Faber, 1961).

5. Penelope Shuttle and Peter Redgrove, *The Wise Wound* (London: Gollancz, 1978).

CHAPTER 9: THE HOLY GRAIL

1. Penelope Shuttle and Peter Redgrove, *The Wise Wound* (London: Gollancz, 1978).
2. Andrew Tomas, *We Are Not The First* (London: Sphere Books, 1972).
3. W. W. Skeat, *An Etymological Dictionary of the English Language* (London: Oxford University Press, 1946).

CHAPTER 10: THE LAND OF WOMEN

1. Robert Temple, *The Sirius Mystery* (London: Sidgwick & Jackson, 1976).
2. H. B. Alexander, ed., *The Mythology of All Races* (New York: Cooper Square, 1964).
3. Ibid.
4. Felix Guirand, *New Larousse Encyclopedia of Mythology* (London: Hamlyn, 1969).

CHAPTER 11: ARTISTS, POETS, AND PRIESTS

1. Robert Graves, *The White Goddess* (London: Faber, 1961).
2. Ibid.
3. Ibid.
4. Peter Redgrove, *In the Country of the Skin* (London: Routledge, 1973).
5. Penelope Shuttle and Peter Redgrove, *Deepening.*
6. Carl Sagan, *The Dragons of Eden* (London: Hutchinson, 1978).
7. Ibid.
8. Ibid.

CHAPTER 12: SCRYING

1. Russell Targ and Harold Puthof, *Mind-Reach* (London: Paladin, 1978).
2. Francis Hitching, *The World Atlas of Mysteries* (London: Collins, 1978).

3. Stan Gooch, *The Double Helix of the Mind* (London: Wildwood House, 1980).

CHAPTER 13: NEANDERTHAL NOW

1. Yuri Zerchaninov, "Is Neanderthal Man Extinct?," *Moscow News*, February 22, 1964.
2. Francis Hitching, *The World Atlas of Mysteries* (London: Collins, 1978).
3. Dmitri Bayanov and Igor Bourtsev, "On Neanderthal vs Paranthropus," *Current Anthropology* 17 (1976).
4. Ibid.
5. Emanuel Vlcek, "Old Literary Evidence for the Existence of the 'Snow Man' in Tibet and Mongolia," *Man* 59 (1959).
6. B. F. Porshnev, "The Troglodytidae and the Hominidae in the Taxonomy and Evolution of Higher Primates," *Current Anthropology* 15 (1974).
7. Ibid.
8. David B. Burr, "Rhodesian Man and the Evolution of Speech," *Current Anthropology* 17 (1976).
9. Geoffrey Goodman, *Psychic Archaeology* (New York: G. P. Putnam's Sons, 1977).
10. Stan Gooch, *Personality and Evolution* (London: Wildwood House, 1973).

CHAPTER 14: THE CHRIST

1. Ian Wilson, *The Turin Shroud* (Harmondsworth: Penguin Books, 1979).

CHAPTER 15: NEW WISDOM FOR OLD

1. Nigel Hawkes, "How Fad-Fed Babies Go Hungry," *Observer*, February 4, 1979.

APPENDIX 2: INNER SPACE AND OUTER SPACE

1. Robert Temple, *The Sirius Mystery* (London: Sidgwick & Jackson, 1976).
2. Ibid.

3. Ibid.

4. Francis Hitching, *The World Atlas of Mysteries* (London: Collins, 1978).

5. C. G. Jung, *Flying Saucers: A Modern Myth* (London: Routledge, 1977).

6. Jacquetta Hawkes, "In Pursuit of Strange Gods," *Sunday Times,* September 15, 1974.

7. L. D. Kusche, *The Bermuda Triangle Mystery Solved* (London: New English Library, 1975).

8. Stan Gooch, *The Double Helix of the Mind* (London: Wildwood House, 1980).

Bibliography

Alexander, H. B., ed. *The Mythology of All Races*. New York: Cooper Square, 1964.

Ashe, Geoffrey. *The Ancient Wisdom*. London: Macmillan, 1977.

Bayanov, Dmitri, and Igor Bourtsev. "On Neanderthal vs Paranthropus." *Current Anthropology* 17 (June 1976).

Burl, Aubrey. *The Stone Circles of the British Isles*. London: Yale University Press, 1976.

Burr, David B. "Rhodesian Man and the Evolution of Speech." *Current Anthropology* 17 (1976).

Carlson, Rick. *The Frontiers of Science and Medicine*. London: Wildwood House, 1975.

Cavendish, Richard. *The Black Arts*. London: Pan Books, 1969.

Däniken, Erich von. *In Search of Ancient Gods*. London: Souvenir Press, 1974.

Donahoe, James A. *Dream Reality*. California: Bench Press, 1976.

Eiseley, Loren. *The Unexpected Universe*. London: Gollancz, 1970.

Elen, Richard. *Radical Occultism*. London: Wildwood House, 1980.

Frazer, J. G. *The Golden Bough*. London: Macmillan, 1922.

Freud, Sigmund. *The Interpretation of Dreams*. London: Allen & Unwin, 1954.

Gooch, Stan. *The Double Helix of the Mind*. London: Wildwood House, 1980.

———. *The Paranormal*. London: Wildwood House, 1978.

———. *The Neanderthal Question*. London: Wildwood House, 1977.

———. *Personality and Evolution*. London: Wildwood House, 1973.

———. *Total Man*. London: Allen Lane, 1972.

Goodall, Jane. *In the Shadow of Man*. London: Collins, 1971.

Goodman, Geoffrey. *Psychic Archaeology*. New York: G. P. Putnam's Sons, 1977.

Graves, Robert. *The White Goddess*. London: Faber, 1961.

Grossman, S. P. *A Textbook of Physiological Psychology*. New York: Wiley, 1967.

Guirand, Felix. *New Larousse Encyclopedia of Mythology*. London: Hamlyn, 1969.

Hafez, E. S. E. *Comparative Reproduction of Non-Human Primates*. Springfield: Charles C. Thomas, 1971.

Harlow, H. F. "Love in Infant Monkeys." *Scientific American*, June 1959.

Hastings, J. *Encyclopedia of Religion and Ethics*. Edinburgh: T. & T. Clark, 1917.

Hawkes, Jacquetta. "In Pursuit of Strange Gods." *Sunday Times*, 15 September 1974.

Hawkes, Nigel. "How the Fad-Fed Babies Go Hungry." *Observer*, 4 February 1979.

Heyerdahl, Thor. *Aku, Aku: The Secret of Easter Island*. London: Allen & Unwin, 1958.

Hitching, Francis. *The World Atlas of Mysteries*. London: Collins, 1978.

———. *Earth Magic*. London: Picador, 1977.

Hulse, Frederick S. *The Human Species*. New York: Random House, 1971.

I Ching (the Book of Changes). Trans. Richard Wilhelm and Cary F. Baynes. London: Routledge, 1968.

Jobes, Gertrude. *Dictionary of Mythology, Folklore and Symbols*. New York: Scarecrow Press, 1961.

Jolly, Alison. *The Evolution of Primate Behaviour*. London: Macmillan, 1972.

Jung, C. G. *Flying Saucers: A Modern Myth*. London: Routledge, 1977.

Kusche, L. D. *The Bermuda Triangle Mystery Solved*. London: New English Library, 1975.

Lacey, Louise. *Lunaception*. New York: Warner Books, 1976.

Lethbridge, T. C. *Witches: Investigating an Ancient Religion*. London: Routledge, 1962.

Michell, John. *The View Over Atlantis*. London: Garnstone Press, 1969.

Murray, Margaret. *The Witch Cult in Western Europe*. London: Oxford University Press, 1962.

———. *The God of the Witches*. London: Faber, 1952.

Needham, Rodney. *Right and Left*. Chicago: University of Chicago Press, 1973.

Porshnev, B. F. "The Troglodytidae and the Hominidae in the Taxonomy and Evolution of Higher Primates." *Current Anthropology* 15 (1974).

Radford, E., and M. A. Radford. *Encyclopedia of Superstitions.* Christina Hole, ed. London: Hutchinson, 1961.

Redgrove, Peter. *In the Country of the Skin.* London: Routledge, 1973.

Redgrove, Peter, and Penelope Shuttle. *The Terrors of Dr. Treviles.* London: Routledge, 1974.

Reynolds, Vernon. *The Apes.* London: Cassell, 1967.

Rose, Ronald. *Living Magic.* New York: Rand McNally, 1956.

Russell, Jeffrey Burton. *Witchcraft in the Middle Ages.* New York: Cornell University, 1972.

Sagan, Carl. *The Dragons of Eden.* London: Hutchinson, 1978.

Sandars, N. K. *Prehistoric Art in Europe.* Harmondsworth: Penguin Books, 1968.

Sassoon, G., and R. Dale. *The Manna Machine.* London: Sidgwick & Jackson, 1978.

Shuttle, Penelope, and Peter Redgrove. *Deepening.* Unpublished.

———. *The Wise Wound.* London: Gollancz, 1978.

Singer, June. *Androgyny.* London: Routledge, 1978.

Skeat, W. W. *An Etymological Dictionary of the English Language.* London: Oxford University Press, 1946.

Smith, Don. *Why Are There Gays At All?* London: Quantum Jump Publications, 1978.

Solecki, Ralph S. "Shanidar IV, a Neanderthal Flower Burial in Northern Iraq." *Science* 190 (1975).

———. *Shanidar: The Humanity of Neanderthal Man.* London: Allen Lane, 1972.

Sparks, John. *Bird Behavior.* London: Hamlyn, 1969.

Spengler, Oswald. *Man and Technics.* London: Allen & Unwin, 1932.

Stephens, W. N. *The Family in Cross-Cultural Perspective.* New York: Holt, 1963.

Swedenborg, E. *Heaven and Hell.* London: Swedenborg Society, 1896.

Targ, Russell, and Harold Puthof. *Mind-Reach.* London: Paladin, 1978.

Temple, Robert. *Sons of the Future.* London: Sidgwick & Jackson, 1980.

———. *The Sirius Mystery.* London: Sidgwick & Jackson, 1976.

Teng, E. L., et al. "Handedness in a Chinese Population." *Science* 193 (1976).

Tomas, Andrew. *We Are Not The First.* London: Sphere Books, 1972.

Vlcek, Emanuel. "Old Literary Evidence for the Existence of the 'Snow Man' in Tibet and Mongolia." *Man* 59 (1959).

Watkins, Alfred. *The Old Straight Track*. London: Garnstone Press, 1971.

Wilson, Colin. *Mysteries*. London: Hodder & Stoughton, 1978.

Wilson, Ian. *The Turin Shroud*. Harmondsworth: Penguin Books, 1979.

Wolfe, Charlotte. *Bisexuality*. London: Quartet Books, 1978.

Yerkes, R. M., and A. W. Yerkes. *The Great Apes*. London: Yale University Press, 1929.

Young, Arthur M. *The Reflexive Universe*. London: Wildwood House, 1977.

Zerchaninov, Yuri. "Is Neanderthal Man Extinct?" *Moscow News*, 22 February 1964.

Index